THE
DARK MAN

Australia's first serial killer

THE
DARK MAN

Australia's first serial killer

JASON K. FOSTER

www.bigskypublishing.com.au

Big Sky Publishing Pty Ltd
PO Box 303, Newport, NSW 2106, Australia
Phone: 1300 364 611
Fax: (61 2) 9918 2396
Email: info@bigskypublishing.com.au
Web: www.bigskypublishing.com.au

Cover design and typesetting: Think Productions
Printed in China by Asia Pacifica Offset Ltd.

National Library of Australia Cataloguing-in-Publication entry (pbk)
Author: Foster, Jason K., author.
Title: The dark man : Australia's first serial killer / Jason K. Foster.
ISBN: 9781922132260 (paperback)
Subjects: Ashe, Richard, 1861-1897.
            Serial murderers--Australia--Biography.
            Serial murders--Australia--History.
            Murder--Investigation--Australia--History.
Dewey Number: 364.152320922

National Library of Australia Cataloguing-in-Publication entry (ebook)
Author: Foster, Jason K., author.
Title: The dark man [electronic resource] : Australia's first serial killer / Jason K. Foster.
ISBN: 9781922132277 (ebook)
Subjects: Ashe, Richard, 1861-1897.
            Serial murderers--Australia--Biography.
            Serial murders--Australia--History.
            Murder--Investigation--Australia--History.
Dewey Number: 364.152320922

Contents

Part III

Prologue

28 July 1896

Row upon row of miners' tents stretched out across the West Australian outback, their white canvas reddened by thousands of miles and hundreds of campsites. Coolgardie's population had exploded since Bayley and Ford had discovered a rich vein of gold, netting them thousands and thousands of pounds. Searching for the dream, for the easy life, men had come from every corner of the country prepared to tough it out for that one small chance of a life of luxury, but for now, their lives were simple as they scratched, dug and sluiced in the soil and the dust.

Dawn was breaking as the sun crept higher in the eastern sky, spilling golden rays across the barren landscape. Flocks of pink and grey galahs squawked loudly in the craggy gums as dozens of men collected their gear in preparation for heading out for the day's toil hoping, praying, that today would be the day they struck it rich. One man, Richard Ashe, sat with several other miners making small talk by a small fire, a worn black billy bubbling away on top of it.

'I have been to many places, a few around Kalgoorlie in particular, where I have come good,' Ashe said as he held up a small bag. No one paid any attention as they devoured the last of their breakfast; they'd heard it all before. Ashe's reputation for telling tall tales was well known, and one miner, having finally had enough, snapped, 'I bet there's nothing but pebbles in there.'

'Oh, no!' Ashe protested, as the other miners sniggered. 'There's at least two thousand pounds' worth.'

'In that case, you're mad!' another miner commented. 'I certainly wouldn't be walking around with that much gold in my pocket!'

'Yeah,' another heavily bearded miner added as he folded his arms. 'We all know you're stupid, Ashe. After all, you stole and sold some copper's horses and then signed your own name on the receipt!'

A chorus of derisory laughter ensued as the miners picked up their gear and headed off to the goldfields. Ashe, unfazed by his colleagues' ridicule, moved to collect his equipment from his tent, keeping a keen eye on the others as he did. The miners, bags strapped onto their backs and shovels in hand, made their way down the sandy road that wound its way through scattered and stunted eucalypts until they eventually disappeared from view. Ashe watched and waited, and when he was satisfied the miners were far enough away, he set to his own prospecting. Moving from tent to tent, he rummaged and searched, taking whatever took his fancy. Jewellery, cash, papers; it all went into his bag. Then he found the items that most excited him, several professional certificates belonging to a Mr Frank Harwood, certificates of good character issued at Broken Hill by the Broken Hill Proprietary Company and a certificate from the Ballarat School of Mines stating that Harwood had passed examinations in chemistry, metallurgy and assaying.

That was it; his next move became clear. Today, Richard Ashe would die, and a new Frank Harwood would be born. Hurriedly dismantling his tent, he collected his possessions and, his bag now full of trinkets and treasures, quickly departed, catching the first train back to Perth, and then on to Fremantle.

As the train pulled into the port town he stood, bags slung over his shoulder, on the carriage step, and leapt down onto the platform before the train had come to a complete halt. Threading his way through the crowds, he hurried from the station and down to the seaside. Amongst the backstreets, full of sailors, drunks and prostitutes, he felt safe and comfortable, and nestled in between the brothels and the saloons, he soon found a suitable hotel.

'Good evening, sir, how may I help you?' the clerk asked politely as Ashe entered.

'Just a room, thank you.'

'Certainly, sir, if you would just sign the register.'

Richard Ashe picked up the quill pen and signed. The clerk turned the book around and read out loud, 'Frank Butler Harwood.'

'Yep, that's me,' he replied.

'Well, Mr Harwood, here is your key. How long will you be staying?'

'Just overnight. I'm catching a boat to Sydney in the morning.'

'Very good, sir. I'm afraid I'm going to have to ask you to pay your bill in advance. We get a lot of people trying to slip out without paying.'

'Certainly,' said Harwood as he reached into his coat and withdrew a large wad of bills, the sight of which made the clerk's eyes light up.

'Excellent, sir,' the clerk said enthusiastically. 'And if there is anything else you need, anything, you just ask me, alright?'

'Thank you, I reckon I could do with a good bottle of whisky. Just bring it up to my room,' Harwood said as he took his room key, picked up his bags and made his way upstairs.

Once inside his room, he tossed his belongings onto the bed and sat in a chair at a desk by the window. He was staring out the window at the busy port below when a knock came on the door. 'Enter,' he called.

The clerk entered, brandishing two large bottles of whisky. 'Do you want a glass?' he said, placing them on the table in front of Harwood.

'No,' Harwood replied as he reached into his pocket and withdrew several shillings and gave them to the clerk.

'Thank you, sir, enjoy your stay, sir,' the clerk said as he dipped his head and departed.

Frank Harwood opened the first bottle, drank heartily and wiped the remnants from his mouth and thick moustache before grabbing the bag full of stolen booty and tipping it onto the bed. The contents scattered across the bed, and he began to examine each piece of ill-gotten loot, but they were nothing more than cursory glances; he was more interested in the mining certificates, which he picked up and took back to the desk, where he studied them while continuing to sip from the bottle of whisky.

Looking out the window and down at the ships below, it suddenly came to him; the best way to use them, the way to silence the voice that whispered to him, begging him to experience that thrill once more. Leaning back in his chair with a self-satisfied smile, he took another heavy swig, and proceeded to finish both that bottle and the other before falling into a contented sleep, his dreams filled with images of the faces of men long gone.

The next morning, he awoke early, his head clouded by the whisky, packed and hurriedly made his way out the door and down to the docks, where he asked around until he found his ship, the *Marlborough*. It had been readied for an early departure, and now its sailors were rushing around finishing the last of their tasks. 'You there,' Harwood said to the nearest sailor.

'Yes, sir?' he replied.

'When do we sail? Soon, I hope.'

'Yes, sir, we sail shortly.'

'Excellent, I have some urgent business I want to get to in Sydney.'

FRANK HARWOOD (Alias Butler).

Frank Harwood, *The San Francisco Call*, 9 January 1897.

PART I

1

A New Path

7 August 1896

As the *Marlborough* entered Sydney Heads, Frank Harwood stood at the bow examining the sandstone cliffs and rugged bushland lining the coast. Night was descending, and the majesty of the harbour intensified as the setting sun sent glistening sparkles skipping over the crests of the small waves. A cool evening wind blew, and the clouds began to thicken in the skies above. The harbour was quiet, with most ships preferring to sit the night out and set sail in the morning. The *Marlborough* docked in Circular Quay with Harwood still standing at the bow, watching the residents of Sydney moving to and fro along the waterfront, silhouetted under the street lanterns, some making their way home, others to an inn for a quiet drink after a hard day's labour.

The *Marlborough* eventually moored, and the passengers soon disembarked. Walking down the gangway, Harwood had a spring in his step as he entered the crowds, sensing opportunity with every new face; his prey, his next victim, was somewhere among them. Turning down Pitt Street, he examined several hotels before finding one that took his fancy: *Gilham's Hotel*.

Inside the entrance, he found a slightly rounded, middle-aged lady sitting behind a large wooden desk.

'Good evening, sir,' she said. 'I am Mrs Gilham. How may I help you?'

'Good evening, madam, my name is Frank Harwood. Do you have any beds?'

'Yes, sir, we do. Do you have any idea how long you will be staying for?'

'Not really; a few days, a week maybe.'

Mrs Gilham smiled and asked for some identification. Rummaging through his bag, Harwood pulled out the certificates and handed them to her. She took a slight interest in the clinking and clanging that came from his bag, but paid little attention, as travellers who were carrying everything they owned were a familiar sight in her establishment. After reading the certificates and recording his name in her ledger, she handed them back to him.

'Thank you, Mr Harwood. Are you intending to do some mining whilst you're in New South Wales?'

'Yes, ma'am, I intend to head out west shortly.'

'Well, best of luck,' she said as she handed him his room key.

'Thank you, but I doubt I'll need it!' he replied jovially as he took the key and headed upstairs to find his room.

Over the next few days, Harwood familiarised himself with the centre of the city, its grid-patterned streets making it easy to find his way around. With each passing day, the voice inside him grew stronger; it was time to set the first stage of his plan into motion. He walked along Pitt Street until he reached George Street, which he followed to Hunter Street, and then proceeded to the corner of Phillip Street, where he entered *The Sydney Morning Herald*'s advertising offices, spoke briefly to a clerk while he placed his ad, and then returned to the hotel to wait. The ad read:

Mining partner wanted to go equal shares. Expedition to western goldfields. Apply Gilham's Hotel, Pitt Street.

12 August 1896

After enjoying a roast lamb dinner, Frank Harwood sat in the drawing room smoking a cigarette as he read through the dozens of responses to his ad. One in particular intrigued him, and he read it over and over again.

Dear Mr Harwood, would love to join you on this expedition. Happy to go half shares. Meet you at Mrs Gilham's Hotel tomorrow night at 6 pm. Mr Burgess.

Many respondents had come and gone over the last few days, but none had been suitable; they either knew too many people or had large families. Several had appeared over the course of the last hour, and each time a new man had entered the room, Harwood had looked up to see if it was Mr Burgess. Unfortunately for them, they were travellers looking for a room, and Mrs Gilham had politely turned each one away, as her hotel was full. Now the bell above the door jingled once more, and Harwood looked up expectantly. A young man in his late twenties, slim with blond hair and a neat, tidy moustache stepped through the doorway. Harwood had seen his kind before, in the Scandinavian countries, and something inside him sensed that this was his man.

'Good evening, madam,' the man said. 'My name is Mr Burgess.'

'Good evening, sir,' Mrs Gilham replied. 'I am sorry, but I cannot offer you a room, as we are currently full.'

Burgess looked slightly confused, but before he could utter any response, Harwood was at his side. 'It's all right, Mrs Gilham, he's with me.'

Burgess smiled, revealing several gold fillings.

'Will you be checking out tomorrow then, Mr Harwood?' said Mrs Gilham.

'Yes, ma'am, I believe I will be.'

'Well, seeing as this man is a friend of yours, I think I can muster up a spare room for one night. It is only a tiny single that I rarely use. I hope that will be acceptable.'

'Any room is fine, ma'am,' Burgess said politely.

'Very good then, gentlemen, I will have your bills ready in the morning.'

The two men retired to the drawing room, with Harwood repeating the same line of questioning that he'd used with the previous applicants.

In the course of their conversation, Burgess revealed that he didn't have any family in Australia, and had few friends. Harwood duly informed Burgess that he was the perfect man for the job, and the next morning the younger man was up early and pacing up and down the lobby while he waited for Harwood, who appeared soon after carrying two large bags.

'Surely we will need more gear than that if we are to be successful,' Burgess stated quizzically as he looked down at his own bag.

'Ah, Mr Burgess, you are with a man who knows his business. This will be enough, I assure you.'

Harwood said his farewells to Mrs Gilham, and the two men boarded the wagon Burgess had purchased. Burgess shook the reins, and the horses began trotting along the streets of Sydney. The men drove for most of the day, their small talk mostly focused on the finer points of prospecting. Harwood answered Burgess's every little question with good humour and, whilst he was no expert, he knew enough to make himself sound like one – anything he didn't know, he simply improvised.

They made camp near Parramatta, and continued the next morning towards Penrith. Burgess suggested they stay the night in one of the many inns but Harwood declined the request, citing that too many fellow miners were likely to be there; they didn't want too many people knowing where they were headed.

Camping by the river, they had a simple, early supper, and were up at the break of dawn. Harwood drove as they made their way up Mitchell's Pass and along the Great Western Road.

Travelling through Springwood then on to Lithgow, they made camp once more. The next morning, they packed their belongings into the cart and continued their journey out west.

'So tell me a little more about yourself, Mr Harwood,' Burgess said, taking the reins and whipping the horses into action as they made their way out of Lithgow and along the road leading through the thick eucalyptus forests of the upper Blue Mountains and down into the western plains. 'You are obviously from England, given your accent, but how did you come to be in Australia?'

'I have seen many a thing, Mr Burgess, many a thing, and you are correct in saying that I am an Englishman. I once served in the Royal Navy on HMS *Sultan*. "Darkey," my friends used to call me.'

'A sailor! You are a long way from the ocean. Did you not like the seas? Is that why you turned to prospecting?'

'Yeah. There was not enough money in being a sailor, so I decided it was time to stop roaming the oceans. I'd like to get together enough money to settle down to a quiet life somewhere, maybe here, maybe England. Either way, I should like to see Old Blighty again.'

'In that case, I hope we find that one big strike, and we can live our lives in the way we want,' said Burgess.

'We will, Mr Burgess, we will!' Harwood said as he slapped Burgess on the back, almost knocking him from the cart. Burgess steadied himself and gripped the reins tightly. The miles continued to pass as they made their way towards Bathurst, and the landscape gradually began to change, the high eucalypts and dense scrub giving way to yellow grassland and mulga trees.

'You must have had some exciting times at sea,' Burgess said as they descended into a small valley and crossed a dry creek bed.

'You don't know the half of it,' Harwood smirked.

'Care to regale me with a story to help pass the time?'

Never in need of a second request to boast, Harwood was only too happy to oblige. 'I remember one time back in '82, in Alexandria in Egypt. I think it was summer, because I remember it being damn hot. Some Egyptians had killed some Europeans, so we were ordered to bombard the city. Pretty much destroyed the whole place without losing a single ship. The Gypos put up a bit of a stoush at Tel el-Kebir. They were good fighters, but in the end we only lost fifty-seven to their two thousand.'

Burgess listened intently as the miles continued to pass by. Harwood moved on to tales about his time in the American Army, the Canadian Mounties and his various other jobs. He told Burgess of how he had become a sailor, and of all his adventures around the world, particularly in Chile and Brazil. Burgess, despite having seen some things in his time, was in awe and wonderment at all he was hearing and, had he paid more attention to Harwood's boasting about his dubious activities in Brazil, may have decided to pull the cart in at Bathurst and part company. However, when Harwood began boasting about his huge gold finds in the west, Burgess completely forgot about everything else, his mind consumed with dreams of riches as they drove through the town and continued out west towards Parkes.

2

A Lust for Gold

23 August 1896

The afternoon sun cast an orange glow across the land as it began to set on the flat horizon. Rounding a bend in the road, the two men spied a camp in the distance, and as they came closer, they could see half a dozen white canvas tents arranged in a neat circle with all the entrances facing inwards towards a centrally placed fire. Harwood pulled the cart in behind the tents whilst Burgess stepped down and started unloading their gear. In a few minutes, he'd erected their tents, whilst Harwood set about preparing the billy.

In the centre of the tents were a group of three men who were engaged in light conversation. Burgess nodded to them, but Harwood simply kept his head bowed as he went about his work. When they'd finished setting up everything, Burgess was the first to make conversation.

'Hey, fellas,' he said as he moved over and stood at the edge of the circle.

'G'day, mate. Grab a seat,' said one man as he waved his hand in the direction of an empty spot on one of the logs surrounding the fire. Burgess sat down, but made a point of shaking each man's hand before he did so.

'So, where you blokes headed?' one man asked.

'Out west to do some prospecting; what about you?' Burgess replied.

'We just move around looking for work. We'll probably head towards Parkes; try and get some work on the railways.'

Harwood, who'd paid little interest to their new companions, now became strangely animated as he came to sit next to Burgess on the log. 'Hi, fellas,' he said as he too shook their hands. 'Anyone got a smoke?'

The nearest man reached inside his coat. 'So how far have you guys travelled today?' he said as he retrieved a cigarette and handed it to Harwood.

'Oh, a fair few miles,' Burgess answered. 'We're making good progress, aren't we, Frank?'

Harwood nodded as he began to look around the camp. 'Hey, fellas, there's seven or so tents here. Where are the other boys?'

'Out hunting,' another man replied. 'Some good roo shooting around here.'

Harwood became enthused by the prospect and, as he rose from his seat, said, 'Think I'll go and have a look around.' He went to the back of the cart, retrieved his rifle and headed off into the scrub.

The men watched him until he disappeared from view, one man reaching for the billy and pouring a cup of tea, which he handed to Burgess. 'Oi, fella, what's the go with your mate?'

'Him?' Burgess replied. 'He's a bit of a queer chap. He doesn't say much, but he thinks a lot.'

'Hmm,' the man said. 'I'd keep your wits about you, mate.'

'Nah, he's alright.'

'If you say so, mate, but I'd still keep your wits about you.'

Burgess continued to make conversation, mostly about the landscape and what life was like in the country, while he prepared a rabbit that Harwood had shot earlier in the day. Making a stew of it, he set the billy on the fire. No sooner had he done so than Harwood returned. 'How was your shooting?' Burgess asked him as he came up next to the fire.

'Didn't see much,' Harwood said as he sat down and lit a smoke. 'I might have another crack in the morning.'

The rest of the night was spent swapping stories over the fire, mostly with Harwood repeating the boastful tales he had told Burgess during their journey.

The next morning, the two men said their goodbyes and went on their way, headed towards Parkes. As they came into town Harwood said: 'I'm just going to go into the store and get some tobacco for my pipe.'

'Okay,' Burgess said. 'I'll stay here and watch the cart.'

Burgess watched Harwood disappear into the store when he heard a voice from the other side of the wagon.

'G'day, mate, the name's Lawrence,' said a tall, blond, athletic man who stood examining the mining equipment. 'Doing some prospecting are ya'?'

'Burgess. Yeah, hopefully we'll strike it rich.'

'Where have you come from?'

'All the way from Sydney and across the Blue Mountains.'

Lawrence went to say more when Harwood returned.

'G'day, mate,' Lawrence said as he reached over to shake Harwood's hand but he received nothing more than a grunted acknowledgment.

'Where you thinking of heading?' Lawrence asked Burgess. 'There's some good gold country if you just keep going west for a coupla' hours.'

'Thanks, mate,' Burgess said as Harwood whipped the reins and the cart began to move.

After an hour's drive, they came to a creek running through a small ravine. 'This looks like a good place to camp. Good water,' Harwood said.

Burgess simply nodded his head in agreement as he reined the horses in. Harwood jumped down from the cart and began pulling down the canvas tents and billy. Burgess tied the horses to a nearby tree, placed the chaff bags over their noses and began collecting firewood. Soon, he had a roaring blaze going. Harwood set up the simple tent, collected three sticks and hastily constructed a frame for the billy. Burgess fetched water from the nearby creek whilst Harwood cut some slices of preserved meat and placed them on two tin plates. Burgess returned, placed the billy on the frame, took a plate and sat back on a nearby log.

'You know,' Harwood said as he looked around at the thick yellow spinifex grass, 'I reckon this looks like a good place to have a go. You see the way that creek runs down there and how those small hills in the distance are placed? Means it's a good spot.'

Burgess nodded excitedly as he ate, and in between mouthfuls, said, 'Well, we'd better get to bed early tonight so we can get to it.'

'It's good to see you're keen, but I reckon I should give you a quick run-down on how to do things before we get at it.'

Burgess sat back while Harwood retrieved a gold pan from the cart and headed down to the creek, where he collected some soil and water in the pan before returning and sitting back down beside Burgess.

'Right, so you start with a little soil in the pan. Make sure you remove all the large rocks, otherwise you won't see anything. Then you swirl it around like this and the larger parts will separate. The gold is heavier than the rest of what's in there so,' he said giving the pan a few more spins, 'once you separate it you should see some…gold.'

Two small specks of gold gleamed in the pan as Harwood passed it to Burgess. 'And that's just the start of it.'

'Can I have a go?' Burgess asked excitedly.

'Just a sec,' Harwood said as he retrieved a small vial filled with water, stuck his finger in the pan and dropped the specks into the vial. 'Here.'

Moving down to the creek, Burgess retrieved some soil and water and then came back and sat beside Harwood and tried to imitate his actions. With every turn, he continually asked whether he was doing it right, his excitement increasing with Harwood's every affirmation. When he was done, he gazed down into the pan, disappointment spreading across his face when he realised it was empty.

'Better luck next time!' Harwood laughed. 'Don't give up.'

Burgess spent the rest of the daylight hours trying time and time again, repeatedly enquiring as to the correctness of his technique, until Harwood decided it was time to call it a night.

The next morning, they were up with the sun and, after a light breakfast of bread and jam, Burgess was straight down to the creek bed resuming his search for gold. Harwood went too, but did not launch himself into the task with as much gusto as his student. By mid-morning, after failing to find a speck, Burgess's enthusiasm had begun to waver, and finally he said, 'What do you reckon we take a break?'

Harwood nodded, and the two men climbed out of the creek bed, Burgess with a billy full of water in hand. After boiling the tea and pouring himself a cup, he sat on a log and queried Harwood about their lack of success.

'I thought you said this was a good spot. Shouldn't we have found at least a few more specks, or maybe even something a bit more substantial?'

'You have to understand,' Harwood said through a mouthful of biscuits, 'prospecting is a difficult proposition. It can be hit and miss. One spot might fail, but another will yield a load. It's a big creek. We'll try a few different places. Don't worry, we'll find something, never you mind.'

After they'd finished their breakfast, Burgess immediately picked up the sieve and shovel and was straight back down to the creek and prospecting again. Harwood leant against a nearby eucalypt and watched on.

Before long, they both heard a rumbling. Harwood looked back up the road and saw a lone traveller driving a rickety cart.

'G'day, George Woodford's the name,' called the traveller as he halted his cart, hopped down and made his way towards the fire.

'G'day, Mr Woodford,' Burgess said enthusiastically as he ascended from the creek bed and shook the man's hand. 'Would you like a cup of cocoa?'

'That would be great, thank you,' Woodford said as he sat down next to the fire.

Harwood, annoyed by the intrusion, merely grunted a begrudging acknowledgement as he grabbed his gold pan, sieve and pick and headed down to the creek to resume prospecting.

'So, you guys looking for some gold, hey?' Woodford asked as he rolled a cigarette, lit it and watched Harwood.

'Yeah,' Burgess said eagerly as he handed Woodford the cocoa. 'Frank reckons this is a great place.'

Woodford inhaled deeply on his cigarette, exhaled, and leant forward to pay closer attention to Harwood's activities. 'Mate, that's not the way,' Woodford called out. 'You need to separate more of the big ones out and keep the fine soil.'

'Allow me to know better!' Harwood snapped back. 'What are you? Some kind of expert! Don't tell me about things you don't know about. I studied at the Mining School in Ballarat. I know what I'm doing!'

Woodford shot Burgess a concerned look.

'It's okay,' Burgess said, nodding. 'My mate is a strong fellow. He partly represents the government, and partly a Sydney syndicate. If we find anything good, it will be a good thing for all of us.'

Woodford, somewhat taken aback by Harwood's rebuttal, looked at Burgess's cap and a gold ring that was attached to a chain hanging from his shirt pocket. He looked back down to Harwood, who was still panning away. 'Mate, I'd lose that bloke if I was you,' Woodford said as he leant in close to Burgess. 'Seems like he's got a bit of a temper. You're welcome to travel with me if you want.'

'Nah, Frank's alright. He knows what he's doing. I need someone who can help me prospect.'

Woodford simply shook his head, rose to his feet, boarded his cart and headed off down the road.

Harwood continued to pan, keeping one eye on his work and one eye on the departing Woodford. When he was out of sight, Harwood came back up to the camp and sat down.

'What was that bloke on about?' Burgess asked.

'*Phhft!* Fella didn't know what he was talking about. I get it all the time. Every bloke in the world thinks he knows a thing or two about prospecting, but they don't have the same qualifications that I do. Stick with me, and I'll make you rich. Speaking of prospecting, what do you think about having another crack?'

Burgess jumped up enthusiastically. 'Excellent. Let's get to it!'

Harwood greeted Burgess's enthusiasm with a smile. 'Grab a shovel. We'll dig a shaft and see if we can find something a bit bigger, ay?'

Burgess hurried to the cart, retrieved a shovel and headed off down to the creek bed. Harwood lingered behind, glancing up and down the road several times before making his way down to the bank of the creek, where Burgess stood like an obedient dog waiting for instructions. 'So where do you think?' Burgess said as he tapped the ground with the shovel. Harwood moved closer and examined the earth, took a look towards the distant hills, and then gazed back at the earth again. 'Here,' he said, pointing to the designated spot with his foot.

Burgess removed his cap, placed it to one side and fervently set to work. He dug a rectangular hole which, in accordance with Harwood's instructions, measured about five feet long and three feet deep.

'Yep, that's good enough. I'll just go up and get the panning gear. Be right back,' said Harwood. Burgess stood in the hole, looking down at it with a sense of pride. Harwood returned shortly after. 'Righto, mate, just kneel down and I'll pass you the sieve and pan.'

Burgess did as asked, and reached out to take the sieve from Harwood. He started to shovel the soil in enthusiastically, fervently shaking the sieve about, then turned to Harwood and said, 'Am I doing it right?'

The adrenaline pulsed through Harwood's body. His nerves tingled as his finger caressed the trigger. Slowly, he raised the rifle and moved it from side to side until he found his preferred spot and fired. The bullet smashed through the doomed man's skull, shattering it into hundreds of pieces. Exploding out through the back of his head, the bullet scattered pieces of skull and brain into the creek bed. Burgess's body slumped forward as Harwood carefully placed the rifle down to one side, retrieved the shovel and manoeuvred the body into the foetal position. He reached for the dead man's cap and tossed it into the thick pool of blood that had seeped from Burgess's skull. Harwood began to fill in the grave, first covering the head. Within ten minutes, he'd completely buried the corpse, and gave the grave a final pat with the shovel before making his way back up to the camp, gathering up all the gear and heading west.

24 August 1896

Harwood travelled for the rest of the day, made camp for the night, and then continued on the next morning. Not far out from Parkes, he came across a farm owner fixing the gaps in the fence surrounding his property. He pulled the cart up alongside him, stepped down and introduced himself. 'G'day, Frank Harwood's the name.'

'G'day,' the man said as he wiped his dirty hands with a rag. 'John Williamson. Where have you come from?'

'All the way from Sydney. Picked up the horses and the cart in Lithgow.'

'That's a mighty fine cart and some good horses you've got there,' Williamson said.

'You think so? I don't really need them anymore, so they're up for sale if you want them.'

Williamson continued looking the cart over, kicking the wheels and attempting to bend the wooden slats. 'How much do you want?' he asked.

'Fifteen pounds. That's what I paid.'

Williamson pondered the proposal. 'Done,' he said. 'We'll just have to drive up to the house so I can get you the cash. Then I'll take you in to Parkes.'

The two men climbed onto the cart and drove up to the farmhouse. Williamson disappeared inside, retrieved the cash and returned a short time later. 'Here you are,' he said as he handed Harwood the money and lifted himself into the driver's seat. 'Let's get on our way to Parkes, hey.'

The men exchanged small talk as they rode, but the further they went, the more Williamson began eyeing Harwood, who was continually playing with his Martini rifle. 'What have you got that for?' he eventually asked, just as they reached the town's outskirts.

'Mining's a tricky business, my friend. There's many a guy that would just as soon kill you and take your gold as look at you.'

'Fair enough,' Williamson said, still unconvinced, as they pulled up outside the Railway dining rooms.

'Thanks for the ride,' Harwood said as he leapt down from the cart and gathered up his belongings.

'Not a worry. Nice to meet you,' Williamson said, relieved to be rid of his strange passenger.

Harwood reached over and shook Williamson's hand, and then headed into the dining rooms, where he sat down and ordered lunch. Lost in his meal and deep in thought, he failed to notice a man who entered shortly after him, paused at the door and took an extended look in his direction.

As Harwood neared the end of his meal, the waiter came over to his table. 'Everything's fine, I do not wish for anything else,' Harwood said.

'Excellent, sir, but I have come to give you a message.'

'Yes, what is it?'

'Sir, there's a Mr Lawrence upstairs; he says he knows you.'

Pushing his plate away and jerking his head towards the stairs, Harwood said nothing, but simply snatched up his bags and rushed from the dining rooms and out onto the platform, continually looking behind him as he hurried towards the ticket office.

'Excuse me,' he said to the clerk.

'Yes, sir?'

'When is the next train to Sydney?'

The clerk looked up to his left and ran his finger over the timetable.

'You're very fortunate, sir. There is a train in an hour.'

Harwood purchased a ticket, picked up his bags and headed off to the furthest end of the platform, keeping a close eye on the dining rooms as he went. For the next hour, he divided his time between watching the dining rooms and examining the tracks and the countryside to see where his best chance of escape lay. No one appeared, and when the train to Sydney arrived he was the first aboard. It was not until the train had pulled away from the platform and was far from Parkes that he sat back in his seat and relaxed.

3

The Next One

24 August 1896

Mrs Gilham was busy behind the counter, and didn't notice Frank Harwood until he was standing directly in front of her. When she eventually sensed that someone was there, she looked up. 'Oh, Mr Harwood, you're back,' she said with some surprise.

'Hello, Mrs Gilham. Yes, I'm back. I don't suppose you have any free rooms?'

'Fortunately, I do, sir,' she said, looking past him. 'Where is your companion?'

'He decided to continue on out west,' said Harwood.

'Will you be looking for a new friend?' said Mrs Gilham.

'Yes, I believe I just might.'

'I hope you find one to your liking,' she said as she checked the ledger. 'I happen to have your old room free; that is, if you want it.'

'Yes, Mrs Gilham. That would be lovely. Thank you very much.'

Harwood picked up his bags and carried them up the stairs. Arriving at his room, he placed them beside the bed, retrieved the rifle, which he carefully placed under his pillow, and moved over to the desk. Looking out the adjacent window, he could see the city streets below and dozens of well-dressed men making their way to and from whatever business it was they had to conclude. He tried to make out their faces, but few men stood still long enough to allow him to form a definitive picture. In his mind, however, his purpose was clear. Somewhere down in that throng of humanity, was the next man to answer his ad, his next victim. Prior to Burgess, it had been some time since he had killed, and the thrill of murder had been reignited, the feeling of power, of control, and he needed to feel the rush again. He needed to take another man's life, and soon. Opening the desk drawer, he retrieved a sheet of paper and a pen, and quickly wrote out a new ad that he would take to the newspaper in the morning.

The following morning, he delivered his ad to the newspaper office in plenty of time for the afternoon edition, and then made his way back to the hotel, where he ordered a bottle of whisky and settled into the drawing room to wait. The first of the respondents began to appear early in the evening. Half a dozen came and went, but none of them were to his liking. Frustrated, he continued to sip whisky, and had just begun to draft another ad when Mrs Gilham called out to him. 'Mr Harwood,' she said as she entered the drawing room. 'There is another man here to see you.'

'Thank you, ma'am,' Harwood said cordially as he rose from his seat and gestured for the man, who was of medium height and build with carefully manicured hair, to join him at the table.

The man bounded over and enthusiastically shook Harwood's hand. 'Sawkins,' he said as sat down. 'I am responding to your ad. I'm very interested in joining you on your next expedition.'

As Sawkins spoke, Harwood sized him up, and soon decided that he was perfect. 'Ah, Mr Sawkins, lovely to meet you. So where do you come from?'

'Western Australia originally, but I moved over here a few years ago to try and make a better go of things.'

'Western Australia!' Harwood said gleefully. 'I spent time in Western Australia. I was a constable for a while, you know, but the pay was no good so I chucked it in. Turned my hand to prospecting instead. Studied mining and engineering down in Ballarat. I've made a pretty good go of things too. A few leases of mine have come up trumps.'

The mention of making a 'good go' of things sparked Sawkins' interest even further, and he leant forward with his elbows resting on his knees as Harwood continued.

'Just been out west to have a look, but there wasn't much doing. I thought we might try something a bit closer to home. Do you know of Penrith?'

'Yes, yes, I know of it. Haven't heard much about there being any gold out there though.'

'That's just what the successful ones want you to think,' Harwood said with a wink. 'After all, what smart miner is going to go around telling everyone where he struck it rich?'

The response seemed to placate Sawkins, who listened intently as Harwood outlined the proposed expedition and its costs. 'So, it would be ten pounds on your behalf,' Harwood said eventually. 'Is that acceptable?'

Sawkins paused for a moment, rubbing his chin with his thumb and forefinger as he weighed up the proposal. 'Yes, ten pounds should be fine,' he said.

'Let me ask you,' Harwood said, 'why do you want to go on this trip?'

'Well, I do alright, but I'd like to get that big find so I can set myself up for good.'

'That's just like most fellas, but most blokes don't have me on their side,' Harwood said with a broad smile.

'When do you plan on departing?' Sawkins asked with increasing delight.

'Well, as soon as possible, unless you have any reason to delay things further.'

'No, no, I can go whenever you please.'

'How about tomorrow then?'

Sawkins looked a little surprised, yet pleased, at Harwood's haste. Seeing a slight reticence in his new-found partner's countenance, Harwood quickly moved to assuage any doubts. 'You're right about not hearing about Penrith. It's because the big strikes are almost at an end, and only the truly astute miner knows where to find them. I want to make haste so that we don't miss out while the going is still good.'

'It all sounds fine to me,' said Sawkins. 'Meet me at my home in Summer Hill tomorrow morning and we will head out from there. Here's the address.' Reaching inside his coat pocket, Sawkins retrieved a piece of paper, which he handed over before rising, shaking Harwood's hand, and departing.

The next morning, Harwood left Mrs Gilham's hotel, bags in hand, and headed out to Summer Hill. After paying for a buggy, he sat back as the streets of Sydney passed by; contemplating all the ways he could kill this new victim. The way he had set Burgess up was beautiful, poetry, but it had all been over too quickly. Maybe he would toy with Sawkins a little, make him beg for his life before he took it from him.

The buggy continued on as Harwood mulled over all the ways he could make the joy of murder last, but as the buggy pulled into Summer Hill he resolved that merely disposing of this man was good enough; clean and quick was the way to go. It was time to get this one over with, and then disappear to find a new killing ground.

He began walking the streets of Summer Hill, piece of paper in hand as he looked up and down, stopping and turning one way before turning back in the other direction.

'Excuse me, sir, can I help you?' a passer-by asked when he noticed Harwood's strange behaviour.

'Yes,' Harwood said as he held out the piece of paper. 'I'm looking for this address.'

The passer-by examined it carefully. 'This is very nearby. You need to follow this street down for a few blocks and then take a right. You should find it easily enough.'

Harwood nodded in appreciation and set off at a brisk walk in the instructed direction. He found Sawkins' house, and knocked with an inappropriate loudness. The door opened, and he was greeted by a woman whom he took to be the maid.

'Yes,' she said abruptly, her annoyance plain. 'Can I help you?'

'Yes, ma'am,' Harwood said politely as he doffed his hat. 'I'm here to see Mr Sawkins. We're going on an expedition together.'

'Hmm, yes, my husband told me about that. Come on in, won't you?'

Deep down, Harwood was smarting that Sawkins had a wife, but he bottled up his displeasure and forced himself to smile. Maybe he'd still get to kill, but after this one he'd just have to disappear sooner than expected. Mrs Sawkins looked at him with doubtful eyes, and the sweep of her hand inviting him inside did nothing to diminish her obvious discontentment.

'Frank,' Sawkins said as he emerged from one of the back rooms. 'Glad to see you made it. Come, let's have some tea before we leave.'

Harwood followed the couple as they made their way out to the rear of the house and into the sitting room. Whilst Mrs Sawkins made the tea, he sat talking with Sawkins about what they could expect. 'We shouldn't be gone for long; a week or so at the most. I know some places where we're sure to find gold. All we can hope for is that we find some big nuggets, but we will definitely come back with a few thousand pounds' worth.'

From the kitchen, unseen by Harwood, Mrs Sawkins was watching him intently, studying his every move as she went about making the tea. When she entered the sitting room, she placed the tea set down and poured cups for her husband and his guest before pouring one for herself and then sitting down so that she was facing Harwood.

'So, Mr Harwood, what qualifications do you have in this field?' she asked.

'I'm sorry, madam?'

'I asked what qualifications you have. You are talking about large amounts of money here, so I assume you are highly qualified?'

Without even the slightest flinch or hesitation, Harwood delved into one of his bags and retrieved one of the stolen miner's certificates, which he handed to her. After taking it from him, she read it carefully.

'You see,' he said, 'I have studied at the finest schools.'

'Hmm,' she said as she handed the certificate back. 'Dear husband, may I speak with you in the next room, please?'

Sawkins looked slightly perplexed, but agreed. 'Excuse me for one second, Frank, I shall be right back.'

Leaving Harwood to peruse the various ornaments, decorations and pictures in the sitting room, Sawkins and his wife moved into their bedroom.

'I don't like that man!' she said resolutely. 'There is something about him that is just not sitting right.'

'Aw, he's alright; just another guy trying to make a go of things.'

'No, there's something to him. Something dark. I don't want you going anywhere with him.'

'It's only for a short time. What could possibly go wrong? And, besides, for a week's work, we could be set for life.'

'I don't care about money. I care about having you. I forbid you to go.'

For his time, Sawkins was an enlightened man when it came to his relationship with his wife. Where others' wives were seen and not heard, this man respected his wife's judgement and intuition. He returned to the sitting room to deliver the news. 'I'm sorry, Mr Harwood, I think I have rushed into this thing a little too hastily. My wife has reminded me that we have several very important business matters that require our attention over the next few weeks and months. I may be able to join you on a later expedition, but I cannot go on this one. I wish you the best of luck, sir.'

Harwood rose and shook Sawkins' hand. 'I understand,' he said as he pondered killing both of them there and then, but decided against it. The setting was too public, and there was too much potential for witnesses. 'You have to do what you have to do. I'll send word of my successes and, as you say, maybe you can join me on another expedition. Shame you're going to miss out though.' With that, he said his goodbyes, giving several sly glances in Mrs Sawkins' direction as he left.

Harwood made his way back to Mrs Gilham's hotel, a scowl on his face as he walked inside.

'Mr Harwood, did you forget something?' Mrs Gilham asked, surprised to see him back again so soon.

'No,' he said gruffly. 'I didn't realise that my business partner had a wife, and when I got to his house, I discovered that she'd forbidden him from going with me.'

'What a shame,' said Mrs Gilham sincerely. 'But after all, there is no arguing with a woman when she makes her mind up. Never mind, I'm sure you will find someone else. You are lucky today in one way; I haven't given your room to anyone else.'

'Thank you, Mrs Gilham. You're a lovely woman.' With that, Harwood headed back upstairs to pen yet another ad.

Wanted. Mining partner to go equal shares on expedition to Grafton area. Apply Gilham's Hotel, Pitt Street.

He then headed to the newspaper offices, intent on lodging his ad in time for it to be published in the next morning's paper.

The respondents started arriving early the next day, but none proved suitable, and as the days passed and his frustration and annoyance intensified, the whispering voice becoming louder and louder, begging, urging him to kill. This time, however, he was particularly careful to screen his potential partners with much more vigour, and so many interviews were over before they'd even begun, as his first questions were always about the presence of relatives, wives, or any other people who were close to them. If a candidate said that they had a wife or brother or sister, he immediately terminated the interview and waited for the next one.

After several days, during which no suitable victims appeared, he packed his bags and left Mrs Gilham's hotel. He was bound for the Grafton goldfields, where he would respond to someone else's ad this time, looking to find another man to murder.

Into the Mountains

7 October 1896

The journey to Grafton, and several other subsequent trips and ventures, came to nothing, and Frank Harwood's desperation to find a new 'mate' increased with every passing day. He eventually returned to Sydney, and to Mrs Gilham's hotel, and as he sat in the bar one afternoon, drinking whisky while he contemplated his next move, he noticed an attractive young lady come to the bar and ask for a sherry. The bartender poured her drink, and the young lady daintily sat herself down and carefully sipped away.

Noticing Harwood sitting alone and looking despondent, she decided to strike up a conversation. 'Hello, sir,' she said. 'Are you feeling okay?'

Harwood looked at her. She looked strangely familiar, but seeing a pretty young girl in front of him, he had little hesitation in picking up his bottle and glass and moving to the seat beside hers.

'Yes, miss, I am fine. I believe I have met you before, perhaps at a social occasion?'

'Oh, yes, I remember you. You were that rather flashy and flamboyant chap I met at that party. So what are you doing with yourself these days?'

'I'm a miner, and I want to go prospecting, but I have been unable to find a suitable partner to accompany me.'

'A prospector! Goodness, have you had much success?'

'Plenty,' he responded with zeal as the whisky began to kick in. 'I have many leases that make me a lot of money. The only problem is finding the right person to help me. I'll tell you what, when I find the right man, he stands to make a lot of money.' Through his hazy eyes, Harwood gleaned that the young lady seemed deep in thought. Eventually, she spoke.

'You know something, sir? I believe I may have someone for you.'

Harwood's interest was sparked and he leant in closer.

'Yes,' she continued. 'My brother. He has just come up from Melbourne. He's waiting for a new job to commence, but I think he would jump at the chance to make some quick money before he starts.'

'When would I be able to meet with him?' Harwood asked. His bloodlust was getting the better of him, and he made the snap decision to disregard his own selection criteria. The time had come to kill. He would do the man in and be long gone before this young lady discovered her brother's fate. He was, however, careful to temper his excitement.

'Right away, if you wish,' she said with a chuckle. 'I just need to go and get him.'

'Would you mind terribly? You see, I have my leases, but some of them run out soon, and I'm eager to get at them.'

'Certainly, wait here and I shall return shortly.'

The young lady excused herself, leaving Harwood sitting at the bar. He poured himself another whisky and drank it through a broad smile. With thoughts and possibilities swirling through his head, he didn't notice when she returned with a strapping young gentleman at her side.

'Sir,' she said after a delicate cough, 'this is my brother I was telling you about.'

Harwood looked up at the young man, who was six feet tall with curly, sandy coloured hair.

'Frank Harwood,' he said, extending a hand.

'Michael Conroy,' said the young man, as he shook Harwood's hand. 'My sister tells me you are a prospector and that you need someone to join you.'

'Yes, that's correct,' Harwood said. 'Won't you join me for a drink?'

Calling out to the bartender for another glass, Harwood moved to the next seat to allow the siblings to sit together. When the bartender placed the glass in front of Harwood, he filled it and passed it to Conroy. 'And whatever the lady is having,' he added.

'Another sherry, thank you,' she said.

'So, my sister told me that you've had some successes and this might be a good opportunity to make some quick money.'

'I own several leases but, to give you an example, I have a mine up in Germanton that I was offered three thousand pounds for but I refused to sell, because I know it will soon be worth five thousand. So, there you have it. My leases are, potentially, worth double what I have paid for them and, as partners, we would go halves in whatever profit we make. What experience do you have?'

'A little. I have been out to the Victorian goldfields a few times.'

Harwood looked Conroy up and down, noting the young man's athletic build. 'Well, you look like a fit young lad. I'm sure whatever inexperience you have will be more than made up for by your physical abilities.'

The talk of such large sums of money and the compliment had made Conroy interested. 'So, where are you thinking of going for this expedition?'

Harwood reached into his bag and retrieved a map, which he unfurled and laid out on the bar. Conroy leant down to examine it. 'Albury?'

'Yes, the river down there means there are lots of gold deposits. Perhaps you could take this map with you and decide on some places you think may be worthwhile?'

'Me?' Conroy questioned. 'But you're the expert.'

'Yes, I know, but it will give me an idea as to whether you have the right kind of mind for this sort of thing. I know where we should be looking, but I want to know if you do.'

Conroy shrugged, rolled the map back up and placed it inside his jacket pocket.

'Just bring it back tomorrow and we'll go from there.'

The Conroys finished their drinks before saying a polite goodbye and departing, leaving Harwood to contemplate what had just transpired as he poured himself yet another whisky. They seemed well-to-do, and he sensed that he could make some good money out of this one, but it still bothered him that his chosen victim had a sister. No, he'd made up his mind. He would leave Sydney immediately afterwards. She could look, but she'd never find him. It had been months since he'd killed, and the voice inside him was insisting on murder.

After finishing the remainder of the bottle, he paid his bill and staggered upstairs. The next day, he woke late in the morning and, even though his head was groggy, he remembered what he had asked Conroy to do. After quickly dressing, he rushed downstairs and asked Mrs Gilham if he'd had any visitors.

'Yes,' she said. 'There was one young man who came here earlier this morning. He left this for you.'

Reaching behind her, she retrieved the map and handed it to Harwood, who hungrily snatched it up. Examining the map, he soon realised that Conroy had not made any markings, instead attaching a note which read:

Sorry, Mr Harwood, I will be unable to go with you; prevented by other business.

Having decided that this was his man, Harwood was furious that his lust for murder would not be assuaged, and headed back upstairs to think about writing yet another ad; one that would, this time, hopefully, be the honey to catch the fly. He was about halfway towards the stairwell when he stopped. It had come to the point where too many people knew he was here, and who he was. It would look odd if he placed yet another ad asking people to come to this hotel. It was time to move on, and time for another change of name.

He turned and addressed Mrs Gilham. 'Thank you for all your hospitality, ma'am, but I think I will be checking out tomorrow. Can you have my bill ready for me?'

'Certainly, sir. By the way, my daughter said to thank you for giving her a photo of yourself.'

'She is a good looking young woman, ma'am. I was glad to do it,' said Harwood, before turning and heading for the stairwell once more.

Mrs Gilham nodded her head as she watched him climb the stairs, glad that this man would soon be away from her establishment and, more particularly, away from her daughter.

After checking out the next day, Harwood walked to Thompson's Railway Dining Rooms, where the clerk greeted him politely. 'Hello, sir, will you be checking in with us today?'

'Yes, if you have rooms,' said Harwood.

'Of course, sir, we have plenty of rooms. Your name?'

'Clare. Frank Clare.'

'Excellent, sir, if you could sign here please.'

Harwood signed the register as Frank Clare, using a false name to avoid any further suspicion. He took his key and headed upstairs to find his room, where he threw his bags down and then sat and penned yet another advertisement. Keeping it simple, he wrote:

Wanted: A mate for prospecting trip on equal shares. Apply 822 George Street.

As he placed the note into an envelope, he resolved to himself that, no matter what, one of the men who answered this ad was going to be the one. The urges were getting stronger and stronger; they had to be satisfied. After placing the envelope into the desk drawer, he set out to find a nearby pub or tavern.

The next morning, he woke early so that he would make it to *The Sydney Morning Herald* offices before the morning deadline. Stepping out into George Street, he set out at a brisk walk, almost running, oblivious to the world around him until suddenly he collided with a passer-by. 'Excuse me, sir,' he said without looking up.

'Frank?'

Hearing his name, Harwood looked up to see the broad-shouldered frame of Michael Conroy. 'Ah, Mr Conroy, how good to see you.'

'So, are you still going to Albury to do some mining?'

'No, after I got your message I sold my lease. Regrettably, you missed your share of the big profit I made.'

'Well, I was otherwise occupied, more's the bad luck for me.'

'Yes, it is your bad luck. You see, I always treat a man as he ought to be treated.'

'Fair enough. Thank you then, I suppose. Good luck with your next venture, sir.'

'Thank you, and good luck to you.'

Watching through irate eyes as an opportunity lost walked off down the street, Harwood's desire to find a victim reached a crescendo, and he hurried as quickly as his legs would take him to the newspaper offices, placed the ad, and then returned to the Railway Dining Rooms to wait.

It was not long after the release of the afternoon edition when potential prospecting mates began to appear. The interviews followed the same routine as usual, and the first few were dismissed. About mid-afternoon, however, three young men entered and proceeded to the counter. Mr Thompson, the owner, greeted them accordingly.

'Good afternoon, gentlemen, are you seeking rooms?'

'No, sir,' the lead man said. 'We are looking for the man who placed an ad for a prospecting mate.'

Upon hearing this, Harwood leapt up from his seat and rushed to the counter.

'These gentlemen are with me, Mr Thompson.'

'Ah, excellent, sir.'

Thinking nothing more of the encounter, Thompson returned to his work as Harwood accompanied the men to a nearby table.

'The name's Frank Harwood,' Harwood said as he sat down, taking a quick glance in Thompson's direction to make sure Thompson hadn't heard him use this alias. 'Would you men like something to drink?' Harwood asked politely as he waited for them to seat themselves.

'No, we're fine,' one man said.

'C'mon, boys! There's always time for a whisky!'

Harwood waved one hand in the air, and the bartender brought a bottle of whisky and four glasses to the table. Harwood poured liberally and handed them each a glass before raising his and saying, 'Cheers!'

The other three men raised their glasses in response and then took a sip, the youngest-looking of them coughing as the warm liquid made its way down to his stomach.

'Ah, lad, it seems like you can't handle your alcohol!' Harwood laughed. 'We'll have to fix that!'

'I'm…Arthur…Preston,' the young man said through his splutters. 'And these are my associates Mr Fielding and Mr Fenton,' he added, pointing to the other two men.

'Pleasure,' Harwood said as he took each man's hand in turn and refilled their glasses.

'So, Mr Harwood, Arthur tells us you're looking for someone to go on a prospecting trip?' Fielding said.

'Yes, are all three of you planning on coming with me?'

'No, no,' said Fielding. 'Arthur is the one that wants to go. We're just looking out for him so we have come along for support and to see what you're all about.'

'Well, I have had so much success and I'd like to keep that going. I just sold a share in a mine for two thousand pounds, but the place I want to go to is a bit rough, so I need someone to help me out.'

'It sounds quite dangerous,' Fielding said with concern.

'Oh, no! Not at all! I know the country well! It's just a bit hard travelling around on horseback all the time, because the country is steep and rocky, but you're alright so long as you travel light and on foot.'

'So, what are your qualifications for this type of thing?' Fenton asked.

Harwood immediately produced the stolen certificates, which both Fielding and Fenton examined closely. In between his jovial comments and boasting, Harwood paid close attention to each man's reactions, knowing that if Preston's friends were not satisfied his next potential victim would not consent to go with him.

'I'm certain this will be a big trip,' he boasted. 'I bought that last mine for three thousand pounds and sold it for five thousand. I've got these new techniques, you see; makes the whole digging and sluicing process that much easier. I'm also thinking about getting this new machine I have heard about which means a man can get through ten times as much work. Could mean ten times the profit!' The word 'profit' had barely left his lips before Harwood snuck a sideways glance at Preston to gauge his reaction. He needn't have bothered.

'Excellent!' Preston said. 'My father in Brisbane sends me an allowance and I have put some of that aside so I will, of course, go half shares in the costs; that would only seem proper. I must also tell you that I think I should be of great assistance to you, as I'm currently studying geology at Sydney University.'

'Very good, that will be a great help and, yes, these things are always half shares of costs; half shares of the profits too, don't forget,' Harwood was careful to add. He took several sly glances at Fielding and Fenton and, seeing that they were still not entirely convinced, said, 'I have had a lot of men applying to go on this trip on those terms, but I like you, Preston, and if you say you will go, you can come with me on Monday.'

'Monday it is then! We are staying at Mrs Clara Williams' boarding rooms in Redfern. We shall see you at Redfern station early!' Preston said eagerly as he rose and enthusiastically shook Harwood's hand before all three men departed.

'Looks like you have a new companion,' Mr Thompson said, having overheard the more boisterous parts of the conversation.

'Yes,' Harwood said. 'We shall be leaving on Monday.'

'Where to first?'

'We will make camp in the Blue Mountains and then head out west, I should imagine.'

'Very good! I need to make a trip out that way soon myself, actually. I have a friend who I haven't seen in quite a while. I will prepare your bill for Monday morning.'

Harwood started up the stairs, then stopped, turned and made his way back to the table to retrieve what remained of the whisky. Grasping the bottle by the neck, he took a swig before heading upstairs.

Monday morning eventually arrived and Harwood set off. He soon reached Redfern station, and only had to wait for a few minutes before the three men arrived carrying Preston's bags.

'Gentlemen!' he said, greeting them eagerly. 'Good to see you! Arthur, shall we be on our way then?' Picking up his bags, Harwood headed to the platform, followed by the others, telling several stories about places out west where he'd struck it big, so that by the time they reached the second-class carriage of *The Western Mail*, Preston was in no doubt as to the fact that he would soon be a very rich man.

The men continued to converse as they stood alongside the train and waited for the 'all aboard' call.

'Where shall we be heading first?' Preston asked.

'We will start in the Blue Mountains and then we will make our way out west.'

'Outstanding!' Preston said eagerly. 'Perhaps we can do some game hunting. I should have brought my shotgun with me.'

Harwood laughed and scoffed. 'Game hunting in the Blue Mountains! I don't think so!'

'Mr Harwood,' Fielding interjected, 'aside from game hunting, I imagine prospecting can be a dangerous business, especially if you are carrying around the amounts of money you are expecting, therefore it may be a good idea for Arthur to bring his shotgun. I imagine it should come in rather handy.'

'Never mind,' Harwood said as he retrieved his rifle from his bag and held it up. 'I'm a pretty good shot.'

Soon enough, the conductor was walking the length of the platform telling the passengers it was time to board. Preston said his farewells before grabbing his bags and boarding the train. They settled themselves in their assigned seats, the train gave a quick toot, and they slowly pulled out from the platform. Frank Harwood rose from his seat and leant out the window, shouting out to the two men who remained standing on the platform. 'We are going a long way out, and it might be six weeks before you hear from us.'

Preston too leant out and gave them a final wave before settling in to quiz Harwood on the ins and outs of the trip and prospecting in general. Harwood continued to give whatever answers came to mind. An hour or so later, the train reached the base of the Blue Mountains and pulled into Emu Plains station.

'This is us,' Harwood said as he rose from his chair and patted Preston on the back. Preston jumped up from his seat, grabbed his gear, and was off the train before Harwood.

The two men were walking along the platform towards the mountains when suddenly a voice called out, 'Frank!'

He was surprised to see Elias Thompson leaning out of a carriage window.

'What are you doing all the way out here, Mr Thompson?' Harwood said as he and Preston moved back towards the train.

'Just on my way up the mountains to visit the friend I was telling you about the other day. Is this your destination?'

'Yes, we'll make for the outskirts of town and camp for the night,' Harwood said.

'Well, good luck to you both,' Thompson said as he leant down from the window and shook both of their hands. The train pulled out of the station to make its slow ascent into the mountains, and Thompson watched the two men walking along the platform and out of the station towards the Great Dividing Range. The train eventually disappeared from view, and Harwood and Preston walked for a good half hour before Harwood suggested they take a break at the foot of the mountains.

'All the roads round here were built by the convicts, you know,' he said as they sat on a large stone. 'Irish ones. One goes all the way out to Bathurst. That's the one we'll take.'

Preston nodded as he sipped from his canteen.

'C'mon,' Harwood said. 'We've got a long way to go, we'd best get to it.'

The two men began the almost vertical ascent up the Bathurst Road, following its various twists and bends. After walking for most of the day, they made their camp beside a small creek, and then continued on the next day, eventually coming to the small mountain town of Linden. Linden, like most towns along the newly built railway line, was nothing more than a few homes and the yellow sandstone stationmaster's residence. Harwood and Preston had already been noticed by and conversed with many locals as they passed through Glenbrook, Springwood and Faulconbridge, and the fact that they were searching for gold had shot through the towns like the wildfires that intermittently ravaged the surrounding landscape. When the two men arrived at Linden, the locals were, therefore, already very familiar with who they were.

Harwood chose a small clearing just outside town to make camp. The following day, the morning sun was just starting to spill through the valleys on either side of the ridge as numerous rosellas darted in and out of the undergrowth and white cockatoos screeched as they emerged from their roosts in the hollows of the towering white ghost gums. Harwood started a fire, placed the billy on it and waited for it to boil, the two men sitting and smoking in the meantime. Out on the road, the first of the locals was already on his way to work.

'You're looking for gold, are you?' he said as he sidled up to the camp.

Harwood nodded, but made no eye contact.

The man laughed heartily. 'You're the first man I've ever heard of that's come along here looking for gold. It's a funny place to look for gold.'

Murmuring under his breath, Harwood simply replied, 'I don't know. I have found traces in the grass.'

Certain in his comrade's knowledge on the subject, and not wanting his companion to come under question, Preston fervently added, 'Oh, yes! We found traces in the grass alright!'

Whilst the stranger's gaze was momentarily fixed on Preston, Harwood reached for his rifle, resting it by his side and within easy reach. As Preston finished speaking, the stranger turned back to Harwood.

'Why don't you go out to Coolgardie?'

Without lifting his head, Harwood merely said, 'Oh, it's played out.'

The passer-by shrugged and continued on his way. The two men spent the day prospecting around the camp and going as close to the steep gullies as they dared. In mid-afternoon, they returned to the camp, and were sitting in the exact same positions as they had been in the morning when the stranger appeared once more. Harwood watched him carefully out of the corner of his eye before looking over at Preston, whose gaze was firmly fixed on the stranger. Harwood slyly reached for his rifle, but his movements did not go unnoticed, and as he came up to them, the stranger said, 'You looking for some shooting, mate?'

Harwood didn't respond but, realising that the stranger was not going to leave, poked and prodded the fire before he finally said, 'Yeah, if there's any good shooting around to be had.'

'Come on then, I'll show you around.'

Grabbing his rifle, Harwood nodded to Preston and the two men followed the stranger back along the Bathurst Road, through the centre of town and further on into some bush on the other side of the railway tracks. Weaving his way along several small, narrow tracks, he eventually stopped on a large, grey-coloured sandstone rock. Harwood and Preston both inched their way towards the edge of the precipice and peered down into the deepest valleys they had yet seen.

'You see up there and there,' the stranger said as he pointed at two ridgelines. 'If you can make your way up, there's some good roo and wallaby shooting. If you're lucky, you might even get a wild boar or two.'

Looking at the two men still staring down into the valley, he continued. 'Tell you what, though, you want to be careful. If you drop anything in there, you'll never find it again.'

The two prospectors moved back from the edge and followed the stranger, who had started to make his way back towards town. When they reached the camp again, he said his farewells.

'Thanks for that,' Harwood said as the stranger set off home.

'Well, what do you think, Frank?' Preston said as he sat down and lit a smoke.

'I think perhaps I would like to do some shooting. I think we should make camp further up the ridge. We'll do some prospecting tonight, and then we'll go out shooting first thing in the morning.'

Preston smiled broadly, not needing to be asked twice before packing together their belongings. In a few minutes they were ready to go, the fire extinguished and their packs on their backs as they headed out along the road. They walked for a couple of miles as Harwood looked from side to side, scrutinising the bush for a suitable campsite and place to shoot. When he found what he was looking for, he headed into the scrub. Finding a small trail leading down into the gully, he said, 'This looks good.'

Preston followed eagerly, and before long they came to a cliff top. Harwood stopped and examined their surrounds. Seeing that the track led down to the left of the sandstone, he said, 'Down here seems good, there may even be a cave.'

Slowly edging their way down, they carefully propped themselves up against the rock wall and held on to tree trunks and branches whenever the descent became too steep. Preston slipped several times, threatening to send them both hurtling down the mountainside. After navigating the trail successfully, they found that it was as Harwood had said it would be; there was a large cave beneath the cliff top.

'This is the spot,' he said as they put their gear down. 'We don't even need to set our tents up.'

Moving to the cave's edge, he looked out at the crimson late-afternoon sky.

'We'd better start prospecting before we run out of light. This is a great spot. I reckon we just might have ourselves our first good strike here. Grab yourself a shovel and start digging.'

The last of Harwood's words had barely left his lips before Preston retrieved a shovel and started digging furiously. Before long, he was kneeling beside a two-feet-deep and five-feet-long hole.

Harwood felt the rush of adrenaline surging through him as he raised his rifle. He slowed his breathing and stretched his hands before resting his index finger a few millimetres from the trigger. Slowly, steadily, he pulled.

The gunshot echoed throughout the valley, sending the cockatoos screeching and cawing as they climbed into the sky. Preston's skull shattered as the bullet tore through it. His body slumped forward, away from the grave, fragments of bone from his skull scattering in the sandy soil. Reaching into his bag, Harwood retrieved a red-and-white-striped towel. Tying one end into a makeshift noose, he knelt down beside Preston's lifeless body and secured it around the dead man's neck. Grabbing hold of the other end of the towel, he wrenched it back until it constricted. Pulling steadily, he managed to turn the body around a full one hundred and eighty degrees. With Preston's head now at the edge of the grave, he propped his feet against the grave wall, and with one final pull, he had Preston's body in the grave. After unknotting the towel, Harwood stood and examined his handiwork. His haste to kill meant that he hadn't waited long enough for Preston to dig the grave to a sufficient length, and his feet were protruding from one end. Squatting, Harwood grabbed hold of Preston's body and flipped him onto his side. Harwood then lowered himself onto the ground on one side of the grave to check the level of the body. Leaning down, he manoeuvred Preston's body a little more until not an inch of him remained beyond the grave's confines. Satisfied, he placed the towel over the body before shovelling the soil back in. When the hole was filled, he collected handfuls of leaves and sticks and scattered them about in an attempt to conceal the grave. His work done, he began rummaging through Preston's possessions. Finding little of value he kept a shirt and a pair of leggings before tossing the rest into the ravine. He then gathered some kindling and several logs, lit a small fire and set about making himself some supper. Afterwards, as he sat smoking, he leant back against the cave wall and listened for the voice inside, but it was quiet; for now.

5

Just One More

23 October 1896

The next morning, he gathered his gear and started the slow ascent back towards the ridge top. Emerging from the bush, he began to look around and, driven by his murderous desires, soon realised he hadn't paid any attention to the route he had taken the previous evening. As he paced up and down the road trying to find his bearings, the increasing heat of the day caused him to sweat profusely. Sitting down on the side of the road, he removed his boots and began to wring the moisture from his socks. Preoccupied with his task, he failed to see a man approaching.

'Certainly is hot weather, isn't it?' the man said as he stopped in front of Harwood.

Keeping his head down, Harwood momentarily considered reaching for his rifle. *No, he's obviously a local; they'll notice him missing,* he thought to himself. Instead, he put on a jovial smile as he looked up and greeted the man.

'You would certainly say it was hot if you had been down where I have been. I've been down there prospecting for gold,' he said, gesturing towards the bush.

The man let out a hearty laugh that echoed through the rolling green valleys.

'Gold? You would have had a better chance if you were prospecting for coal!'

'Yeah, maybe you're right. I'm on my way back to Sydney. Say, you don't happen to know the way to Linden station, do you?'

'Yeah, mate of course. It's about a mile and a half down that way.'

'Cheers, mate,' Harwood said as he rummaged around in his bag and retrieved a small packet of tea and one of sugar. 'Here take these as a present.'

'Thanks, mate. You seem like a good bloke. William Willis is my name,' the man said as he extended his hand.

'Frank Harwood.'

'Come on then, I think there is a train to Sydney soon. Let's see if we can get you there in time to catch it.'

The two men set off down the road, exchanging small pieces of information about themselves, Harwood about his prospecting and Willis about his job as a carpenter. Before long they came to Linden, where Willis pointed toward the railway station. 'Righto, mate, I'd better be off. Best of luck to you,' he said.

'Thanks,' Harwood replied, 'but I don't need luck. I'm one of the luckiest men in the world.'

Willis smiled and headed off down the road. Harwood made his way to the railway station and found a seat on the platform, although he only sat there for a few moments. More and more locals began to arrive, each one taking an extended look as they passed him, causing him to shift uncomfortably in his seat before quickly deciding that the time had come to move on. He rose and walked to the station office, where he stuck his head inside to enquire as to the next station down the line.

'Faulconbridge,' came the response. 'Just follow the road down and you can't miss it.'

Hurriedly, Harwood set off. Wanting to avoid any further attention he kept himself as inconspicuous as possible by keeping to the small trails in the bush beside the main road. As he trampled through the shrubbery he caught himself on several branches and failed to notice Arthur Preston's shirt being ripped from the side of his bag and into the undergrowth.

After about half an hour or so, Faulconbridge station appeared in his sights. Feeling far more comfortable, and anonymous, he made his way onto the platform and sat down. Various locals came and went along the adjacent road, but paid little attention to the lone traveller. Eventually, though, one man stopped. 'Frank,' he called.

Looking up, Harwood was somewhat relieved to see William Willis, and returned a furtive wave, whereupon Willis changed course and made his way up the stairs and onto the platform. 'Why didn't you wait at Linden?' Willis asked.

'When I got to the station I discovered that the train wasn't going to be coming for some time, so I decided to stretch my legs a bit and get on down here.'

'Fair enough,' Willis said as he checked the board. 'The Sydney train shouldn't be too far away now, but we'll have to signal for her, as she doesn't normally stop here.'

Sitting down beside Harwood, Willis couldn't help but notice the previously unseen rifle. 'Been doing some shooting?' he asked casually.

'Yeah, went looking for some pigs but didn't have much luck.'

There was no time for any more pleasantries, as the chuffing of the train could now be heard in the distance. 'Righto, mate, this is you then,' Willis said as he stood and extended his arm to signal the train.

Placing his rifle back into his bag and slinging it over his shoulder, Harwood stood and positioned himself beside Willis. The train slowed and came to a stop. Harwood jumped on board and waved goodbye to Willis, who stood on the platform until the train was out of sight. Comforted by the security of the carriage, Harwood lay back and closed his eyes, drifting into a comfortable sleep that was only interrupted when the train pulled into Sydney.

Harwood hopped down from the train and made his way along the platform and out into the streets of Sydney. He quickly checked into a nearby hotel, deposited his belongings in his room, and then made his way down to the bar for the customary bottle of whisky.

The following morning, he was up at a reasonable hour, gathered up his gear and started to walk back towards the Railway Dining Rooms. When he reached his destination, he found Elias Thompson in his usual position behind the counter.

'Mr Harwood! Back so soon? What on earth happened?'

'Oh, the young fellow got knocked up, so I came back to look for another mate.'

'Dear me, what a shame. I take it you want a room. I think I have your old room available if you wish to have it.'

'Thank you, Mr Thompson. That would be lovely.'

24 October 1896

Over the next few days, as he sat at the bar and in the dining rooms, Harwood sensed that more and more people were talking about him and pointing in his direction. Somehow, he felt that he knew some of them, but he couldn't put names to faces. One evening, as he sat hunched over his whisky bottle, he thought, *I need to kill one more. I need something more substantial,* as he nervously shifted his head from side to side and glared at the other patrons, certain now that they were all staring at him. Regardless of whether they were actually taking any notice of him or whether it was simply a murderer's paranoia, he quickly drained his glass, pushed his seat back and hurried up to his room to pack. After rushing back downstairs and paying his bill to one of Mr Thompson's underlings, he was quickly out the door in search of new digs.

He threaded his way through the city, strangely drawn back to Pitt Street, where he found the Metropolitan Hotel. Stepping through the door, he was greeted by a plump, middle-aged lady dressed in a black dress and white apron.

'Good evening, sir, I am Mrs O'Connell. How can I help you?' she said.

'I'd like a room, please.'

'Certainly, sir. I will get you a key if you would just sign your name in the register.'

Handing him the register, she turned to retrieve a room key whilst Harwood took several glances around before signing himself in as 'Frank Butler.'

Once he had his key, he headed upstairs to pen yet another ad, and the next morning, he was back in the offices of *The Sydney Morning Herald.*

Metallurgist wants sociable young man, mate, prospecting Western district. Equal shares. Experience unnecessary. Butler. Metropolitan Hotel, 401 Pitt Street.

'Frank Butler', *The Nepean Times*, 1896.

6

A Change of Fortune

22 August 1896

Captain Lee Mellington Weller was in his late thirties, with thick, dark curly hair and an equally thick and curly beard. He stood on the starboard deck breathing the ocean air as he examined the rugged bushland and sandstone cliffs on either side of Sydney Heads. The salty air calmed his soul, but it was still awash with sadness. His wife and he had planned to come to Australia to start a new life but now she was dead and his world seemed one of confusion and uncertainty. He'd had his own command. He'd come to Australia before and it all seemed so perfect, so much so he'd decided to move here with his wife but she'd fallen ill on the ship and died not long after they'd reached Newcastle. Now, he'd come back down to Sydney to try to figure out what to do with his life now she was gone. *How had it all gone so wrong?* he thought to himself. *Maybe this town will change my fortunes.*

His ship passed Fort Denison and he gained his first glimpses of the centre of Sydney. His grip tightened on the railing, several small tears rolling down his cheeks as the ship rounded Bennelong Point and entered Circular Quay. He bowed his head and moved inside to collect his seachest. Returning to the deck, he began to scan the wharf looking for the friend he was to meet, and when he eventually made out his face, he gave Robert Luckham a brisk wave.

The ship inched its way towards the dock, and when it finally came to a halt the gangway was lowered. Numerous passengers made their way off the ship in single file, but Weller waited for the crowd to clear before getting one of the seamen to help him with the seachest containing his most treasured memories. He and the seaman proceeded down the gangway and placed the heavy chest on the wharf just as Luckham arrived to meet them.

'How are you, my friend?' he asked as he embraced Weller.

'It's been a rough few months, but only one way to go now,' Weller replied.

'I'm glad to have you back. Here, let me help you with your luggage,' Luckham said as he helped his friend to pick up his seachest. They carried it to an adjacent wharf, where they boarded the Manly ferry, arriving in the leafy beachside suburb a short time later.

After walking a short distance along the promenade, they came to Luckham's home, where he showed Weller to his room. 'I imagine you must be quite tired, so I shall let you sleep, and when you feel ready, we can take some supper,' Luckham said.

'I'm fine, Robert! I have slept much of the way,' Weller said as he stowed his chest under the bed and made his way back to the hallway. 'What I do need is a drink!'

'Excellent! Off to the pub then!'

Weller was quickly out the door and set off at speed, Luckham having difficulty keeping pace. 'Slow down, Lee! What's the rush?' he said.

'Just stretching my sea legs, Bob, just stretching my sea legs.'

Before long, they reached the centre of Manly and entered a nearby tavern.

'Same poison, Lee?'

'Yep, whisky.'

Luckham indicated a table adjacent to the front window, which looked out onto the beachfront. Weller sat down while Luckham went to the bar. He soon returned, and poured two glasses before he said, 'Great to see you again, Lee. Here's to new beginnings. Cheers!'

The two men raised their glasses. Luckham sipped, but Weller drained his glass and immediately poured another. The second glass disappeared even quicker than the first. A third glass lasted slightly longer, but before long nearly half the bottle was gone.

Watching on with a mixture of amazement and concern, Luckham felt compelled to comment. 'Lee, take it easy! This is not like you at all!'

'Yes, yes, I suppose you're right. Sorry, it's been a long few months and a difficult voyage,' Weller responded, sipping his fourth glass now.

'Yes, of course,' Luckham said sympathetically. 'What do you plan to do now?'

'I'm not sure. I've had some time to think about it, but you know, with everything that has happened, nothing seems to fit; nothing seems right.'

'I understand, Lee,' Luckham said with an affirming nod. 'But make sure you keep yourself busy. Too much time to think will only destroy you.'

Weller reached into his pocket and retrieved a brooch, which he stared at as he rubbed it between his fingers.

'I'm sorry for your loss, Lee. I'm sorry that your wife died,' Luckham said as he leant over and placed a gentle hand on Weller's shoulder.

Weller put the brooch back in his pocket and looked up at his friend through his tears.

'Thank you, Bob. That means a lot to me.'

The two men sat reminiscing, with Luckham becoming increasingly concerned as Weller continued to drink two glasses to his one until, after a few hours, it was plain that his friend had drunk way too much.

'Come on, Lee. I think you've had enough. Time to go home.'

With some difficulty, he lifted his friend to his feet, draped his arm around his own shoulders, walked him home and put him to bed.

Over the next few months, Weller's idle hands and idle mind saw him become a regular at the same tavern. The days when Luckham would come home to an empty house, and then find Weller down at the pub, always seated at the table where they'd taken their first drink, became increasingly frequent. One day, Luckham decided he'd held his tongue for long enough. The time had come to say something. Sitting down opposite Weller, he poured himself a drink.

'Lee, I have waited for some time hoping you would pull yourself out of the state you've gotten yourself into, but I cannot hold out any longer.'

'I have no idea what you're talking about!' Weller slurred, almost falling off his chair.

'Yes you do. You have been with me for a bit now, and it tears me apart to see you drowning your sorrows like this. It's not helping. I've told you many times that you needed to keep your mind occupied, and look what has happened. You cannot change things. Do you think this is what your wife would want for you?'

Luckham knew that mentioning Weller's dead wife was a sore point, but he had no choice. He waited for a furious rebuke, but instead Weller began to cry.

Captain Lee Mellington Weller, *The Nepean Times*, 1896.

'You're completely right,' he spluttered through his tears. 'I know she wouldn't want this for me. Robert, I've been thinking about what you said, and you're right. Maybe it's time I moved out and started searching for employment.'

A glimmer of hope came across Luckham's face, and he stood and embraced his friend. 'Wonderful! What were you thinking of, heading back out to sea?'

'No, I think I've had enough of that for the time being. I will go into Sydney. Something will present itself.'

'I'm sure it will, my friend, I'm sure it will. I think it's a good time to try something new. I have a friend, Mrs Tresnan, who runs a lodging house called Queensland House. She will sort you out. I will even pay your bill for the first few weeks.'

MRS. LEE WELLER, Who e Husband Is Said to Have Been Murdered in the Blue Mountains of Australia by Butler.

Mrs Lee Weller, *The San Francisco Call*, 3 February 1897.

The two men spent the rest of the night quietly drinking and reminiscing before eventually heading home to bed.

Weller was up early, and caught the morning ferry across the harbour. After disembarking, he walked the few hundred metres to Phillip Street to his new lodgings. Walking through the wooden doors of Queensland House, he was greeted by a middle-aged lady seated behind the reception desk.

'Good morning, sir. Can I help you?' she enquired politely.

'My friend Mr Luckham has arranged for me to stay here.'

Mrs Tresnan flicked through the ledger on the desk in front of her.

'Ah, yes sir, you must be Captain Weller. Welcome to Queensland House,' she said as she reached behind her for a key. 'Here you go. Your room is up the stairs and to the right. Do you need someone to help you with that chest? It looks awfully heavy.'

'No, thank you, this chest has been around the world with me several times. I am fine with it,' he said as he took the key, lifted his chest with both arms and proceeded up to his room. When he entered the room, he found it to be pleasant enough, simple but adequate. After sliding his chest under the desk, he sat down on the bed and stared out the window. Soon enough, his hand found its way into his pocket and his wife's necklace was draped between his fingers. Bowing his head, the tears flowed freely as he let out a deep sigh before clasping his fingers around the necklace and drawing it him. He thumped his chest resolutely, and then lifted himself from his bed and proceeded down the stairs and out onto the street. He made his way back to the quay before turning left and heading towards the Fortune of War Hotel. He ordered a bottle of whisky, then sat down, gazed out over the harbour and slowly drank his way through the bottle.

Over the next week, he became a regular at the Fortune of War, albeit drinking far less than he had been, and eventually he began to ask around for work.

One afternoon, he met a man who invited him to a party on Castlereagh Street. His mind already clouded prior to leaving the hotel, he spent the night talking to numerous people, but didn't really pay much attention to any of the conversations, nor to names or faces.

When he woke up the next morning, he checked his coat pockets and realised that a large sum of money and his Master's ticket were missing. He immediately marched down to police headquarters, where he found a young constable sitting behind a long desk.

'Can I help you, sir?' the constable asked.

'Yes, officer. I would like to report some stolen property.'

Theft in a burgeoning colony was far from being out of the ordinary, particularly around the docks of Sydney, so the constable was instantly dismissive, simply reaching beneath the desk for a form and handing it to Weller without making eye contact.

'Fill in the form, sir, list the property you have lost and write down as many identifying details as you can.'

Weller wrote down his name and a description of the missing items before sliding the form back across the desk. His eyes still cast downwards, the constable took the form and placed it in a tray beside him. Weller continued to stand in front of the desk as more silent moments passed, before coughing discreetly.

The constable looked up, clearly irritated. 'Yes?'

'Well, aren't you going to do something about my missing possessions?'

The constable stood up and crossed his arms, his body language reiterating his annoyance. 'What would you like me to do, *sir*?'

Weller threw his hands up incredulously. 'What do you mean "What would you like me to do?" I would like you to get out and start looking for my belongings!'

Detecting the English accent in Weller's voice, the constable's tone became derisory and condescending. 'Sir, perhaps you're not familiar with how things work in the colonies. This town is filled with thieves and ruffians whose profession is stealing. I'd wager that whoever took your belongings has already sold them, which makes our task of finding them that much more difficult. Now if you don't mind, sir, I have many more important matters to attend to.' With that, the constable sat down and returned to his paperwork.

Weller stepped forward and leant over the counter. 'Officer,' he began slowly but deliberately, 'money is one thing, and I understand that it is not traceable, but surely a Master's ticket with my name on it should not be too hard to find.'

The constable ignored him.

'Officer!' Weller shouted. 'I need that Master's ticket. Without it, I cannot work! If you do not find it for me, I shall have no choice but to become one of the very people you are supposed to be hunting right now!'

The constable stood up again. 'Sir, we will do our best, but if you continue to make threats, I will have no choice but to charge you with disturbing the peace.' Suddenly, the constable's eyes darted beyond Weller, his expression changed and he hung his head slightly.

'I'm Detective Roche,' a man said in a thick Irish brogue, stepping around Weller. 'Is there a problem here?' Roche was of medium build and was wearing a light-grey suit. His hair was cropped short, and he sported a neat and tidy moustache that covered his entire upper lip. Atop his head he wore a bowler hat, and his shirt and tie were neatly pressed. What caught Weller's attention most was the stern, serious look in his eye that told him this was an officer who would stop at nothing until he got his man.

'Yes, Detective,' Weller said. 'I have come here to report a robbery, and this man is being quite obstinate.'

'It's all right constable, I will take it from here,' said Roche. Withdrawing a small, leather-bound notebook from his pocket, Roche said, 'Tell me what happened.'

'My name is Captain Lee Weller. I went to a function at a house in Castlereagh Street last night. I had a little too much to drink, and when I checked my coat pockets this morning, I realised that some of my belongings had been stolen.'

'Captain Weller, I promise you I will do my best to get your belongings back. Can you please tell me where I can find you?'

'I'm staying at a place called Queensland House. I will be there most of the time.'

'Yes, I know it. If anything comes up, I will come and find you there.'

'Thank you, Detective. This really is greatly appreciated.'

Mid-afternoon a few days later, Weller was sitting in his room perusing the work ads from yesterday's afternoon edition of the *Sydney Morning Herald* when a knock came on his door. 'Yes?' he called.

'Captain Weller. It's Mrs Tresnan. There is a detective downstairs who wishes to speak with you.'

'Excellent,' Weller replied.

Making his way downstairs, Weller found Detective Roche waiting for him. 'Good afternoon, Captain Weller.'

'Detective. Won't you join me in the sitting room?' The two men took a seat at a vacant table, and Mrs Tresnan brought them tea.

'I have some good news for you,' Detective Roche said as he sipped his tea.

'Oh, yes?'

Roche reached inside his pocket and withdrew a sum of money and Weller's Master's ticket, which he slid across the table.

'I don't know what to say,' Weller said, almost speechless. 'I cannot believe you have retrieved these so quickly. Where did you find them?'

'A prostitute had them.'

'Excuse me?'

'A prostitute. I went to the address you gave me. She was working the place, and one bloke stole your belongings before going off with her. It would seem that he'd also had too much to drink, and when he passed out, she stole your, and his, possessions.'

Greatly relieved at the return of his possessions, Weller invited Roche to the Fortune of War for a celebration drink. Roche consented, but only had one drink before politely excusing himself, leaving Weller staring out at the harbour. Suddenly, it came to him. The sea didn't hold the same allure as it once had. Yes, maybe he could find his way aboard another boat and simply lose himself in the oceans, but it didn't seem right anymore. It was time for a change. He began to consider the course of his life. Robert was right. A copy of the Saturday morning edition of *The Sydney Morning Herald*, was lying on the window sill in front of him. He picked it up and began to flick through the advertisements.

Instinctively, he found himself looking at positions on ships or around the docks. Catching himself for not breaking old habits, he started flicking through the pages again, this time searching for something completely removed from everything he had ever known.

There it was, standing out like a lighthouse; the perfect ad.

Metallurgist wants sociable young man, mate, prospecting Western district. Equal shares. Experience unnecessary. Butler. Metropolitan Hotel, 401 Pitt Street.

He quickly finished his drink and, after folding the paper and placing it under his arm, headed straight out of the bar and made his way hurriedly along the quay. He turned right into Pitt Street, and after a few hundred metres he retrieved the paper from under his arm and checked the address again. After pausing several times to check the street numbers above the doors, he soon reached the Metropolitan Hotel. Walking inside, he made straight for the reception desk.

'Yes, sir, would you like a room?' Mrs O'Connell asked.

'Ah, no actually, I am looking for a man named Butler. Do you know where I might be able to find him?'

'Yes, sir. He will be somewhere in the public bar,' Mrs O'Connell said, pointing to her left.

'Thank you,' said Weller, who then turned and walked towards the bar. Stepping through the door, he began to scan the dozens of faces that were present, unsure of how to go about finding the man he sought.

'Hello,' said a man with a thick black moustache who was seated at a nearby table. 'Have you come in response to my ad?'

'Mr Butler?' Weller asked.

'That's me. Come join me for a drink, won't you?'

Not needing a second invitation, Weller was soon seated and drinking.

'So, your ad says you need a mate for a mining expedition,' he said, tapping the paper.

'That is why I placed it!' Butler laughed. 'I'm thinking about heading out west because I've been told there are some good pickings out there. I have had many men wanting to come on this trip so, not that you really need it of course, I need to ask if you have any experience with this kind of thing?'

'No, sir,' Weller responded despondently. 'I'm a ship's captain, but I'm looking for something new, which is why I answered your ad.'

The mention of his profession sparked Butler's interest, and he leant forward over the table.

'You're a captain? I like that. Like I said, I have had many men wanting to come with me, but I was a sailor once, and it would be good to have someone who understands me on this trip. Sailing is a lonely profession, though. Can I take it you have no family?'

'I did,' Weller said solemnly, 'but my wife became ill on the voyage out here and died not long after.'

'Oh, how terrible!' Butler said with as much sincerity as he could muster as he tried to hide his excitement.

'Well,' said Weller, as he polished off the last of his drink and poured another, 'things happen. Time to make a new start; can't dwell on the past forever.'

'That's the spirit,' Butler said emphatically. 'Maybe this trip will be just the thing to change your luck.'

'We can only hope. So, you think I'm the right man for you?'

'Oh, yes, you're the *perfect* man.'

Butler's approval lifted Weller's deflated spirits, and a smile came over his face. 'So when shall we leave?'

'Today is Saturday. It will take a few days to get everything together, so why don't we say…Thursday?'

'Excellent. Thursday it is then!'

Celebrating their new agreement with a drink, they sat for another two hours as Weller quizzed Butler about the details, and by the time Butler had woven his web, Weller was certain that in a few short months he would be a rich man who could retire to a comfortable life.

7

The High Country

29 October 1896

Thursday morning arrived, and Weller was hurriedly packing his belongings when he heard a knock. Turning towards the door, he saw Robert Luckham standing there. 'Robert!' he said with delight.

'Hello, Lee. You said you were leaving today, but I came to see if you really were.'

'Yes, I certainly am. I took your advice. It's time to embark on something new. It's time to turn my luck around.'

'So, you mentioned you have a new venture in mind. Dare I ask what?'

'I was thinking about doing some prospecting.'

'Prospecting?' Luckham exclaimed, rather surprised by the magnitude of the shift away from his former profession. 'So, are you going with anyone?'

'Yes, with someone who placed an ad in the paper. He is a metallurgist who has had some success; he studied mining down in Ballarat.'

'Do you know anything about this man?'

'Not really, just that his name is Butler, but I am sure everything will be fine.'

'If you say so,' Luckham said, unconvinced, 'but make sure you keep your wits about you.'

'I have nothing to lose! It'll all be okay. I'm just going out west to see the country and, while I am at it, try to turn my fortunes around.'

Luckham couldn't argue with his own advice, so he patted Weller on the back as he moved beside the bed and helped him pack the last of his belongings, but no matter how hard he tried, his journalistic instincts told him something wasn't quite right. 'Lee, I want you to promise me two things.'

'Yes, of course,' Weller said as he turned from his case and faced Luckham.

Luckham took a small leather-bound journal from his pocket, gave it to Weller, and said, 'Firstly, I want you to promise me that you will write me a letter every few days.'

'Yes, Robert, I will write to you every few days. Wait,' Weller said as he looked at the journal and realised it had Luckham's initials on it. 'Robert, I can't take this!'

'Lee, I insist. You can give it to me when you get back. There is something else I want you to take,' he said as he reached inside his coat and retrieved a British Bulldog revolver, which he held out in front of him.

'What's that for?' Weller said as he looked at the weapon.

'I want you to take this for protection.'

'Robert, I don't need that,' Weller said dismissively. 'Nothing is going to go wrong.'

'Nevertheless, I've heard stories about miners who strike it rich only to have their lives taken when someone steals their find. Promise me you'll take it.'

'Robert, I really don't see the point,' Weller said as he pushed the revolver away.

'Please, Lee, take it,' he said as he put the revolver in a canvas bag and handed it to Weller, who examined the side of the bag closely.

'R.A.L.?' he read out loud. 'Robert, I can't take your bag as well!'

'Yes you can. And look inside; there's something else to remember me by.'

Weller opened the bag. 'A pipe and a knife. Thank you, Robert.'

'My pleasure,' Luckham said as he sat down at the desk and watched Weller carefully place his wife's jewellery into the seachest. 'So, where to first?'

'All I know is that we will make for Glenbrook and camp there, then move on to Lithgow and out to Bathurst.'

'Lee, I wish you all the luck in the world,' Luckham said as he stood. 'And don't be away too long now, will you?'

'Thank you, my friend, I will write to you, and I promise I shan't be away too long,' Weller said as he shook Luckham's hand. Luckham departed, and soon after, Weller gathered his chest and bag and headed to the railway station, where he checked his seachest into a locker and retrieved his ticket before setting out towards the Metropolitan. On the way, he stopped in at the post office to send a letter to his solicitor.

28 October 1896

Mr A. Donaldson, 37 Bedford Row, London, W.C.

I leave from Sydney tomorrow, and am going up country with a man prospecting for gold. I can't tell you our definite destination, but our first stop will be Glenbrook, then on to Lithgow and Bathurst. I have nothing at stake re money, and should we do any good work we go equal shares. Please send letters as usual, and should I be away longer than anticipated, and out of reach of rail and post, do not be anxious. I will let you know from time to time where I am. My name will be down on the books at the Mining Office in Sydney, which gives me miner's rights to whatever may turn up, and the authorities will also know what district we are prospecting in, so that in the event of anything happening to us, to a certain extent our whereabouts will be known. Perhaps fortune may do me a good turn – it's about time – but it will be a wild, free, open life.

Captain Lee Mellington Weller

With the small beige canvas bag slung over his shoulder, Captain Lee Mellington Weller hurriedly made his way through the streets of Sydney until eventually he stood in the foyer of the Metropolitan, and only had to wait a few minutes before Frank Butler came down the stairs with a similarly styled canvas bag slung over his shoulder.

'Is that all you're taking?' Weller laughed.

'I'm an experienced bushman,' Butler responded. 'This is all I will need. Shall we have some breakfast?'

Weller nodded and the two men walked jovially into the dining rooms. After seating themselves, they didn't have to wait long before Mrs O'Connell came to take their orders. 'Would you gentlemen like some toast and tea?'

Both assented, and as she poured the tea and prepared the toast, she listened in on the conversation.

'Where are we headed first?' Weller asked excitedly.

'We will make for Glenbrook, as I said, then we'll head out towards Bathurst. From there, we'll try a place called Hill End. Good gold country. We should come back very rich men.'

Weller nodded enthusiastically as he took a sip of tea and wiped strawberry jam from his lips. 'Sounds good. Have you been out in that country before?'

'Yes, many times. Had some good success out there. Don't worry. It'll all be fine.'

Mrs O'Connell, having left momentarily, now returned. 'Can I get you gentlemen anything else?' she asked.

Finishing the last of his breakfast, Butler rose from his seat. 'No, ma'am. Shall we?'

Weller finished the last of his toast, wiped his mouth once more and followed Butler out the door. Mrs O'Connell followed, stopping at the front entrance.

'Will we be seeing you again, Mr Butler?' she called out.

'I am going prospecting in the country and I am taking my friend here with me. I expect we may be gone for some time!'

She watched the two men threading their way through the crowds until they disappeared from sight.

They made their way through the city streets until they eventually arrived at Redfern station. Moving onto the platform, they could see the *Western Mail* steaming and heaving as its engine warmed and thick plumes of white smoke billowed into the morning sky. As they walked along the platform, hundreds of people from all walks of life surrounded them, going about their business. Distinguished gentlemen and ladies alike boarded the front carriages, whilst those lower down the societal ladders boarded accordingly. Butler and Weller boarded a second-class carriage and found a seat about halfway along. After loading their luggage into the overhead compartments, they sat back and watched as the carriage rapidly filled. Not wanting too many people to know their business, Butler looked menacingly at any passenger who as much as glanced at the spare seat across from them. A man in blue overalls boarded at the end of the carriage and made his way down the aisle looking for an empty seat. He stopped next to Butler and Weller, having realised that this was the only remaining seat. 'Is this seat taken?' he asked.

Before Butler had a chance to respond, Weller said, 'No, not at all.'

'Joseph McMiles. I work for the railways,' he said as he shook both men's hands.

'Lee Weller.'

'Frank Butler.'

The train pulled out from the station and gradually picked up speed.

'So, where you boys headed?' McMiles asked as the train moved out of the city and into the suburbs. Butler looked out the window and did his best to seem disinterested, but Weller was eager and enthusiastic.

'We're heading out west to do some prospecting! We expect we'll have some good success, don't we, Frank?' Butler merely nodded as McMiles and Weller continued to engage in small talk. Butler answered when asked a question, but for the most part kept himself out of the conversation. More than an hour had passed when the train rounded a sharp bend.

'Look, Frank! The mountains,' said Weller.

Butler nodded as the train passed over the Victoria Bridge and the Nepean River. 'Yes, not far now.'

McMiles said his goodbyes as the train pulled into Emu Plains. The train continued on, the route shifting slightly south as it traced its way along the foothills of the mountains, before turning westwards again as it slowly wound its way through the tall white eucalypt forests and sandstone cliffs. It climbed higher and higher as Weller looked out the window, down into Glenbrook Creek and into the gullies below.

'Beautiful area,' Weller remarked. 'Reminds me of the high country in Wales.'

'Hadn't really thought about it,' Butler replied. 'I suppose you are right. Good gold country down there. Tomorrow we may just go down and have a search around.'

Rounding the last of the ridgeline, the train straightened and moved on another mile before pulling into Glenbrook station. Butler and Weller were among the first off the train, followed by various railway workers, daytrippers and local residents. The stationmaster stood outside his office and watched as the various passengers walked by, tipping his hat as he took Butler and Weller's tickets.

The sun reached its highest point in the sky as the two men continued along to the end of the platform, walked up the stairs and turned towards the town. As they made their way through the village, Butler began filling Weller in about some of the town's details. 'They've not long put the railway line through here, so it's still small. We should find a few people camping up at the lagoon though.'

'How do you know that?'

Glenbrook Lagoon. Photo by Rachel DiGiglio.

'There's always a few there because that's where they get the water for the steam for the trains. There are usually a few prospectors out there too.'

Butler kept up a steady pace, but Weller dragged his heels a little as he took in every new sight. As they made their way through the village, several locals watched with cautious intrigue as the strangers headed towards the lagoon, which was half a mile further on.

As Butler had predicted, there were a dozen or so large white canvas tents strung from lines that ran between the trunks of the tall red and grey gums. Several groups of men sat around their campfires watching the newcomers intently. Butler ignored them and searched around for a few minutes before deciding on a spot to the rear of the camp, deep in the paperbarks and slightly away from the others. The two men set to preparing their camp, erecting their canvas tents before tying some waterproof sheeting above.

A view of the lagoon from Butler and Weller's campsite. Photo by Emily Brooks.

Late in the afternoon, Weller decided to go for a walk around the one-mile perimeter of the lagoon. Feeling better than he had in some time, he listened to the cicadas chirping loudly as they clung to the trunks of the casuarinas and the small saplings in the undergrowth beneath the eucalypt canopy. Walking through the ferns, he looked out at the water lilies, which extended across nearly half the lagoon's surface area. As he made his way further around the circuit, he came to a small tributary that led away from the lagoon and trickled down the mountain. Hearing loud screeching above his head, he looked up to see three black cockatoos slowly flapping their wings as they made their way back to their roosts. Upon finishing his round trip, he found Butler stoking a roaring fire as he prepared the billy. Sitting down beside him, his first question was, 'What's for dinner?'

'I was just preparing a little bit of damper here.'

'Hmm, I think I would like something more substantial,' Weller said as he began unloading the contents of his bag. 'I'm sure they will have a store somewhere nearby. I may just go check.'

Unbeknown to Weller, Butler had taken a great interest in the Bulldog revolver that Weller had taken from his bag. 'What do you need that for?' he asked.

'My friend gave it to me, for protection.'

'Is it loaded?'

'Of course!' Weller said as he packed the revolver away and slung the bag over his shoulder and began walking down the path back towards the station.

'Never mind!' Butler called out after him. 'You won't need that. I will look after you.'

The sun was setting in the crimson western sky as Weller retraced his path back towards the station. Knocking on the door of the stationmaster's house, he was soon greeted by Lewis Beattie. 'Yes, can I help you?'

'Hello, my name is Captain Lee Weller. How do you do this evening?'

'I am well,' Beattie said. 'I remember you and your companion from the station this afternoon. What can I do for you, sir?'

'I'm wondering if you could give me directions to the local store. I need to pick up some supplies.'

'Yes, of course, you follow this road down the hill and turn left. There you will find Howlett's Store. They're probably closed by now, but just knock on the door and they will answer. They're nice people. They will look after you.'

'Thank you, sir, and good night.'

'Take care of yourself, sir. It is a strange evening.' Beattie watched as Weller walked away down the street towards the store before closing the door.

Weller soon reached Howlett's store, and finding the door ajar, he pushed it open and entered. The bell tinkled, and Mr Howlett appeared from the back room. 'Good evening, sir! How can I help you?' he said politely.

'Good evening to you, sir, I'm looking for something tastier for dinner than mere damper, and I would like something that will last for a few days, as I expect we may be camping near the lagoon for a while.'

'Well, we are running a little low at the moment, but I do have some bacon here if you care for it.'

'Yes, that will do handsomely,' Weller said. 'I would also like some cans of tinned meat, and half a dozen candles if you have them.'

Howlett disappeared into his storeroom and returned with bacon wrapped in a moist cloth, several tins and the candles, which he handed to Weller, who handed over several shillings, gave his thanks and headed back to the camp.

The two men spent the next day canvassing the surrounding gullies and ravines in search of a good prospecting spot. Having decided on a place, Butler suggested they return to camp and have and early supper so they could be up before dawn.

The Stationmaster's House as it is today. Photo by Jessica Smith.

31 October 1896

Steady rain was falling as they set out, packs slung over their shoulders, down the dirt road back towards Glenbrook station, passing several more houses on the opposite side of the railway tracks. The sun's early morning rays began to flit through the swaying branches of the eucalypts as the two men entered the bush and followed a small track leading away to the edge of the ridge.

The landscape was in stark contrast to that around the lagoon. Weller examined the medium height of the trees as he walked, noticing the difference in vegetation and the increasing harshness of the scrub, something he communicated to Butler.

'Yeah, the soil's different and there's not as much water up here. Means it's good gold country,' Butler replied.

They were almost through the trees and at the edge of the ridge when Weller caught a glimpse of the surrounding valleys, thickly layered in green.

'This way,' Butler said as he took a sharp right and headed into the bush. The two men soon came to a series of large grey sandstone rocks covered in white lichen. Beside the largest boulder was a small overhang with a cave beneath it that was about seven feet in diameter. Butler crouched and entered the cave to take a look around. 'This looks good,' he said to Weller when he emerged.

Weller nodded excitedly. 'This is a good place for gold?'

'Oh, yes,' Butler said as a smile came over his face. 'This is the perfect place! Put your gear down, grab the pick and we can even have a go right now if you want.'

Doing as instructed, Weller placed his pack against the large boulder, withdrew his shovel and awaited further guidance from Butler. Butler retrieved a stick from the scrub and began to poke in the soil until he found a suitable place. 'Here. This is an excellent spot. We should strike gold here. I'm sure of it.'

Weller was beaming as he knelt down and began digging out the soil, whilst Butler stood behind him and watched. 'Yes, very good,' he said encouragingly. 'The gold's usually a fair way down, so make it a bit longer and about two feet deep. That's where we'll start finding something. I'll just go and get the sieve out of my bag so we can separate the larger rocks.'

Butler returned to the large boulder. Reaching inside Weller's bag, he retrieved the revolver, turned, and slowly raised it to waist height. The voice inside him cried out with encouragement. His finger caressed the trigger as he savoured the taste of murder and the feel of the adrenaline rushing through his body. His senses heightened, his heart was thumping as he aimed the weapon at the centre of the back of Weller's head. Meanwhile, the good captain, the thought of finding his first strike spurring him on, dug furiously. When the hole was deep enough, he started to turn around, hoping to see Butler's nod of approval.

The sound of the gunshot echoed through the valleys, the bullet punching through Weller's skull and brain and exiting near his left ear. His body slumped forward, the blood spurting out into the grainy soil. Butler stepped forward and immediately began rifling through Weller's coat, searching for anything of value. What interested him most was the railway locker ticket, which he quickly pocketed, along with Weller's gun and pipe. He kept the gun but, having no need for the pipe he tossed it back into the grave. He retrieved the miner's pick that Weller had used to dig his own grave and tossed it into the scrub before undertaking a thorough search through Weller's bag. He kept the bacon, candles and tins of meat but tossed the knife back into the grave. He returned to the corpse and pushed and prodded it until it was completely within the confines of the shallow grave. Kneeling down, Butler realised that Weller's body was still protruding above ground level. As he had done with Burgess and Preston, he forced the body into a different position until eventually he was satisfied, and began filling in the soil. When it was done, he patted the earth down and then moved into the nearby scrub, where he found three logs that he carried back to the gravesite and placed over the freshly disturbed dirt. Satisfied that he'd concealed the grave sufficiently, he picked up both bags, headed back to the trail, and then made his way towards Glenbrook and back towards the lagoon to destroy their camp and conceal all evidence that they had camped there by whatever means.

The track leading to where Weller was murdered. Photo by Emily Brooks.

A view of Butler's killing ground, Weller was buried under the ledge on the left. In the distance is Glenbrook Gorge. Photo by Jessica Smith.

Butler's 'Prospecting grounds'. Weller's grave is under a ledge on the right-hand side. Photo by Emily Brooks.

The cave overhanging Lee Weller's grave. Photo by Emily Brooks.

Lee Weller's Grave today. Photo by Tamara Walton.

Photo by Jessica Smith.

A. J. O. PRESTON.   CAPT. LEE WELLER.

Two of Butler's victims, Arthur Preston and Captain Weller, *The San Francisco Call*, 3 February 1897.

8

A Wolf in Sheep's Clothing

31 October 1896

Peter Farrell was sipping on an ale in the front beer garden of the Orient Hotel when he looked to his left to see a man walking down the road. The man's socks were pulled up over his trousers, and it was plain that he had been walking in the early morning rain.

'Good morning, sir,' the traveller said as he walked past Farrell and into the bar, Farrell nodding in acknowledgment. The traveller soon emerged again, and approached the table where Farrell was sitting. 'Do you mind if I join you?' he asked.

'Not at all,' Farrell replied with an outstretched hand.

The traveller put his bags beside the table, placed his glass of whisky on it and sat down. 'Frank Butler,' he said happily as he shook Farrell's hand.

'Peter Farrell.'

'So, what are you doing out this way?' Butler asked.

'Mate, I just travel from place to place, taking whatever work comes along. Labouring, mostly.'

'Are you hard up?'

'It looks like it,' Farrell said as he stared down at his simple clothes.

'Well here,' Butler said as he began unpacking several items from his bag. 'You might find these useful.'

Farrell took the remaining bacon, still wrapped in a wet cloth, and a few cans of tinned meat and the half dozen, unused, candles.

'Thank you,' Farrell said gratefully as he carefully placed the items into his own bag.

Butler took several sips of his whisky.

'Were you out in the rain last night?' Farrell asked, looking at Butler's soaking clothes.

Butler looked down and grasped a handful of his wet shirt.

'Yes, I was out shooting with a mate of mine, but we couldn't find anything to shoot. If I had seen you on the road, I could have given you a lot of other things.'

'Yeah, what's that then?'

'There's some waterproof sheeting up there and a tent. It's a good tent although it is a bit torn from being blown down,' Butler said as he pointed towards the mountains. 'If you go to the lagoon at Glenbrook, I have left a camp there, where you can obtain some clothes and more provisions. Here, I will make a sketch of the place.'

Reaching inside his bag, Butler withdrew a pencil and a sheet of paper and began drawing. When he was finished, he handed the map to Farrell, who took it, carefully folded it and put it inside his shirt.

'There's a shaft here,' Butler said as he pointed to the map. 'If you look about you'll find a lot of things there.'

'Thanks.'

'No problem,' Butler said with a smile as he finished the last of his whisky. Behind him, a loud toot sounded. Butler turned to see the steam engine puffing its way towards Emu Plains. 'Well, that's me. Nice to meet you,' Butler said as he extended his hand.

'Yeah, you too.'

The train pulled into the station, and the passengers had barely disembarked before Butler hopped up into the second-class carriage. The remaining passengers boarded, and the train started to move again, Butler giving Farrell a quick wave as the train gathered speed. Butler then settled back in his seat, closed his eyes and let out a deep breath. The train crossed back over the Nepean River, stopped at Penrith, and then continued on. Not long after leaving Penrith, Butler heard a voice say, 'Hello.'

Opening his eyes, he was confronted by the large frame of Joseph McMiles standing before him. 'Hello,' Butler said, startled.

'Where is your friend?' McMiles asked.

Butler paused momentarily and glanced quickly out the window before responding. 'Oh, he decided to continue on out west. I have some urgent business I must attend to in Sydney, so I had to leave him.'

'That's a shame. Well, all the best to you,' McMiles said as he continued on his way and found a seat further down the carriage. The train moved closer and closer to Sydney, but Butler never took his eyes off McMiles. He shifted uncomfortably in his seat, and the more glances he exchanged with the labourer, the greater his unease became. When the train eventually pulled into Blacktown, he took one last look at McMiles before collecting his gear and hurrying off the train.

He waited for the next train to Sydney, which he boarded, and then got off at Redfern and walked back into the city centre. He momentarily contemplated returning to the Metropolitan, but soon realised that Mrs O'Connell would ask too many questions about his missing companion. Finding himself on George Street, he paused outside the Coffee Palace and checked their sign. Seeing that it said 'Vacancies,' he headed inside and was greeted by a thin clerk.

'Would you like a room, sir?' the clerk asked.

'Yes, if you have one available.'

'Certainly, sir. If you would just complete the register.'

After Butler had signed his name, the clerk read the register before handing Butler his key. 'There we are, Mr Weller. Enjoy your stay. Will you be with us long?'

'Not too long, I shouldn't think.' Butler then turned and headed upstairs. As soon as he was in the safety of his room, he opened Lee Weller's bag and began to withdraw the contents, carefully laying out each item on the bed. There was a small amount of cash, as well as various papers and identity documents. He examined each one closely, but one document immediately sparked his interest, and after studying it closely, he tucked it safely in his pocket. In his eagerness to rifle through Weller's belongings, he'd completely forgotten about the locker ticket. Pulling it out of his pocket, he snatched up some of the money and then rushed downstairs and out the door, hurrying back towards Redfern station. When he reached the station, he headed inside and wandered around until he eventually found what he was looking for.

He walked to the luggage storage area and handed the ticket to the clerk, who disappeared into a back room before returning a short while later carrying a large seachest.

'There we are, Mr Weller,' said the clerk as he slid the chest through the lower door.

'Thank you,' Butler replied, trying to hide the grin on his face.

Taking the chest in his arms, Butler hurried back to the Coffee Palace, rushed upstairs to his room and laid the chest on the bed. The only thing keeping him from his ill-gotten booty was a small lock, which he broke by smashing it with the butt of Weller's revolver. Tossing the remainder of the lock aside, he unlatched the chest, opened the lid and peered inside. First he removed Weller's books, and then his clothes. Beneath them was something that caused the smile on his face to grow even wider; Mrs Weller's jewellery. After removing the jewellery and the remainder of Lee Weller's identity documents, he placed them in the desk drawer beside the bed before closing the chest and rushing back outside and exploring the nearby streets until eventually he found what he was searching for. Rushing back to his room, he refastened the chest's latch as best he could before grabbing his rifle, grasping the chest by one of its handles and hauling it downstairs, out the door and through the streets until he came to Moss Woolf's second-hand shop.

He pressed his back against the door to keep it ajar, causing the bell to jangle at length as he dragged the chest inside. Woolf, upon hearing the bell's insistent call, soon appeared at the counter and watched Butler as he pulled the chest across the floor, lifted it onto the counter and began to remove the contents. Woolf watched on intently as Butler placed all of Lee Weller's clothes, two prayer books, a blanket, some printed cards with Weller's name inscribed on them and, lastly, the Bulldog revolver on the counter. 'How much will you give me for this lot?' Butler asked.

Woolf examined everything closely, stroking his chin as he did so, and then took another quick glance over everything. 'Two pounds.'

Butler's contorted facial expression was a clear indication that he was not impressed. 'Surely this must be worth at least five,' he protested.

'Sir, this revolver is worth a bit, but the rest of it is not worth much at all, so I will not go over two pounds.'

Eager to offload his stolen treasure, Butler decided not to argue, but now retrieved his Martini rifle from inside his coat. 'What about if I throw this in?'

Woolf took hold of the weapon in both hands and looked it up and down. 'I will give you another five shillings.' Butler said nothing, merely nodding his assent. Woolf gathered everything up and handed the now much lighter chest back to Butler. Weller's possessions now his, Woolf reached into his till and counted out the required amount. Butler hurriedly snatched up the cash. 'Pleasure doing business with you, sir,' Woolf said.

'I don't think you have given me enough here, so I insist that you come and buy me a drink!' Butler commanded.

Letting out a deep sigh and bowing his head before looking back at Butler, Woolf offered his apologies. 'Sir, I have a business to run. I can't just go off for a drink in the middle of the day.'

Despite Woolf's pleas, Butler was insistent. 'Sir, you know you have somewhat swindled me. I demand you come and buy me a drink!'

Knowing he had come out much the better in the deal, Woolf relented. 'Just give me a second.' He went out to the back room, before returning with his shop keys in hand. Butler stepped out onto the street and waited while Woolf locked his premises. When he'd finished, he turned to Butler. 'Where shall we go?'

'Where is the closest hotel?'

'The Square and Compass, just down the road,' Woolf said with an outstretched arm.

'Perfect,' Butler smirked.

The two men set off down the street, and were soon in the pub. Finding a seat near the front window, Butler sat down while Woolf remained standing. 'So, what'll it be?' Woolf asked.

'Whisky,' Butler said eagerly. Woolf set off towards the bar, while Butler stared out the window and contemplated where the next chapter of his life would take him. It was probably time to get out of Sydney. *Three is a good count, but I've been lucky so far. Best not to push it,* he thought. Woolf soon returned with a bottle of whisky and two glasses.

'You have taken me for a ride, it would seem,' Butler said as he began sipping on his whisky.

'My friend, you were plainly too eager to sell,' Woolf said, before sipping his own drink.

'Perhaps you are right.'

'You have somewhere you need to be?'

'Yes, I am on my way to Newcastle. I am a sea captain you see, and I shall try to get myself onto a ship there.'

'Hmm, a good place for it,' Woolf agreed as he drained his glass and poured another, which he consumed just as quickly. 'Well, I have done what I have said I would do. Now, I must return to my store. I have a large family I must take care of. Time is money. Best of luck to you, sir.'

'I do not need luck,' Butler grinned, realising there was still three-quarters of a bottle of whisky to be drunk. 'I make my own.'

9

A Strange Encounter

16 November 1896

The Newcastle Sailors' Home was a haven for men whose vocation was to sail the seven seas. Some sought adventure, mostly the young ones, while others found solace and mateship in their companions, having sacrificed family life for a marriage to the sea. Charles Booth, the home's manager, had seen them all. Knowing that the most important thing for a sailor was to find the right ship, he took his job finding berths for the men very seriously.

It was nearing midday, and Booth sat behind his desk in the front foyer catching up on paperwork. Hearing the door open, he looked up from his books to see a man wearing a soft hat and sporting a trim moustache. Booth's gift, from years of meeting many a man, was to gauge a man simply by examining his face. There was something in the slight unevenness of the man's sideburns and the way the bridge between his eyebrows was slightly scrunched that made him feel uneasy. What bothered him most was the deepness of the man's eyes. It was as though they held a dark secret. With every slow step the stranger took, dragging a large chest behind him, Booth's uncertainty increased. As the stranger reached the front desk, seemingly sensing the manager's concern, his face changed, a jagged smile appearing.

'Good day, sir,' Butler said.

'Good day,' Booth responded curtly.

'I'm wondering if you could find me a berth on a ship heading towards the Hawaiian Islands and then on to San Francisco?'

Knowing the movements of every ship in and out of the port, Booth did not need to check his records to know which ships were available. He also knew that sailors were, at present, in short supply, but something inside made him question whether this man was a sailor.

'I'm sorry, sir, you are too late. A ship has just left on that route. I imagine there shan't be another one for some time yet.'

'Oh,' Butler said, making no attempt to feign his disappointment. 'Then may I trouble you for a room then?'

Booth, his suspicions now confirmed even more, stood up.

'I am sorry, sir, but this home is for sailors only.'

'Oh, but I am a sailor. Can't you see my seachest here?' Butler said.

It was unconvincing, and Booth was not about to be taken in solely by a man's word, or merely by the fact that he carried a seachest. 'What proof do you have? In order for you to stay here, I must see some sailor's discharge papers.' Confident in the fact that the stranger would not possess such documents, Booth allowed a wry smile to come over his face.

Butler, beginning to understand Booth's disposition, returned a similar smile before rustling around in his canvas bag and withdrawing a piece of paper. 'I've got a Master's certificate.'

'You're a captain?' Booth asked dubiously.

'Oh, yes, sir. Of course, my father was in the navy, and I did my apprenticeship on board the *Worcester*,' Butler grinned as he handed the Master's certificate over and recounted details that Weller had told him.

Booth took the certificate and examined it carefully. His demeanour changed slightly and, despite his reservations, he was obliged to offer a room. He pushed the register towards Butler and offered him a pen, which he took and used to sign his name.

'Thank you, sir,' Booth said as he turned the register book around and looked at the name. 'Captain Lee Weller.'

'Yes, that's me,' Butler replied.

'I'm sorry, Captain, but I get a lot of men trying to lodge here when they are not sailors. I have to check everyone stringently,' Booth said by way of apology as he retrieved a key and handed it to Butler.

'No need to apologise. I know what some of these vagrants can be like. It's no bother, no bother at all,' Butler said as he took the key, retrieved his chest and bag and made for his room. After depositing his belongings, he smiled in satisfaction. 'Time for a drink,' he said to himself as he locked his room and headed off down the stairs and out the door.

Once he was back on the foreshore, he looked up and down its length. Drinking was, as in most ports, a thriving business, and Butler had a multitude of choices. Seeing that there appeared to be more choices to his left, Butler set off in that direction, determined to have a drink in whichever establishment took his fancy, or several of them if he so desired. He had made it about halfway along the length of the foreshore when he heard someone call out.

'Hey, Darkey!'

He knew it was directed at him, but not wanting to have anyone question his new identity, Butler kept walking.

'Hey, Darkey! Darkey Ashe!'

Butler quickened his pace, but the voice's owner soon caught up to him.

'Darkey,' the man said through slightly laboured breathing as he tapped Butler on the shoulder. Butler turned around to see who had recognised him. Although he couldn't remember the man's name, the face was familiar. 'Hello! Good to see you! How are you?' he said.

'It's me, Brownie,' the man said, seeing the lack of recognition in Butler's face. 'I'm good, mate. I'm good! What are you doing here in Newcastle?'

'Well, I was trying to find a ship to the States, but there doesn't seem to be anything at the moment, so I was on my way for a drink, if you would care to join me.'

'Ah, Darkey! Always were one for the drink, weren't you. Let me guess, you're on your way for a whisky?'

'Of course!'

'Well, what are we waiting for? I know the perfect place. Come on.'

The man wrapped his arm around Butler's shoulder and set off down the street.

A few hundred feet later, they came across a tavern, which was quiet, seeing as it was the middle of the day, although there were already several sailors seated at various tables scattered around the room. Maritime paraphernalia, such as shark heads and large stuffed fish, adorned the walls.

Butler made his way to the bar and ordered a bottle of whisky and two glasses, and then returned to the table that Brown had chosen, filling both glasses before seating himself. Butler raised his glass, followed by Brown. 'Cheers!' Butler offered.

'Cheers!' Brown said before taking a hefty swig. 'So, Darkey, what have you been up to since the Suez?'

'I have been all around, America, Chile, here. What about you?'

'I have just been getting on whatever ship I can. I like the open sea, not many responsibilities out there; just do your job and that is all you need worry about.'

'How long have you been in Australia for?'

'Only a month or so.'

'And when are you heading out again?'

'Pretty soon I reckon, 'coz I'm not really fussed where I go.'

Upon hearing that this old acquaintance whom he had unexpectedly encountered would soon be out of the country, Butler allowed himself to relax a little. He drained his glass and poured himself another.

'So, what about you, Darkey? How long you been here?'

'Um, a year or so, I guess.'

'And how have you made your way?'

Before responding, Butler realised that Brown's glass was empty, and so he topped him up. 'Mostly, I have been all over Western Australia, fossicking and prospecting, buying claims and selling them again, and at all sorts of games since I saw you last.' Reaching inside his waistcoat pocket, Butler fiddled around a little before withdrawing two spent bullet cartridges and throwing them on the table. 'This is how I made my living,' Butler said with a broad smile as the cartridges clattered loudly over the table before coming to rest.

Brown picked up one cartridge and rolled it in his fingers, examining it closely, then placed it back on the table as he smiled to himself. 'Ah, Dick, you're as bad as ever. That sort of thing wouldn't suit my book.'

'So, what would suit your book?' Butler asked, sensing an opportunity. *Maybe there is time for one more murder before I leave Australia*, he thought to himself as he rested his elbows on the table and leant in closer. 'Would you be interested in coming prospecting with me?'

'Nah, that wouldn't suit my book either. I will be on a ship soon. I thought you were here to get yourself on a ship.'

Butler sat back in his chair and knotted his hands behind his head. 'I was going to, but there don't seem to be any ships that suit me for a bit, so I think I might do some more prospecting. There are some good spots north of here. It's a shame you don't want to come with me. There's easy money to be made.'

'Like I said, not my book, Dick, not my book,' Brown said as he smiled, then rose from his chair, giving Butler a hearty slap on the back before moving to the bar to get another bottle.

The two men spent the rest of the afternoon and much of the evening reminiscing about their adventures before eventually stumbling out of the tavern and helping each other back to the Sailors' Home.

However, on their way home, Butler came across a familiar face.

'Captain Petrie!' Brown called out.

Upon hearing the name Butler shied his head away and tried to remain inconspicuous.

As the captain came over it was plain he was displeased about being taken away from his business.

'Captain Petrie!' Brown slurred as he draped himself over the man.

'What? What do you want?'

'How are you? Captain Petrie, you know Ashe?' Brown said as he pointed to Butler.

Even in the dim streetlight Petrie still knew his man.

'Yes, I remember him very well. Now, if you'll excuse me I must be going!'

Petrie strode away down the foreshore while Brown drunkenly looked at Butler, 'what was all that about?'

'Nothing, I first came to Australia with him. I had a problem with me leg but he kept trying to force me to work so I gave him a piece of my mind. I got put in gaol for threatening him.'

'Ah, Dick, you're as bad as ever,' Brown said as he started to stagger back towards the Sailor's Home.

'Yeah, well, next time I see him I'm gonna blow his brains out.'

17 November 1896

After rising mid-morning the next day, Butler's urge for one more killing got the better of him, and after he'd gone downstairs for breakfast, he returned to his room and penned another note, which he then took to the offices of the *Newcastle Herald*.

It read: *Metallurgist wants agreeable mate, prospecting; mining experience unnecessary, equal shares, Butler, this office.*

Over the next few days, Butler discovered that finding a prospecting mate and a fresh victim would not be easy, as men here seemed to be more interested in the open seas than the Australian bush. Given the lack of responses, he determined that getting on a ship as soon as possible was his best course of action, no matter where it went. Having made his decision, he made his way downstairs and sought out Booth who, in the course of the last week, had changed his attitude towards the affable Lee Weller. 'Mr Booth,' Butler said, upon finding him at the front reception desk working on the books.

'Ah, Captain Weller, how are you this morning?'

'Fine, fine. I was wondering if you'd had any luck securing me a ship?'

'I've heard there are going to be some ships available shortly. I will keep you informed.' Butler's disappointment and agitation was plainly apparent, compelling Booth to add, 'You look like you need a drink.'

'I think you're right,' Butler said, nodding. 'Care to join me?'

Booth thought on it for a moment, tapped his pen on the book in front of him, and then said, 'You know what, I've had enough of this bookwork for now. I think I just might.'

Just as Booth stepped out from behind the reception desk, he and Butler were joined by one of Butler's new-found acquaintances, Alfred Hill. 'You boys off for a drink?' Hill asked with a broad smile.

'Sure are. Care to join us?' said Butler.

Not needing a second invitation, Hill consented, and the three men made their way out onto the promenade. They walked along the footpath, and then turned down Scott Street, passing an interested spectator who remained unseen by Butler.

'Hello, Mr Hill, I haven't seen you since you were on the *Francis Fisher*,' the man said.

'Hello, Detective McHattie. How are you this fine morn?' Hill replied.

Upon hearing the word 'detective', Butler stepped slightly back from Hill's side and bowed his head.

'I'm well, Mr Hill. I'm well. So, where have you been?'

'On this ship and that.'

'You shipping out shortly?'

'I should think so.'

As the two men conversed, Butler strode on briskly, keen to put some distance between himself and McHattie, Booth following in his wake. Seeing that Butler was now some way ahead of him, Hill excused himself and hurried to catch up with the other men. McHattie continued to watch them as they went on their way, curious as to the identity of the third man.

10

Bon Voyage

18 November 1896

The near run-in with Her Majesty's constabulary had spooked Butler, and he was now keen to remove himself from Newcastle, and Australia, as soon as possible. He was sitting in the dining room of the Sailors' Home perusing the few responses that he'd received to his ad when Booth came in and sat down beside him.

'How are you doing today, Captain Weller?' Booth said jovially.

'I'm good. Any news about a ship?' he said, putting the responses to one side.

'I knew you'd ask me that!' Booth laughed. 'And that's precisely why I came to see you; a Captain Fraser came in yesterday and told me he needed five sailors for a ship called the *Swanhilda*.'

Several days of heavy drinking had clouded Butler's mind and made his body weary, but upon hearing Booth's words he immediately perked up, his body language and general demeanour changing entirely. 'Oh, yes?' he asked keenly.

'Yes, indeed, you need to be down at the shipping office within the hour. I was looking for you this morning to tell you, but I was unable to find you.'

'Excellent, Mr Booth, thank you so much,' Butler said as he feverishly shook Booth's hand. 'I best be off then so I don't miss out!' With that, he rushed out the door and was soon entering the shipping office, but found himself at the end of a long line of men that extended from the counter to just a few feet short of the doorway. Butler shifted from side to side as he waited impatiently for the queue to move. Looking along its length, he could see a man who he presumed was the Captain Fraser to whom Booth had referred standing to one side.

Fraser was a man of medium height and build, but even from some distance Butler could see from his stance that he was a man who stood his ground. His crisply pressed uniform also spoke of a man who took great pride in his appearance. Butler waited for a few more minutes until his impatience eventually got the better of him, and then rushed forward from the end of the line and marched straight up to Fraser. 'Captain Fraser?' he said.

'Yes?' Fraser said with a slightly puzzled look on his face.

'My name is Captain Weller. Is this ship going to San Francisco?'

'Yes, it is. Now, if you would kindly wait in the line with the rest of the men, and then you can sign on.'

'What will the ports of call be? Will there be many, or are we going to sail direct?'

Fraser was now becoming impatient, and Butler's antics had attracted the attention of the other sailors.

'Captain!' he said, the annoyance in his voice clearly apparent. 'If you would only wait in line with the others, you can sign on with that clerk over there.'

Butler reached inside his coat pocket and retrieved Lee Weller's Master's ticket, which he shook in front of Fraser's face.

'You see here, Captain. I am also a captain, a great asset for your ship. You must make sure you get me on this voyage.'

Fraser gave Butler an unconvinced look, but took the ticket nevertheless, glancing at it only briefly before handing it back. Realising that he would get no joy by continuing on his present tack, Butler did as he was told and returned to the rear of the line. More minutes passed, and Butler continued shifting from side to side and looking up and down the queue. When his turn finally came, Butler quickly signed on and then marched back over to Fraser. 'So, Captain, when will the ship sail? How soon will we be able to get out of Newcastle?'

Fraser shot Butler an undisguised look of displeasure, and paused for several moments before responding. 'I'm not sure. Sunday, or Monday morning maybe.'

'Can't we go any sooner?'

'No, Captain, we cannot,' Fraser replied bluntly.

Butler frowned, and then turned and marched out of the office, slamming the door loudly behind him.

After he'd left, another captain, who'd been watching proceedings intently, remarked to his companion, 'If I were Fraser I wouldn't take on that man. He'll make trouble before the voyage is over.'

The near run-in with McHattie and the delay in his ship leaving now caused the previously jovial 'Captain Weller' to become withdrawn and surly, and he barely left the Sailors' Home as he counted down the days and hours until the *Swanhilda* set sail.

CAPTAIN DONALD FRASER.

Captain Donald Fraser, *The San Francisco Call*, 3 February 1897.

23 November 1896

Word came through that the *Swanhilda* was due to sail, and so Butler packed the last of his, and Weller's, belongings into the seachest and then proceeded downstairs, where he said a polite goodbye to Booth before making his way outside, where Hill was waiting for him.

'Morning, Lee. How are you?'

'Very well, Alfred.'

'You excited about getting underway?'

'You don't know the half of it.'

'Here, let me give you a hand with that,' Hill said as he leant down and tried to lift the seachest. Finding it rather weighty, he exclaimed, 'What the bloody hell have you got in here, a dead body?'

'No, just everything I need, Alf, just everything I need.'

'Well, you'd better give me a hand with it,' Hill laughed.

The two men slowly made their way down the foreshore to the port. Pausing at the beginning of the first wharf, Butler asked a passing sailor for directions to the *Swanhilda*. Much to his relief, the sailor pointed to a position about halfway down the adjacent wharf, meaning that they only had to lug the chest a few hundred feet further.

Out in the harbour, the *Swanhilda's* half-red, half-white hull bobbed and swayed in the light swell. Its three masts carried half a dozen sailors, busy rigging scores of ropes as the ship's engines warmed up and its smokestack sent thin plumes skyward. Butler and Hill made their way to a smaller wharf where, beneath them, a man stood in a rowboat holding on to a pylon as he tried to keep his boat steady.

'You there!' Butler called out.

'Yeah?' the man replied gruffly.

'Take me over to the *Swanhilda* immediately.'

'Righto, but a "please" would be nice,' said the man curtly. Butler slung his bag over his shoulder and moved to a ladder leading down to the boat.

Hill put the chest down and shook Butler's hand. 'Best of luck to you, Lee.'

'You too, Alf. You too.'

Butler moved towards the ladder and handed his bag down to the waiting arms of the boatman, who took the bag and put it to one side. Hill started to slide the chest over the edge of the wharf. 'Gees, this is heavy! What have you got in there, a dead body or something?' the boatman exclaimed as he took hold of the chest.

'Everything I own is in there,' Butler responded, his voice earnest, 'and I don't imagine I'll ever be back in Australia again.'

Just then, a sudden wave rocked the rowboat, and the chest toppled from the boatman's arms and into the ocean.

'Quick! Grab it! Don't let it sink!' Butler cried out in horror. The boatman's hands were instantly in the water, but the chest was too heavy, and was on the verge of sinking. The boatman needed to muster all his brute strength just to keep it near the surface. Butler leapt down into the boat and quickly plunged his hands in the water, grasping the other side of the chest.

'Pull it in! Pull it in!' he cried.

'I'm trying,' said the boatman angrily. 'It's too bloody heavy!'

Each man gave an almighty heave, and the chest broke the surface. Another heave, and it was scraping against the boat's hull. With one last, desperate pull, the chest toppled into the boat, knocking both men onto their backsides, where they lay breathing heavily.

The boatman was the first to recover, and made sure the chest was secure before casting off and rowing out towards the *Swanhilda*. Butler turned to wave to Hill on the wharf, and after that final parting gesture, he nestled against the rowboat's stern, watching as Australian soil moved further and further away. Knotting his hands and placing them behind his head, he let out a sigh of relief. This was it. He had done it! Another country, another series of successful murders. Soon he would be in America, where Lee Weller would die and a new man would be born.

PART II

11

First Clues

20 November 1896

Inspector-General Fosbery's day started out like any other, the only difference being that he was more tired than he remembered being in a long time. Dispensing with the obligatory morning pleasantries to his staff, he hurried across the main office and into his own, barely having time to sit down and gather his thoughts before one of his receptionists knocked on the door. 'Excuse me, sir,' she said as she cautiously peered around the door.

'Yes, what is it?' Fosbery responded indignantly.

'Sorry to bother you, sir,' she apologised, 'but I just received a letter.'

'Can't someone else take care of it?' he rumbled.

'Um, I'm very sorry, sir, but you specifically instructed me that if anything came in from the press, you wanted to see it immediately.'

Unable to argue against his own edict, Fosbery extended his right arm begrudgingly and flicked his fingers back and forth, gesturing to her to bring it to him. 'Who is it from?' he asked.

'Ah,' she said, checking the name of the sender on the back of the envelope. 'It's from a Robert Luckham…from *The Bulletin*.'

'Luckham, yes I know of him,' Fosbery said as he took the letter and turned it over and over in his hand. *Luckham's a good journalist, a damn persistent one*, Fosbery thought to himself, as the receptionist left the room. *Whatever's inside, he's going to hound me until I see to whatever it is he wants.*

Reaching out to the top right-hand corner of his desk, he retrieved his letter opener, slid it under the top fold and carefully sliced the envelope open. After removing the letter, he unfolded it and began to read.

To Inspector-General Fosbery,

My name is Robert Luckham. I write to you as I am rather worried for the safety and wellbeing of my friend, Captain Lee Mellington Weller. On 29 October, Captain Weller embarked on a journey out west with a fellow who goes by the name of Frank Butler. I gave my friend a revolver to take for his protection. He was wearing a blue and white spotted silk shirt, dark blue trousers and a blue coat, if that helps. I asked that he write to me every few days. I have received no letters from him, which leads me to believe that Captain Weller may have fallen victim of some form of foul play.

Captain Weller informed me that his movements were to be from Sydney to Glenbrook and then out towards Bathurst in search of gold. Prior to his departure, he was to meet his companion at the Metropolitan Hotel.

Not having heard anything since his departure, I now hold grave concerns for Captain Weller's safety and wellbeing. I would be greatly appreciative if you could investigate this matter for me.

Yours faithfully,

Mr Robert Luckham

In a still wild colony, Fosbery knew only too well that people disappeared all the time, only to be found soon after in another part of the country. Communications were not always consistent or current, and the chances were that this Captain Weller was merely unreachable, or his letters had become lost in the post. Nevertheless, Fosbery re-read the letter. No, he had to do something, otherwise Luckham would continue to send letters until action was taken. Raising himself from his chair, he moved to the door. 'Detective Roche,' he called out across the office. 'Would you come in here please.'

'Yes, sir,' Roche replied, and duly arrived at Fosbery's door, by which time Fosbery had returned to his chair.

'Come in, would you?'

Roche stepped inside Fosbery's office and sat down in the chair opposite Fosbery.

'What is it, sir?' Roche said, seeing the letter in Fosbery's hand.

'I received this letter from a journalist, Robert Luckham. Do you know of him?'

'Yes, sir, he's given me some good leads before. Damn persistent bugger.'

'Precisely,' Fosbery said as he handed the letter to Roche. 'That is why I want you to look into this.'

'Certainly, sir,' Roche said as he took the letter.

'Keep me informed, won't you?'

'Of course, sir.'

'That'll be all.'

'Thank you, sir.' Roche returned to his desk, sat down and read the letter. When he'd finished, he rubbed his hand back and forth across his head, ruffling his hair. He rubbed his face with his hands, and then leant back in his chair. Something was there, something familiar, but he couldn't put his finger on it. Then, suddenly, it came to him, and he rushed back into Fosbery's office.

'What is it?' Fosbery said as he looked up from his desk.

'I know the name mentioned in this letter.'

'You what?'

'Weller…the name is familiar to me. He had some items stolen, and I retrieved them for him.'

'So, you know what this man looks like?'

'Yes, sir, I do.'

'Very good, then you'll be able to give a positive identification when we find him. They two men have probably just got lost up in the mountains somewhere. They wouldn't be the first and they won't be the last. Just see what you can find out so we can get Luckham off our back.'

'Yes, sir,' Roche said as he turned and left Fosbery's office. Roche retrieved his notebook from his desk drawer, and then re-read the letter. His first port of call was immediately apparent. He left the building and threaded his way through the streets until he arrived at the Metropolitan Hotel, where he found Mrs O'Connell at work behind the counter. 'Excuse me, madam,' he said as he reached inside his pocket and withdrew his badge.

'Yes?'

'My name is Detective Roche. I wonder if I may ask you a few questions.'

'Of course,' Mrs O'Connell said as she slowly made her way out from behind the counter.

'Do you mind if I make notes?' Roche asked politely as he took his notebook out of his coat pocket.

'No, not at all.'

'Can I start by asking your name and position here at the hotel?'

'My name is Mrs Bridget O'Connell. I am the owner.'

'Have you had any men in here that you'd immediately recognise as prospectors or miners?'

She put her palm to her cheek and looked upwards as she pondered the question.

'Now, let me see, we have so many people coming through here. It's hard to remember them all.'

'Anything, anything at all, would be a great help.'

'I've had quite a few men come through here who are on their way to the mines out west.'

'Did any stand out as being slightly odd or peculiar?'

'In my experience, all miners are a little bit odd, Detective!' she laughed.

'Maybe so,' Roche chuckled. 'But do you remember anyone who may have had meetings with many different men?'

The rephrasing of the question sparked Mrs O'Connell's memory. 'There is one man I remember who fits that description. He was always talking to this person and that.'

'Do you remember his name?'

'I think it was Butler, or something like that. Let me just check my register.'

Mrs O'Connell headed back behind the counter and started to peruse the register, running her finger up and down several pages until she found what she was looking for. 'Yes, Detective, here it is. Mr Frank Butler. It was a few weeks ago.'

'Thank you, ma'am. That's a great help. Do you remember him going off with a man, someone who was perhaps dressed like a sea captain?'

Mrs O'Connell emerged from behind the counter again and stood in front of Roche. 'Now that you mention it, I do. I remember Mr Butler meeting with a man who looked like that.'

Roche's face lit up. 'Did they happen to say exactly where they were going?' he asked, wanting to confirm the accuracy of Luckham's information.

'As a matter of fact, they did. Glenbrook first, and then out to somewhere near Bathurst I think.'

'Could you tell me anything else?'

Mrs O'Connell proceeded to inform Detective Roche of every single detail she could remember, including detailed descriptions of both men. 'I hope that is of some help to you, Detective,' she concluded.

'Yes, ma'am, extremely helpful. Thank you. You have a good day, Mrs O'Connell,' he said as he tipped his hat. He'd barely reached the door when she called out to him.

'Detective?'

'Yes?' he said, turning back to her.

'Has something bad happened?'

'No, we're just making preliminary investigations, ma'am. We think they may have just gotten themselves lost. Nothing to worry about, nothing at all.'

'Oh, good,' she said as she returned to her work.

Roche made his way back to the office and immediately sought out Detective Hector McLean, who was busy taking beige-coloured files from one side of his desk, flicking through them, and then placing them on the other side. At first he didn't notice Roche, who had to cough to gain his attention. McLean looked up. 'John, how are you?' he said as he rose.

'Good, good,' Roche said as he sized up McLean's bulky frame. 'You look like you've put on some weight. Too much good food?'

'Something like that! What's up?'

'We received a letter from a journo telling us that his friend has gone missing. His companion was on his way out to Bathurst via Glenbrook in the Blue Mountains.'

'Is there any suspicion of foul play?'

'I am not sure, but the boss asked us to check it out so we can be certain.'

'So, what do you want me to do?'

'Jump on the next train out to Glenbrook and have a look around. If anything turns up, telegraph and let me know. Here are the descriptions of the two men.'

'Right then,' McLean said as he snatched up his coat from the back of his chair. 'I'll get straight on it.'

McLean made his way from the office rushed home to pack his suitcase, before he hurried towards Redfern station, taking tea while he waited an hour or so for the next train. Upon boarding the train, he sat back and let his investigative mind tick over. The inner-city suburbs soon gave way to the countryside and, after another hour, the train arrived at Glenbrook station. He stepped onto the platform and was welcomed by the local stationmaster, Lewis Beattie.

'Good afternoon, Detective,' Beattie said as he shook McLean's hand. 'Detective Roche telegraphed ahead that you were coming. I'm Lewis Beattie, the stationmaster.'

'Mr Beattie,' McLean said as he returned the handshake.

'I've taken the liberty of organising some accommodation for you at the local inn. I hope that will suffice.'

'I'm a simple man, Mr Beattie, one who is content with simple things. Can you tell me about the night when you met the two me we are searching for?' McLean asked as he walked beside Beattie.

'I saw Captain Weller and his companion when they arrived here on the 29th. The Captain came to ask about buying some supplies that night so I sent him to Howlett's store. I saw them several times over the next few days but, after that, I never saw them again. We get a lot of people who stay here before they continue on out west. I figured they had done the same. Do you think something bad might have happened?'

'We're still in the preliminary stage of our investigations. Right now all we know is that we have two missing men.'

'Detective,' Beattie said as he stopped and turned to face McLean. 'It is not unheard of for people to set off into the bush never to be seen again. The mountains are rugged and unforgiving to the uninitiated.'

'In that case,' McLean replied. 'I will need to organise as many locals as possible to help in the search. I think it might be a good idea to telegraph back to headquarters and organise some blacktrackers. Could I use your telegraph machine?'

'Of course, Detective. Follow me,' Beattie said as he walked back to his office.

McLean tapped away before he said, 'done. We'll have some trackers here tomorrow. Now, if you would kindly take me to the inn I would greatly appreciate it.'

'Of course,' Beattie said as headed towards the door. 'Follow me.'

The following morning, six blacktrackers arrived early and milled around the front of the inn as they waited for McLean and the other officers to appear. The burly detective soon emerged, followed by a small entourage of officers who'd come down from Springwood.

McLean immediately addressed his men.

'Righto, boys, we're searching for two missing men. At this stage, we're assuming that they've probably just got lost, but if you find anything, let me know straightaway. Constable Tate here has descriptions of the two of them.'

McLean swept his hand in the direction of a young, blond man of solid build who proceeded to hand out the descriptions whilst McLean went over to the blacktrackers.

'Which one is you is Jimmy?' McLean asked.

'Dat be me,' said a greying Aboriginal man wearing light-coloured trousers, a red flannelette shirt and a worn, broad-brimmed brown hat.

'Righto, mate, is this your country?'

'No, mate, dis not my country, my country Wiradjuri country, out near Dubbo. Dis not a problem but, we find lost people 'round here all da' time.'

'Good. Good. The two men we are looking for were seen camping up near the lagoon.'

'Hey, dis no worries, ay. If dem boys been up there, Jimmy find 'em.'

'Right, let's get to it then,' McLean said. The assembled party snaked its way along the road adjacent to the railway line, the trackers taking the lead. The group passed several locals who had emerged from their houses to investigate the cause of the commotion, some joining the rear of the party, others watching on intrigued. After a quarter of an hour, the party reached the edge of the lagoon, coming first to the worker's camp. The men camping there looked up from their billies or out from their simple canvas tents. Some began shifting nervously from foot to foot as soon as they saw the uniformed officers.

McLean ordered several of his subordinates to begin to interview the men, while Jimmy and the other trackers began searching in and around the camp. McLean watched on as they checked in between the paperbarks and red gums. For almost quarter of an hour, the trackers surveyed every inch of ground, pausing several times to discuss things among themselves in Wiradjuri. They pointed in every direction before they seemed satisfied, and then Jimmy approached McLean. 'Kay, policeman, we reckon we got some tracks. Dem whitefellas was here alright. Dey camped just over der,' he said, pointing to the rear of the camp.

Just as Jimmy was about to elaborate, one of his companions called out to him. 'Ay, Jimmy, come look at dis.'

McLean, Jimmy and several others rushed over to where the man was standing. 'What you got?' Jimmy asked.

'Jimmy, I was following dem whitefellas' tracks and den I looked in da scrub and found dis old mine here. See, look down der, a tent been shoved down der.'

McLean inched closer and peered down the shaft. 'Shit, you fellas go alright, don't ya,' he said to the trackers. 'Boys,' he called out to his officers, 'get this tent out of there.'

'We take bit more of a look around I reckon,' Jimmy said. 'We find more here, very sure.'

The trackers, all of whom had been standing together around the shaft, now fanned out and began looking deeper and deeper into the scrub, each man bending down several times as they followed various paths. One thing immediately struck McLean; from the way the tent had been shoved into the shaft, he was certain someone had something to hide.

He looked from side to side, and noticed a makeshift fireplace. Inside the circle of stones was an inch-high stack of coals. At first glance nothing seemed out of the ordinary, but when McLean squatted down, reached for a stick that was resting nearby and started scraping through the coals, he found something that interested him. It appeared to be a small block of charred wood, but when he turned it over he knew he was definitely onto something. He reached down and picked up the object, tapping it lightly to remove the excess charcoal before turning it over. Before he could investigate further though, Jimmy called out. 'Ay, policeman, dis fella find something. You come look.'

Still holding the object in his hand, McLean walked over to where one of the trackers was squatting in the scrub. 'What is it?' he asked.

The tracker reached into the bushes and pulled out a pair of trousers, which he handed to McLean. McLean placed the object he'd found in the fire to one side and turned the trousers over and over in his hands, searching for any hint as to the owner's identity. Inside the top part of the rear waistband, he could clearly make out the initials 'F.H.'. He took his notebook from his pocket and recorded the initials.

'Ay, policeman, what dis thing?' Jimmy asked as he picked the object up from the ground.

'Not sure yet, I just found it in the coals.'

Jimmy turned it over with one hand and started brushing away the soot with the other. 'I reckon dis be some sort of book, look,' he said as he handed it to McLean.

McLean examined it closely. 'Think you might be right, Jimmy. Look here, there's some writing.'

'What him say?'

McLean had to squint to decipher it, but soon made out the words 'F. Luckh…'. After recording it in his notebook, making particular reference to the fact that the F could also be an R, he addressed the officers and the trackers. 'Righto, boys, I don't think we're searching for two missing men anymore. Something unpleasant has happened here. I'm going to head down to the post office to telegraph the bosses and await further orders. You boys keep looking around the lagoon and see what else you can find.'

The trackers and officers spread out and began sifting through the bush while McLean and Tate hurried back towards the village centre.

≈

'Detective Roche,' the telegraphing officer at police headquarters called out.

Roche was seated at his desk engrossed in the witness statements he'd already collected when he heard his name called.

'What is it?' he asked the officer as he made his way into the telegraph room.

'I'm receiving a telegraph from Detective McLean.'

'What does it say?' Roche asked.

'One second, sir.'

The telegraphing machine beeped furiously as the officer recorded the message. When done, he handed his notepad to Roche.

Detective Roche. Stop. Have found camp at lagoon. Stop. Tent located. Stop. Also burnt notebook with "F. Luckh". Stop. Awaiting orders. Stop.

Thousands of thoughts ticked over in Roche's mind: a hidden tent and a burnt notebook. Like McLean, he was certain they were now dealing with a case of foul play. The only question was, had two men been murdered, or had one murdered the other?

'Sir?' the telegraphing officer asked.

'Yes,' Roche said, snapping out of his thoughts.

'What would you like me to send back?'

'Tell him to widen the search and report back with anything new.'

'Sir.'

Returning to his desk, Roche sat down and started to read the afternoon editions of the papers. The first one he picked up was *The Sydney Morning Herald*, which carried the story of the investigation on the front page.

A mysterious affair is being inquired into today in Glenbrook by New South Wales police and some of the local residents. They have gone to Glenbrook Creek to search for a man named Captain Weller, who has been missing for about a fortnight.

Shit, doesn't take them long, Roche thought to himself as he put the paper down and closed his eyes. He leant back in his chair and paused for a moment, before opening his eyes and reading through the case files again. The media pressure had begun, and was only going to intensify; this one had to be solved, and quickly.

12

A Jigsaw Puzzle

26 November 1896

Roche had spent the last few days searching for something, anything, to break this one wide open. Every morning he was in the office early, and every morning, with a hot cup of coffee in hand, he would sit down and begin to read the papers. It had started with a few, but the story had spread across the country like wildfire and now dozens and dozens of morning editions were spread across his desk. He didn't particularly like journalists, but he knew they served a purpose. He was tired of reading through papers, but knew he had to; perhaps one good journalist had found something he'd missed, and a good lead would present itself. Every single paper carried the story of the Glenbrook disappearances on their front page, and on the second and third pages as well. Some carried decent reporting, but most of the stories were mere sensationalism, centred on all the weird and wonderful theories as to what fate had befallen the two missing men. Flicking through yet more papers, nothing caught his interest; there was nothing he didn't already know. Besides, he'd soon be out in Glenbrook to see things for himself. He put the last paper down just as a constable walked into the detectives' office.

'Sir, there's a man waiting out the front who I think you might want to talk to.'

'Okay, I'll be right with you.' Roche rubbed his eyes. He was weary and frustrated, and the last thing he wanted to deal with was another nut case claiming to know the whereabouts of the men. Lifting himself out of his chair, he made his way out to the front office.

Half a dozen people were seated on the other side of the main counter. Unsure as to who it was who wanted to see him, he looked at the front-desk officer, who nodded to his left towards a tall man who now rose from his seat and stepped forward.

'Detective?' he asked.

'Yes,' Roche said as he shook the man's hand. 'I'm Detective Roche.'

'My name is Fielding.'

'Pleasure to meet you, Mr Fielding,' Roche said, immediately unimpressed by the visitor. 'What can I do for you?'

'I've been reading the papers over the last few days, and I believe I may have some information about the Glenbrook disappearances.'

Roche was still unconvinced, but he reminded himself that, as a detective, he had to try to take every witness seriously, even though his patience was beginning to wear thin.

'Yes, what is it?' Roche asked, trying his best to hide his disinterest.

'Can we talk in your office?'

Reluctantly, Roche consented, indicating the way to the detectives' office with his hand. He led Fielding to his desk and gestured towards a chair. 'Take a seat, Mr Fielding.'

'Thank you.'

'Now, what have you got for me?' Roche asked as he half-slumped into his chair behind the desk.

'Well, Detective, regarding the Glenbrook mystery. I think I may know one of the men you are looking for.'

Roche leant forward slightly, but his facial expression made it clear that he still wasn't giving Fielding his full attention.

'Detective,' Fielding said with more conviction now, 'I read the papers, so I know you must have had many people coming through here with all sorts of tales, but last month a friend of mine, Arthur Preston, went prospecting out west with a man.'

At the mention of the word 'prospecting', Roche sat up and rested his elbows on the desk. 'Go on.'

'Arthur answered an ad to go prospecting with a man calling himself Harwood.'

'You met this 'Harwood'?'

'Yes, sir, I did. I had some reservations about him too, but Arthur had his heart set on it.'

'We believe this man Harwood is now going by the name Butler. You haven't seen your friend since he left with this "Mr Harwood," as he introduced himself to you?'

'No.'

'Do you remember what this Harwood fellow looked like?'

'Oh, yes, very clearly. He was about forty, and almost six feet tall. He was solid, quite muscular actually. He had dark hair with a little bit of grey in it. He had a trim, dark-brown moustache with small sideburns. He had a weird nose. It was flat at the top but then pointy towards the end. I think he may have had it broken a few times. He was well dressed and spoke with an accent.'

'An accent?'

'Yes, it was definitely English, maybe from the north, maybe from the Midlands, but I couldn't be sure.'

'So, what did he say and do?' Roche said, looking up after scribbling furiously in his notebook.

'We met him at Thompson's Railway Dining Rooms. Myself and another of my friends, Mr Fenton, had a few reservations, as I said, so we quizzed him rather heavily. He told us how he had been prospecting all over the place and he showed us his miner's certificates.'

'So, when you saw them, you were satisfied that he was who he said he was?'

'Mostly. He seemed on the level and Arthur was very excited about it all.'

'Interesting. Then what happened?'

'We saw them off at the railway station. Harwood told us they would be gone for about six weeks, but we have not heard from Arthur since.'

'So when did this all take place?'

'It was early October.'

'And can you give me a description of Mr Preston?'

'Um, he was in his early twenties. Medium build, brown hair.'

'Can you tell me what he was wearing the last time you saw him?'

'Yes, he was wearing a white shirt, a coat, and some light-coloured leggings.'

'Does he have any tattoos, scars or other distinguishing marks?'

'Not that I can think of.'

'Is there anything else you can tell me?'

'Hmm, no, I think that is about the extent of it.'

'Well, if there is anything else that you remember, please let me know.'

'I will do,' Fielding said as he rose from his seat.

'Thank you, you've been very helpful,' Roche said as he stood and shook Fielding's hand.

He sat back down as he watched Fielding walk out, and then re-read the descriptions and details Fielding had given him, tapping his pen on his notebook and smiling to himself. He grabbed his coat from the back of his chair and rushed out the door, heading for Thompson's Railway Dining Rooms. When he arrived, he found Elias Thompson clearing away the tables. After depositing the last of the plates he'd collected, he turned and noticed Roche standing just inside the door.

'Hello,' he said. 'I'm sorry, sir, but we have just finished lunch. I think I might be able to get the missus to put something together for you though, if you want.'

'Mr Thompson,' Roche said as he showed his badge. 'I have not come here for lunch, but I thank you for your kind offer nevertheless. My name is Detective Roche, and I was wondering if it would be okay to ask you a few questions?'

'Certainly,' Thompson said with a surprised look as he pulled out two chairs and gestured for Roche to sit down. 'What's this all about?'

Taking out his notebook, Roche began. 'Mr Thompson, do you remember a man who may have stayed here, a man going by the name of Harwood, or Butler perhaps?'

'Harwood, no I don't remember a Harwood, nor anyone named Butler.'

Roche, realising that the man he was looking for may have used several aliases, read out Fielding's description.

'That sounds like a man we did have here, but his name was Frank Clare, not Harwood or Butler. What about him?'

'Could you please describe him for me, perhaps his personality?'

'He was always jovial, seemed pretty happy. He used to meet a lot of people here.'

'And his physical appearance; is there anything you could add to what I have already told you?'

Thompson gave almost the exact description of the suspect as Fielding had, and told of how Mr 'Clare' had met many men in the Dining Rooms.

'And that is about all I know,' Thompson said.

'Thank you, Mr Thompson, you have been very helpful. I shall be talking to you again, if that is okay,' Roche said as he rose and shook Thompson's hand.

'Of course, Detective. Anything you need.'

By the time Roche arrived back at the office, his desk was covered with the afternoon editions. Scanning through them, he found that they carried little more than the morning editions had. He picked up the *Evening News*, and suddenly his excitement heightened. As quickly as he'd entered the office he was out the door again, hurrying through the city and down Pitt Street until he arrived at Mrs Gilham's Hotel. A very attractive young lady with flowing blonde locks sat behind the reception desk, focused intently on filing her nails.

'Hello, miss,' Roche said politely as he doffed his hat. 'My name is Detective Roche.'

'Hello, Detective,' the girl said, a little alarmed at finding a policeman standing in front of her. 'Is there some kind of trouble?'

'No, miss, I'm looking for Mrs Gilham. I just need to ask her a few questions.'

'Oh, that would be my mother. I shall just go and get her.' Miss Gilham disappeared into the back rooms and returned shortly after, accompanied by a much older woman.

'Hello, Detective,' she said. 'I am Mrs Gilham. My daughter tells me you would like to ask me some questions. Would you like a cup of tea?'

'Yes, tea would be wonderful. Is there somewhere a little quieter where we could talk?'

Indicating the dining room with her right hand, Mrs Gilham nodded to her daughter to fix the tea while she and Roche moved to a table and sat down. 'So what is it you want to talk to me about, Detective? Is it the same thing the newspapers have been asking me about?'

'You are an astute woman, Mrs Gilham,' Roche said, just as her daughter arrived with a tea set and poured two cups. Roche sipped his tea, smiled up at Miss Gilham, and retrieved his notebook from inside his jacket. 'So, Mrs Gilham, I read what you said in the papers, and I was wondering what you could tell me about the man we are looking for.'

'Certainly. As I said to the papers, he has stayed here before.'

'Can you tell me what you remember?' Roche said excitedly.

'He always appeared to be light-hearted, whistling and jolly, and made himself popular. He shouted whisky and wine for the waiters, and no one had the least suspicion he was a bad character. Personally, I thought him a blowhard.'

'A blowhard?'

'A blowhard who was taking people down floating mines, for he was always talking big. On one occasion he showed me a wire he had received making an offer of two thousand pounds for a mine, and he said it was worth six thousand pounds. I suppose he sent it to himself. He was always trying to be everyone's friend. He was one of those people who talks himself up, but one where you know his stories are just that; talking himself up.'

'Could you describe what Mr Harwood looked like?'

Her expression became confused, and she looked at Roche oddly. 'Describe him? Why, Detective, I have a photograph of him.'

'Excuse me?' Roche said, unable to believe his luck. 'You have a photo of him?

'Of course,' she said, as she rose and walked to the reception desk, returning with a small black-and-white photograph in her hand. 'I think he took a fancy to my daughter, and he gave her a photo of himself. Here you go.'

Roche took the photo and examined it closely, amazed at the correctness of both Fielding and Thompson's descriptions. He finished his tea and thanked Mrs Gilham before hurrying back to the station and rushing into Fosbery's office, forgetting to knock. He found the Inspector-General signing off on several piles of paperwork, and in his excitement he failed to notice the three men standing beside Fosbery's desk. 'Inspector! You would not believe the day I have had!' he proclaimed.

'Detective Roche, take a seat, please,' Fosbery said calmly.

Roche sat down, and finally noticed the presence of the other men. Two of them he recognised, Superintendent Camphin and Sergeant Thorndike, but he hadn't seen the young man with neat black hair and a small, tidy moustache before. He looked him up and down, observing a strapping young man wearing a clean and crisp constable's uniform.

'Hello, sir, sergeant,' Roche said politely to Camphin and Thorndike.

'So what's with all the excitement?' Thorndike asked.

'I have interviewed three witnesses who have positively identified one of the men we're searching for. Better yet,' he said as he reached inside his jacket, 'I have a photo.'

He handed the photograph to Fosbery, who took an extended look before passing it on to the other men. Roche watched the young constable, still curious as to his identity and the reason for his presence. He assumed that he was merely someone's assistant, but when the young man took the photograph and it became clear that the other men were eagerly awaiting his reaction, Roche's intrigue increased. The young constable scrutinised the picture carefully before handing it back to Fosbery.

'Constable Conroy,' the Inspector-General asked, 'Is that the man you met with?'

'Yes, sir, there's no doubt about it. That's the man.'

'Outstanding!' Fosbery said as he clapped his hands together.

'What's going on?' Roche asked, now somewhat bemused.

'Sorry, John,' Fosbery said. 'May I introduce you to Probationary Constable Michael Conroy?'

Conroy bowed, a gesture returned by Roche as Fosbery continued.

'Our elusive Mr Butler has made one very grave error…well, two now, considering we have a photo of him. Would you care to enlighten the detective as to what I am referring to?' Fosbery asked Conroy.

'Certainly, sir. Detective Roche, it is quite simple really. My sister met this Butler, who was calling himself Harwood at the time, at a party, and then again at Mrs Gilham's hotel. He told her he was going prospecting. I was looking for something to occupy me until my police training began, and she thought it would be a good opportunity for me, so she fetched me and I met with him.'

'And you obviously didn't go?'

'No, he asked me to map out certain spots in Albury. I took the map home, but the more I thought about it, the more I thought it strange that a man who claimed to be an "expert" was asking me to decide on potential places to prospect.'

'Quite wise,' Roche commented. 'And it would seem that such discretion has possibly saved your life.'

'That would seem to be the way of things,' Conroy said with a wry smile.

'And we now have another man to identify Mr Butler,' Fosbery said confidently. He handed the photograph back to Roche, and addressed the group. 'I'm sure all of you understand that the pressure's building, especially with the increasing media attention. Detective Roche, you continue with your investigations around Sydney. Sergeant Thorndike and Superintendent Camphin, you will go out to Glenbrook to help Detective McLean find these men. We must bring this thing to an end, and soon.'

13
Deep Down Below

26 November 1896

Hector McLean stood on the platform of Glenbrook station awaiting the arrival of the next steam train. Despite being a burly, hardened man, he couldn't help but be a little nervous, as he was all too aware of the intense pressure that would be on him for the foreseeable future. Yes, the media had taken hold of the case, with more and more journalists arriving in Glenbrook every day, but dealing with them was part of the job. What made him more nervous was the fact that his superiors were on their way to oversee things.

Straightening his suit one more time, his anxiety grew as the steam train came into view and slowed as it approached the platform. Before it came to a complete stop, Superintendent Camphin and Sergeant Thorndike were already alighting and McLean hurried down the platform to meet them.

'Superintendent, Sergeant,' he said as he shook their hands. 'How are you both?'

'Well, well,' Camphin said. 'So how's the search coming along?'

'Not too bad,' McLean replied as they walked along the platform towards the stairwell and exit. 'I've had the blacktrackers searching in and all around the lagoon but we haven't yet found anything more than what I already reported. Do you want to get settled in first before I show you around?'

Camphin's look immediately conveyed his answer, but he still verbalised his thoughts. 'Detective,' he said as he looked back at the score or more journalists following them, 'as I'm sure you are aware, the media are all over this. I don't have time to "settle in". They expect results, as do our superiors. This, as I'm sure you're aware, means we have little time.'

'Yes, sir, of course, sir. Where would you like to begin?'

'I'd like to have a look at the lagoon.'

'Certainly, sir, we'll make our way there now.'

As the three men and accompanying officers walked the mile and a half to the lagoon, their conversation revolved around the possibilities in relation to what had happened to Captain Weller. The locals, already in a heightened state of excitement, became even more animated with the arrival of high-ranking officers, the group of a dozen men swelling to triple that number by the time they reached the lagoon. McLean immediately set about showing Camphin each item, and exactly where they'd been found, all the while with the journalists peering over their shoulders.

Camphin nodded to the local constables, who quickly stepped in and moved the journalists back more than a hundred feet, while he began moving his head from side to side as he looked over the expanse of the lagoon.

'Sir?' McLean asked when he realised something was brewing in Camphin's mind.

'If they camped here, there's only a few ways back down the hill. Assuming Captain Weller has fallen foul of murder, I'm wondering about our mysterious Mr Butler's next move. Have you asked the stationmaster whether he saw anyone fitting Mr Butler's description catching a train back to Sydney?'

'Yes, sir, I asked him, but he said he hadn't seen anything.'

'This is pretty rough country,' Camphin said as he examined the surrounding landscape. 'I don't think he would have tramped through the scrub. He must have taken one of the roads down the hill. How many are there?'

'Only two, the Zig Zag Road and Mitchell's Pass.'

'As we came up on the train, I had a thought,' Thorndike interjected.

'Well, what was it, man?' Camphin asked.

'I was thinking, if I was a murderer, the gullies around that bridge we came across, Knapsack Bridge I think it's called, would make a good place to dispose of a body. You could get rid of the body in the scrub, and then hurry down to Emu Plains.'

'Hmmm,' Camphin said. 'Go on.'

'With you permission, sir, I'd like to take a team down to the bridge and conduct a thorough search.'

'Sounds like a good idea; get on to it right away.'

With a nod of his head, Thorndike set off back towards the station with two dozen men in tow, including several locals and half a dozen journalists. He and his men collected as much gear as they could carry, and then set off through the scrub towards the old Lucasville station, soon arriving at the bridge. Standing at the top of the steep gully, Thorndike twirled the end of his moustache with his right hand as he surveyed the scene below.

'What do you think, sir?' one of his officers asked.

'Hmm, this is going to be harder than I thought. There's so many places where a man could hide a body and no one would ever find it.'

'Excuse me, sir,' a voice came from behind, causing both men to whip their heads around.

'Yes,' Thorndike said, unsure as to the voice's owner.

The man stepped forward and offered his hand. 'My name is John Howlett. I'm a local.'

'Yes, Mr Howlett, so?'

'I've lived here my whole life, sir, and I've spent a lot of time walking around this area. There are a few shafts around the base of the bridge; perhaps someone could have shoved a body down one of them?'

Thorndike's demeanour immediately changed. 'Interesting,' he said as he stroked his chin. 'Do you reckon you could show me some of these shafts?'

'Certainly, sir, I'd be happy to.' With that, Howlett set off down a narrow track that snaked its way down the gully towards the bridge. As they descended, Thorndike examined the Roman-style arched viaduct, the sunlight casting an eerie glow as it reflected off the bridge's large rectangular yellow sandstone blocks.

Howlett stopped several times to warn the men following him to be very careful with their step but eventually they reached the base of the bridge.

'On the other side of that pillar there are several deep shafts. I'm not sure who dug 'em; I think they might be miner's shafts. All I know is they go a long way down. I used to throw stones down there when I was a kid.'

'Hmm,' Thorndike said. 'Seems like a perfect place to dispose of a body. Officer,' he said to the nearest of his subordinates, 'get some rope and prepare yourself to be lowered down so we can have a look.'

'If you don't mind, sir,' Howlett offered, 'I'd like to volunteer. I've done a lot of climbing around here and, like I said, I know this country well.'

'Sure, if you want to. It's all yours.'

The officer who had been tying ropes together now handed them to Howlett, plainly relieved that he didn't have to descend down a dark shaft. Howlett immediately looked over the ropes and shot the officer a look as if to say, 'Lucky you didn't use these knots to go down that shaft, otherwise you wouldn't be coming back.'

After undoing the knots and retying them, Howlett secured the rope around his waist and buttocks, moved to the side of the shaft and sat down, securing his feet flat against the top lip.

'Remember, if you find something,' Thorndike said, 'don't touch it. Just let us know, and we'll take it from there.'

'Okay, sir, just make sure you bastards don't drop me,' he said, looking up at the officers holding the other end of the rope before starting to inch his way down the shaft. The reporters and locals occupied every vantage point and peered down at Howlett until he disappeared from view, the only light coming from the small lantern he was carrying in his left hand.

'Anything?' Thorndike called after pushing his way through the reporters and peering down the shaft.

'Nope, there doesn't seem to be anything down here, came the reply.' With that, they pulled Howlett up and moved on to the next shaft, where they repeated the process.

Meanwhile, back at the lagoon, Camphin and McLean were making preliminary examinations around the trees lining the lagoon's circumference, although thick patches of scrub rendered several places they wanted to check unreachable. The two men, associated officers and the media were almost halfway around the lagoon when they came across Jimmy and his companions, whom McLean immediately introduced to Camphin.

'How do you do, sir. My name is Superintendent Camphin,' he said as he offered Jimmy his hand.

'Good der, fella, you big boss man?'

Camphin chuckled. 'I'm one of the boss men, but not the big boss man. He'll be up here later today I should expect.'

'Jimmy, dat's me, and des fellas my mob.'

'Pleased to meet you all,' Camphin said. 'And the NSW Police Force would like to thank you all for your assistance.'

'We happy to help, no problem, we help you catch dis murdering man.'

The other Aboriginals nodded.

'So, what have you found, Jimmy?' Camphin asked as he moved nearer to the shore.

'Mr Camphin, we searched dis lagoon. I went diving in dere meself but, apart from dem things we find the other day, we not find nothing. Der some holes near da whitefellas' camp. I reckon you might want look down der.'

Camphin nodded. 'We will. Keep up the good work, boys.'

The trackers set off to continue their search as Camphin turned on his heels and headed back towards the miners' camp. 'Let's go and check out these holes he mentioned. Do you know what he is talking about?'

'Yes, sir,' McLean said, trailing behind. 'They're old air shafts from the look of them. I was just waiting for more men and equipment before we went down into them.'

'Alright, we can have a quick look, but Sergeant Thorndike has most of the equipment, so we'll have to wait until he returns before we can do anything.'

They soon arrived at the camp, where several locals sat tending their billies. Camphin and McLean took cups of tea, along with bread and jam, and sat down to eat their lunch. They were discussing the next stage of the search when Thorndike arrived.

Camphin and McLean stood up and looked at Thorndike expectantly, but he said nothing, instead taking several sips from a cup of tea that one of the locals had given him. Camphin and McLean stamped their feet impatiently while they waited. 'Well, come on man, don't keep us in suspense! Did you find anything?' Camphin finally snapped.

Thorndike, still slaking his thirst, shook his head to indicate that he hadn't found anything. Putting his tea to one side, he said, 'What about you, found anything?'

'Nothing more than what we already knew.'

Thorndike took several looks around before walking down to the water's edge, where he squatted down and gazed out over the still waters and large green lilies. 'Superintendent,' he said as he picked up a handful of dark sand.

'Yes?' Camphin replied as he joined Thorndike.

'Do you think the body, or bodies, might be in the lagoon?' he asked as he tossed the sand to one side and stood up.

'What do you mean?'

'Well, we found their belongings around the shore. It seems to me that it would be pretty easy to tie a rope and a rock around someone's feet, chuck 'em in and leave 'em for the fishes; or the eels.'

Camphin scanned the water just as the wind picked up and small waves began to travel from one side of the lagoon to the other.

'Sir,' McLean offered, 'the trackers have been diving all over the lagoon, but they haven't found a thing.'

'With your permission, sir,' Thorndike responded, 'it would be nigh on impossible for the trackers to dive down and search every inch of the bottom. I think we should drag the bottom of the lagoon, to see if the trackers missed anything.'

'Do we have the equipment for that?' Camphin asked, interested in Thorndike's idea but unsure as to its viability.

'I'm sure they'd have something down at Penrith. There must be dozens of boats on the river that we could use. Wouldn't be too hard to load one on a train and get it up here.'

'Not a bad idea. See if you can make it happen.'

Thorndike nodded, grabbed several men, and headed off in the direction of Glenbrook station.

'Thorndike!' Camphin called out.

'Sir,' Thorndike called back.

'Wait one second. Inspector Latimer's train will be here soon. Probably best if we come to the station with you.'

They made their way to the station and while they waited on the platform the officers chatted with Beattie, asking him various questions about the local area and, more specifically, its topography. Latimer's train pulled in a short time later.

'Good afternoon, gentlemen,' Latimer said as he disembarked and shook hands with Camphin, McLean and Thorndike. He didn't recognise the fourth man, but quickly introduced himself.

'Lewis Beattie,' the stationmaster replied.

'Pleasure to meet you, sir.'

'Would you like some tea, Inspector?'

'That would be lovely,' Latimer replied as the men made their way into the stationmaster's office.

'I think I will forego some tea,' Sergeant Thorndike said as he lingered at the doorway. 'I am going to go and telegraph Penrith to see if I can organise a boat to be brought up.'

Thorndike disappeared into an adjacent room and Beattie put the kettle on the stove while Latimer and the others sat down.

'Mr Beattie?' Latimer said.

'Yes, sir?'

'How long have you worked here?'

'Oh, many, many years.'

'So, you know the locals and this area very well?'

'Of course, sir. Why do you ask?'

'Well, I was looking at the gorge and the river as the train made its way up the mountain, and I think we're going to need more manpower to conduct a thorough search.'

'This is a sleepy town, sir. It may be difficult. How many were you thinking?'

'I will take whatever you can muster, Mr Beattie.'

'I shall get onto it right away then, sir.'

'Excellent, Mr Beattie. We'll come back later this evening and you can update me on your progress. Superintendent, would it be possible to go up to the lagoon, and would you mind terribly filling me in on the details on the way?'

The policemen made their way back to the lagoon, and by the time they arrived Latimer knew every detail. He started his own search of the scene by walking the lagoon's full kilometre circumference, stopping numerous times as he examined beneath the scrub and in several holes. When he arrived back at the main camp he ordered tea for himself and his senior officers before nodding his head towards a small series of logs surrounding a disused fire off to the left and well away from everybody else. The officers sat down with their elbows resting on their knees, their hands wrapped tightly around their cups. It began to rain just as Latimer began to speak.

'This really is pretty rugged country. There are so many places where we could be looking. I'd say it was like looking for a needle in a haystack, but I'm not sure if that would be apt.'

McLean looked at Camphin, and the two men could see the forlorn expression on Latimer's face as the magnitude of the task dawned on him. It was McLean who attempted to alleviate Latimer's discontent. 'Sir, you know those air shafts we showed you?'

'Yes.'

'Some of the officers found a couple more while we were searching the lagoon's edges. Might be worth a look.'

'Really?' Latimer said, his mood immediately lifting. 'Best show me then.' They rose and walked the few hundred feet to the shafts.

'There, sir,' McLean said as he pointed to the first shaft. Latimer moved near to the edge and peered down into the darkness before examining the remaining shafts.

'As dark as night down there. Can't see a bloody thing. Best we get some of the men searching them. Round up some volunteers, if you can find any, and get them to do it.'

'Save yourself the trouble, sir,' McLean interjected. 'I'd like to volunteer.'

Latimer looked up and down McLean's frame. 'Ah, those shafts look pretty narrow. Are you sure you're going to fit?' he sniggered.

McLean glanced down at his body while Camphin held his hand to his mouth, trying his best not to burst into raucous laughter. McLean smiled and looked back at Latimer. 'Well, sir, if I get stuck, you'll just have to find some volunteers to dig me out!'

The three men chuckled before McLean's countenance became more sombre. 'Seriously though, sir, I'd rather you let me go down, because if we do find something worthwhile, the last thing I'd want is for an inexperienced officer to go messing up the evidence.'

Latimer stroked his chin with his thumb and forefinger as he screwed up his face. 'I think you might be on to something there, Detective. Right then, I guess you're it.'

Needing no further invitation, Camphin set off to retrieve the ropes and other equipment from Thorndike. By the time he returned, McLean had already removed his coat and was standing beside the first shaft.

'Put your feet and back up against the walls and use your feet to lower yourself down,' Camphin said as he tied the ropes around McLean's waist. 'We'll have half a dozen of the locals on the other end, so when you want to come back up give a few tugs on the rope and we'll help haul you out.'

McLean looked over Camphin's shoulder at the six men before looking back down at his own frame. 'Ah, are you sure that's enough?' he said nervously.

Camphin smirked as he turned his head. 'If it makes you feel better, we'll tie the other end to that eucalypt over there.'

Scrutinizing the tree in question, McLean said, 'Are you sure that's big enough?'

With that, Camphin gave McLean a hearty slap on the back, all but pushing him into the shaft. McLean carefully manoeuvred his way down into the shaft, and only half of his body was still visible when Camphin called out to him. 'Wait! You'll need this,' he said as he retrieved a miner's light, turned it on, and placed it atop McLean's head.

'Thanks,' McLean said. 'Wouldn't be much point going down there without this.'

Camphin slapped McLean on the back once more, and then nodded to the men to begin feeding the rope. Soon enough, McLean's body disappeared from view, leaving Camphin staring down at the flickering light.

'More rope,' McLean yelled up to him.

'More rope,' Camphin ordered.

The six volunteers let the rope slide slowly through their hands.

'That's it,' McLean called as he felt his feet find the base of the shaft. Seeing the light tracing a circle, Camphin called down, 'Anything?'

'Nothing in this one. Pull me up.'

The six men braced themselves and began hauling on the rope. It took all the effort they could muster to bring the large detective back to the surface, and by the time the top of McLean's head emerged from the shaft, eventually followed by the remainder of his body, the volunteers were wiping beads of sweat from their brows.

After lifting himself out of the shaft, McLean slowly walked to the next one. The men untied the rope from the original eucalypt, found one closer to the second shaft and retied it. McLean then descended in the same manner. Camphin watched the light moving further and further down the shaft, until he was sure McLean was near the base.

'Anything?'

'One sec. Just about at the bottom.' Reaching out with his feet, McLean found the base. 'Something doesn't feel right,' he called up. 'It almost feels like the floor's moving.'

'Floor's moving?' Camphin called down. 'What do you mean "the floor's moving"?'

'I mean the floor's moving!' McLean said as he illuminated the base of the shaft with the miner's lantern. 'Fuck! Fuck! Fuck! Pull me up!' he screamed.

Exhausted from their first attempt, and not paying particular attention, it was several moments before the volunteers started to haul on the rope. 'Fucking pull me up now, ya' bastards!' McLean pleaded.

Knowing that something was drastically wrong, but unsure as to what, Camphin echoed McLean's cries. 'Hurry up, boys! Get him out of there!'

Mustering together the last of their strength, the men gave an almighty pull and McLean was soon on his way up. By the time he emerged safely from the shaft, the volunteers had collapsed. McLean now did the same. Breathing heavily, he let out a large sigh before looking up at Camphin who, seeing McLean's ghostly complexion, was rather concerned about his colleague's welfare. 'What happened? Are you okay?'

Through laboured breathing, McLean spluttered, 'Fuckin' black snakes.'

'What?' Camphin said incredulously.

'Black snake. Big bastard, and a whole bunch of little ones surrounding it.'

Disbelief turned to hilarity as Camphin, Latimer and any other officer or local within earshot collapsed holding their sides.

'Shut up, ya' bastards,' McLean grumbled as he lifted himself off the ground and patted himself down before walking over to stand beside the last shaft.

It took a few minutes for the laughter to die down and for the men to retie the rope around yet another tree. Camphin ordered another six men to take the place of the original six, just in case McLean needed to be retrieved quickly again.

'You sure you want to go down another hole?' he asked seriously as he stood next to McLean and tried to see if there was anything moving at the base of the shaft.

'Let's just get this over and done with,' McLean growled as he positioned himself at the edge. When he was certain the new volunteers were ready, he lowered himself down.

'Watch out, Detective!' several onlookers called as he began to descend.

'Yeah, don't get your arse bitten off!' another cried.

Ignoring their jibes, McLean nervously inched his way down. When he could feel he was near the bottom, he braced his legs against the walls and examined the ground carefully before putting his feet down.

Much to his relief, the floor wasn't moving, but with his attention firmly fixed on searching for snakes, he hadn't noticed that there was indeed something else on the ground. After conducting a second survey of the base of the shaft, his nerves rapidly evaporated, only to be replaced by a rush of adrenalin as his excitement peaked. 'Boss! Boss!' he yelled.

'What, more snakes?' he replied. 'Quick, pull him up!'

Feeling the rope becoming taut around his waist, McLean shouted, 'No! No! Don't pull me up! I've found something!' The rope slackened, and as he looked up to the shaft's entrance, he could see the outline of Camphin and Latimer's heads.

'Did you say you've found something?' Latimer asked in clarification.

Recognising the voice, McLean replied, 'Yes, Inspector, that's right. I have found something. Several things, actually.'

'Put them in the bag and bring them up so we can have a look.'

Placing every visible item in the canvas bag that was hanging from his waist, McLean got as close to the ground as he dared and carefully scanned the area with the light to make sure he hadn't missed anything. Satisfied, he tugged on the rope twice, signalling to the men above to start hauling him up.

Camphin and Latimer shifted about uneasily while McLean slowly ascended, and his head had barely appeared before they were badgering him about what he had found. After emerging from the shaft, McLean reached inside the bag and meticulously laid out a blue and white spotted silk shirt. Men began to gather round as McLean carefully unfurled the shirt, and a collective gasp came from the crowd as more than a dozen empty golden cartridges were revealed.

After the din died down, McLean commented on the find to the others. 'Didn't Fosbery say that Weller was wearing a shirt like this one? We're close, real close. Weller's got to be around here somewhere. Come on, there's one more shaft to go. Lower me down into it.'

Repeating the process once again, McLean went down the last shaft and upon reaching the base, he became animated once more. 'Pull me up! Pull me up!' he yelled.

Once again, McLean was hauled back to the surface, more quickly this time.

'What is it?' Latimer asked as he and the other men gathered around. McLean, not about to be hurried, lifted himself out of the shaft, untied the ropes around his waist and stepped away before unloading the contents of his bag onto a small patch of grass. There was a roughly drawn map of the lagoon and a pair of leggings that had plainly been set on fire. Latimer and Camphin moved closer to examine them, the other men forming a respectful semicircle behind them.

After examining McLean's haul, they bagged what they'd found and went on searching around the lagoon until the clouds began to thicken in the sky. It began to sprinkle, then rain, then pour down, the heavy rain making it impossible to go on. Darkness also began to settle, so Latimer ordered a halt to the day's work, the officers and journalists heading off to the local inn whilst the locals returned home to discuss the day's events over their dinners.

The following day, the sun had barely begun to illuminate the rugged hills before the search parties started to head out, but before they set off to traverse the steep ravines and gullies, Latimer indicated that he wanted to brief everyone.

Outside the inn, more than two hundred people stood assembled in the steady rain waiting for Latimer to begin. Despite the dire weather, a sense of excitement permeated the mob, the locals keenly sensing that they were part of the most exciting thing to hit Sydney town in decades. Many fidgeted as they waited to get underway, each man secretly hoping he'd get to be the hero, the one to find one or more bodies.

'First of all I would like to thank everyone for volunteering and giving up their time,' Latimer began. 'The New South Wales Police Force is very aware that your efforts make our work so much easier. We believe we are looking for the bodies of at least one, but quite possibly two or more men. You people know this land better than anyone, and so I want you to use all your knowledge and do your best to help bring this mystery to a close. If you find anything, please report it directly back to us. Good luck.'

With the last of his words, the crowd dispersed in every direction, spending the rest of the day descending into every gully and every valley between Glenbrook and Linden. The afternoon sun had begun to sink in the west when the search parties started to return home. Some had found several items of interest, but for the most part their efforts had yielded little.

The same pattern continued for the next few days, but still they found nothing. The heavy rain served to dampen the spirits of the volunteers, and more and more decided to abandon the search and return to their quiet lives. The officer's spirits too were dejected, and so Latimer, deciding that Glenbrook had been covered, moved their base of operations further up the mountains to Springwood.

They'd had no luck in finding Weller's body. Now it was time to focus on finding Preston's.

14

Promising Leads

30 November 1896

Roche sat down at his desk and ran his fingers through his hair before letting out a deep sigh. The sheer number of interviews was beginning to take its toll, and he felt like he was taking two steps forward and one step back. He was certain he had a murderer on his hands, and not only that, he was certain the man they were hunting was not just a two-time murderer but a serial killer. Nothing had been found to lead anyone to this conclusion, but the nauseous feeling in the pit of his stomach convinced him that this was the truth, and that Butler had to be found before he claimed more victims, but he had no real clues as to where to begin.

'Detective Roche!' Michael Conroy called out as he bounded across the office with a package in his arms, which he placed on Roche's desk and quickly unwrapped.

'What's this?' Roche asked as he leant forward and picked up the piece of clothing.

'I just got these, after the forensic guys had finished with them. They're the items that Detective McLean found down two air shafts near the lagoon at Glenbrook.'

'Hmm,' Roche said as he put the shirt down and picked up the burnt leggings, turning them over and examining them closely. 'This is interesting.'

'What is?' Conroy asked as he stooped down and looked at the leggings.

'Look at this maker's tag,' Roche said as he held it up.

'A Brisbane company,' Conroy said.

'That rings a bell for some reason,' Roche said as he began flicking through the pile of papers on his desk. He was halfway through them when it came to him.

'Conroy, remind me, where did Mr Fielding say that Arthur Preston came from?'

The question was largely rhetorical, and Conroy immediately caught on to Roche's train of thought. 'Brisbane!'

'There we go!' Roche said with more excitement in his voice than he'd had in days. 'Where was Arthur Preston staying again?'

'Mrs Williams' boarding house in Redfern.'

'I think we should have a chat with her. Let's go,' Roche said as he snatched up his coat and rushed out the door. Conroy had trouble keeping up, but caught the detective just before he stepped outside the building, the two of them arriving at the boarding house soon after.

Roche entered and found the middle-aged landlady busying herself with cleaning.

'Excuse me, ma'am, my name is Detective John Roche. Are you Mrs Williams?'

'Yes, I most certainly am,' she replied, perplexed as to why a detective had come to her establishment. 'What can I do for you?'

'I just wanted to check something with you. Do you remember having a boarder here by the name of Arthur Preston?'

'Arthur? Yes, I remember him.'

'Did he say anything to you before he left here?'

'Yes, he was very excited. Something about a prospecting trip out west.'

'Do you remember what he was wearing when he left?'

'Yes, I most certainly do.'

Reaching into his bag, Roche withdrew the leggings.

'Was Mr Preston wearing these when he left?' he asked.

Mrs Williams took the leggings and examined them carefully.

'Yes, I believe he was wearing these. Has something happened? I've been reading about something terrible happening in the mountains in the papers.'

'Yes, he's gone missing in the mountains but we're not sure what's happened to him. Right now we're doing our best to locate him. Thank you, Mrs Williams. We'll contact you again if we need anything else.'

The two men rushed back to headquarters to report the positive identification to Fosbery.

'How is the investigation coming, John?' Fosbery asked as he looked up from his desk after hearing Roche knock.

'We've got several good leads, plus the boys have found some good evidence around the lagoon.'

'Any bodies yet?'

'No, sir, but we have found possessions which we believe may belong to both Arthur Preston and Captain Weller.'

'So, you found their possessions. This is not, in itself, proof that either man is a victim of foul play. They may have simply rid themselves of their own belongings.'

'Yes, I am aware of that, sir.'

'Good, now that's out of the way, what do your instincts tell you?'

'They tell me that we have at least two dead men. I also feel that this could be just the tip of the iceberg.'

'I've trusted you in the past, John, and you've never let me down. So, what next?'

'With your permission, I'd like to make copies of the photo that Mrs Gilham gave us and circulate them around every town and village in the mountains from Penrith to Katoomba and see if anything comes up. I would also like to send them to every police station in the country. I'm certain that someone, somewhere, must have seen something.'

'Good idea,' Fosbery said. 'Get onto it.'

'Also, I think it would be a good idea if we were to offer a reward,' Roche added.

'How much are we talking here? You know it's never that easy to get rewards approved.'

'Yes, sir, I know, but I'd say twenty-five pounds for anyone who finds Captain Weller or Butler alive, and if something has happened to Weller, fifty pounds to find the body.'

'That's a fair bit of money, John. Are you sure?'

'Sir, you know as well as I do that greed is a great motivator. Any less, and people may not bother. I understand that with all the media coverage people might want the fame, but I'm sure that offering the money can't hurt. It will also demonstrate to the media how serious we are about putting this one to bed.'

'Hmm,' Fosbery pondered. 'You're right. I'll make sure it happens. I think the photo and descriptions need to go to the papers too. We'd better give them something; they've really been on my back about all of this.'

'Sir, I'll get it done.'

Butler's description was sent to the media, along with the offer of the reward. The description read:

About 40 years of age, 5'9" or 5'10" tall, stout build, muscular appearance, dark hair slightly tinged with grey, dark-brown moustache and small side whiskers, peculiar nose – flat on bridge, large on point, and turned to left side as if it had been broken; rather high shoulders; dresses well; an Englishman.

≈

Meanwhile, McLean and Thorndike sat, maps spread out over several desks, in the Springwood police station. Having received telegraphed confirmation that the leggings did indeed belong to Arthur Preston and that the police were looking for bodies and/or a murderer, the police widened their search.

'We've been concentrating our efforts along these ridge lines here,' McLean said to Thorndike, pointing to a spot on one of the maps, 'but something tells me Butler wouldn't have killed Preston around Springwood.'

'Why do you reckon that is?' Thorndike asked as he examined the maps more closely.

'Too many people. Too much chance of being seen.'

'Seems to me that his plan was to come up here, commit the murders, and then disappear again. If it's worked for him before, he'll try it again. He probably thinks he's smarter than us, and will get away with it,' Thorndike said as he contemplated the maps.

'Maybe you're right,' McLean offered. 'I still think we should shift our search further up the mountains.'

'Okay, but where do you suggest?' Thorndike said.

'You see how the train line snakes its way through here, past Faulconbridge and up to Linden?'

'Yeah,' Thorndike offered as he watched McLean trace the railway line with his finger.

'We've had reports of someone fitting Butler's description walking from Linden, so I reckon it's worthwhile shifting our search up there.'

'Hec, mate, we've already had a few parties up there, but if you think it's worth another look, then it's probably worth another look,' Thorndike replied. He was about to say more when he was interrupted by a knock at the door.

'Enter,' McLean said.

The door opened and a well-dressed local man in his late forties with neat, slightly greying hair entered the room.

'Yes,' McLean said as he and Thorndike looked up.

'Gentlemen, Mr Pritchard asked me to bring this to you,' the man said as he held up a shirt.

They knew the local innkeeper was busy organising all the supplies and provisions for the search parties and police officers and they were somewhat perplexed as to why Pritchard would send them a shirt.

The man handed the shirt to McLean who traced his fingers down a large tear near the collar.

'This looks like it has been cut by a knife,' he said.

'Maybe someone has just tossed it in the bush, could be nothing, Thorndike said as he took a closer look at the tear and the collar. 'Wait! Look at these initials!'

'A.T.O.P.,' McLean said as he took the shirt and examined the collar. 'Arthur Thomas Osborne Preston. That's the full name that Roche sent us from Sydney.'

'Where exactly does Mr Pritchard live?' Thorndike asked as McLean picked up the shirt and locked it away.

'Up at Linden,' the man replied.

'Looks like you might have been right, Hector. I think we best move the search up there, starting with the area around Mr Pritchard's house, even though Butler may have tossed Preston's shirt into the bushes, or Preston simply lost it.'

'Either way, at least we have confirmation that Preston was at Linden,' McLean said as he hurried outside and ordered his men to be ready and assembled in ten minutes. Soon, dozens of men were assembled outside the police station carrying an assortment of shovels, ropes and picks. The news of the shirt find had spread quickly and, however weary they were from weeks of searching, the men felt a renewed sense of hope, and were now impatient for the search to get underway. McLean, understanding the men's desire for haste, soon appeared at the front of the station and addressed them.

'Okay, boys, as I'm sure you've all heard, Mr Pritchard discovered Arthur Preston's shirt in the bush, so we're going to shift our search up to Linden. I want you to split up into groups of three or four. Half the groups will search the northern side, while the other half will search the southern side. Sergeant Thorndike and I will search around Mr Pritchard's house and then we will base ourselves at Linden station. If you find anything, I want you to report back to us immediately.'

The various search parties set off along the road, and after a solid half hour of walking they reached Linden station, where they assembled along the platform and awaited further instructions. McLean quickly positioned himself halfway up the stairs.

'Right,' he began. 'The parties standing to my right, you fan out and search the north side. The parties on my left, you search the south.'

The groups duly set off in their assigned directions. McLean and Thorndike set off to examine the area around where the shirt had been found but, finding nothing more of interest, they returned to the station to wait for news from the other search parties who spent the entire day moving up, down and along the ridgelines, searching in any place that looked remotely promising. Dozens and dozens of men scoured every bush, behind every tree and beneath every overhang, but when twilight came and the sun began to set, McLean sent the order around that they were all to return to Springwood and resume the search the following day.

As the men trudged back to their lodgings, their spirits were low. The new evidence had raised their hopes and given them renewed enthusiasm, but after days of searching they were exhausted and, in reality, their efforts had returned very little.

15

To Arthur Preston

3 December 1896

Three more days passed, during which the men searched further afield, as well as going back over ground they'd already covered. The next morning, the search parties trudged out towards Linden once again for another long day of searching.

'Sir,' a young constable said to McLean as he watched the other officers disperse and disappear in the same fashion as they had done over the past few days.

McLean turned. 'Yes, Constable Delaney?'

'Sir, Constable Hardiman and I have been scouring one of the south ridges.'

'And?'

'Well, there is a ridge closer to here that we'd like to have a look at.'

'Why is that?' McLean wasn't questioning Delaney's policing abilities, but rather was interested as to the young officer's thoughts.

'Well, sir, when we were walking back here yesterday, the ridge looked a little easier to walk. I dunno, sir, just a hunch.'

'Hunches are a key part of police work, young Delaney. You go search that ridge, and tell me what you find,' McLean said encouragingly.

The two officers duly set off and traced a few ridges. After stopping for a brief lunch, they walked a few more kilometres to the track that had caught Delaney's interest the previous day. The lip of the gully sloped away steeply as a thin track wound its way through the dense bush. Reaching the base, the two men came across a creek where several small waterfalls trickled down to form a large, deep pool. Delaney squatted down and refilled his canteen before drinking heartily and refilling it once more. Standing up, he looked around at the ferns and moss-covered boulders scattered over the rainforest floor.

'I don't reckon he brought him all the way down here; it's taken us long e-bloody-nough!' Delaney exclaimed as he wiped his brow.

'Maybe that was his plan,' Hardiman offered. 'Maybe he figured no one would come searching around here.'

Delaney circled around, looking up at the thick eucalyptus canopy above them. Even in the semipermanent darkness, he sensed the light was fading. 'We'd better start heading back up,' he said. 'Don't reckon we've got too much light left.'

'Yeah, I reckon you're right,' Hardiman said. He filled his canteen, turned and started to make his way back up the mountainside. After a lengthy vertical climb, the landscape begun to flatten out, and the two men paused beneath a large overhang for several gulps of water in between laboured breaths.

'Remind me,' Hardiman said as he inhaled deeply in an attempt to regain his breath, 'never to go that far down a mountainside again.'

'Right there with you, mate. Right there with you,' Delaney replied as he checked his pocket watch.

'What time is it?' Hardiman asked as he set off along the trail.

'Four o'clock.'

'Come on, or we'll be late for the debriefing.'

'It isn't until five. We'll be right,' Delaney said as he followed Hardiman, the two of them, wearied by the climb, moving at a pace barely above a meander. Not far from the top of the ridgeline, Hardiman stopped for another sip of water. Standing beneath a large, grey sandstone overhang, he gazed out over the tops of the eucalypts towards the rolling green valleys beyond.

'John,' he said, turning around, 'Preston could be anywhere out here. We've got Buckley's chance.'

Delaney walked over to the edge of the sandstone ledge and took one final look down into the valley.

'Yeah, I think you might be right,' he said.

'C'mon, Let's get going,' Hardiman said as he began walking back towards the top of the ridge line. Delaney followed, but only took a few steps before he stopped and began examining a patch of dirt underneath the overhang.

'Hey, John, did you notice this on the way down?'

'Notice what?' Hardiman said as he came back down the track and stood beside Delaney.

'Look over there,' he said, pointing to the patch of dirt.

'What am I looking at?' Hardiman asked.

'The soil.'

'What about it? I don't see anything.'

'There. The soil looks darker.'

'Yeah, actually, you might be right.'

Delaney picked up his walking stick and moved further under the overhang. Hardiman followed until they both stood next to the darker soil. Delaney started to poke and prod the patch of earth with his stick, but had barely turned over a few grains when a horrible stench rose from the ground.

'I think we might be on to something here,' he said as he pulled his handkerchief from his coat pocket and held it to his nose. Hardiman followed suit, merely nodding in reply. The two men continued to carefully remove soil, and the deeper they delved, the more nauseating the stench became, until eventually Hardiman had to step to one side, where he vomited violently.

'You right?' Delaney asked.

Not being able to do much more than nod, Hardiman composed himself as best he could, but a dismissive wave of his right hand indicated that he couldn't continue with the digging. Delaney shifted some more soil, and suddenly some tangled strands of human hair appeared. He delicately scraped some more soil away to reveal a slightly decayed forehead and the top of an ear. Certain that they'd found Arthur Preston, Delaney decided to leave the rest of the digging to the experts.

'John,' he said to his partner, 'I'd better inform Detective McLean. You right to stay here and guard the body?'

'I'd rather you stayed,' Hardiman coughed, still tasting the bile in his throat.

'You'll be right, mate, you'll be right,' Delaney laughed as he withdrew a small hip flask from inside his coat and tossed it towards Hardiman. 'Sit up top if you have to.'

Bending down to pick up the flask, Hardiman took a prolonged sip, closed his eyes, and felt his body recovering as the liquid warmed him. By the time he opened his eyes again, Delaney had already disappeared up the track.

Delaney rushed towards the top of the ridge as quickly as he could, and when his feet eventually reached flat ground he set off at speed towards headquarters.

Half an hour later, he rushed into McLean's office, sweating profusely. 'Sir! Sir!' he said as he struggled to regain his breath.

'What, what is it?' McLean replied.

'We…we…found something,' Delaney spluttered between large gulps of air.

McLean leapt up from his chair, grabbed a jug and poured Delaney a glass of water.

'You right?' McLean asked.

'Yes, sir. Thank you, sir. You know how Constable Hardiman and I wanted to check that ridge?'

'Yes.'

'We went all the way down into the valley, but we didn't find anything, so we came up a different way, and stopped for a breather on a rock ledge not far from the top. I was looking out over the valley, and then I peered down over the edge and noticed a patch of dark soil. We squatted down to have a look, and as soon as we started to dig, the smell came straight up, and after a little more digging, we discovered a human head.'

McLean knew that even though there might be dozens of bodies hidden in these mountains, the chances of this particular body not being Arthur Preston were extremely slim. Either way, they now had a murder victim on their hands, and that required their full investigative attention. 'Send three constables to guard the site. I'll telegraph Sydney to tell them what you found and await further orders.'

'Yes, sir,' Delaney said as he turned to leave. He'd just reached the office door when McLean called out to him.

'Excellent work, Constable. Excellent work.'

≈

'Sir! Sir!' the telegraph officer cried as he rushed into Fosbery's office. The Inspector-General and Roche were deeply engrossed in examining the various Sydney papers, and Fosbery looked up irately, annoyed at the interruption.

'You know there's such a thing as knocking,' he scolded.

'Sorry, sir, yes, sir, but I just received a telegraph from Detective McLean.'

Whilst both Fosbery and Roche knew that McLean had been ordered to telegraph his progress on a regular basis, receiving something from him did not necessarily warrant a disruption.

'And?'

'Sir, I think you had better read this straightaway.'

Fosbery snatched the telegraph from the officer's hand, a clear indication of his annoyance, and read it.

Human remains found at Linden. Stop. Believed to be those of Arthur Preston. Stop. Awaiting further instructions. Stop.

Fosbery's face and mood changed completely and, despite the grim nature of the news, his frown transformed into a broad smile.

'What is it?' Roche asked impatiently, seeing Fosbery's excitement.

'They've found him!' Fosbery said as he looked at Roche.

'Which one?' Roche inquired.

'Preston,' Fosbery said as he handed Roche the telegraph.

'Outstanding!' Roche said as he read. 'What do you want me to do?'

'Take Brennan with you, and the pathologists and Coroner Lethbridge.'

'Yes, sir.'

'I want all of you out there first thing in the morning.'

'Yes, sir.'

'Sir,' the telegraphing officer interrupted, having stood quietly to one side.

'Yes,' Fosbery said, having forgotten about him.

'What would you like me to send back to Detective McLean?'

'Tell him I'm notifying the coroner and sending the pathologist and more staff, and to make sure the crime scene is preserved until they get there.'

'Yes, sir,' the officer said as he departed.

Sitting down at his desk, Fosbery slumped back in his chair.

'Finally,' he said as he sat back up and looked at Roche, who had taken up the seat opposite. 'We'll need to take someone up there to make a positive identification. You've done all the yard work. Who have we got?'

'Preston met Butler at Thompson's Railway Dining Rooms. I have already interviewed Mr Thompson, and he gave me a pretty good description of both men. I could take him.'

'Anyone else?'

Flicking through his notebook, Roche found the page he wanted, and read a summary of his notes to Fosbery. 'At the initial meeting with Butler, Preston took two friends along. One of them was Mr Fielding, who was the one who came in here to report Preston missing.'

'Find him and take him too.'

A knock at the door interrupted them. Fosbery and Roche looked up to see the constable responsible for the front desk.

'Yes?' Fosbery said.

'Sorry to interrupt, sir, but there's a man out the front who'd like to talk to one of the detectives about the Arthur Preston case.'

'Can't someone else handle it? We're kind of busy just now.'

'Ah, yes, sir, but he specifically asked to speak to Detective Roche.'

'Probably just another nut who thinks they can solve the case. I'll deal with it,' Roche said as he rose from his seat.

'Thank you, John.'

'Back shortly,' Roche said with a strained smile.

Following the constable out to the front office, Roche immediately spotted Fielding. 'Mr Fielding,' he said with surprise. 'What brings you here?'

'Sorry to bother you, Detective, but I've just come to inquire whether you've made any progress with locating my friend Arthur.'

Roche shook his head in disbelief.

'Detective?' Fielding said, unsure as to the reason for Roche's response.

'Your timing is impeccable,' Roche said. 'Come through, won't you.'

Leading Fielding through the detectives' office, Roche took him straight into Fosbery's office. 'Sir,' Roche said, 'allow me to introduce Mr Fielding.'

Raising his head, Fosbery's face took on the same look of disbelief. He rose from his seat and shook Fielding's hand. 'How do you do, sir?'

'I have been doing okay, but as I said to Detective Roche here, I have come to inquire about my friend Arthur.'

'Forgive our reaction,' Roche said as he pulled up a chair for Fielding and indicated for him to sit down, 'but we have only just received news about your friend, and we're curious as to how you found out about this so quickly.'

'The evening papers ran a story about a body being found in Linden. As soon as I read it, I had a feeling it may have been Arthur.'

'Gees, those journos don't miss a bloody trick, do they!' Fosbery exclaimed before recomposing himself. 'Mr Fielding, I'm sorry to have to tell you this, but, yes, we do believe the body we found is that of your friend.'

Fielding buried his face in his hands to hide his tears. Roche put his hand on Fielding's shoulder.

'We're very sorry to have to ask you this, Mr Fielding, but in order to be sure that the body is in fact that of your friend, I'm going to have to ask you to accompany me to the Blue Mountains to make a formal identification.'

'Yes, of course,' Fielding said as he wiped his eyes and composed himself. 'When do you want to leave?'

'First thing tomorrow morning, if that's possible.'

Fielding closed his eyes, pondered the request and gave a slight nod.

The following morning, Drs Taylor and Paton, the Coroner, Mr Lethbridge, Roche, Brennan, Fielding, Thompson and several reporters and photographers boarded the early train and arrived at Springwood at 5 am. When the official party arrived, they found dozens of men rushing about placing shovels and bags in neat rows outside the station.

'Good morning, gentlemen,' McLean said to them all. 'Are you ready for the examination of the scene?'

'Yes, sir, that we are,' Paton responded.

'I'll tell the men to collect all the gear and we'll be on our way,' McLean said. 'It's a good half-hour walk through some pretty rough country, so I hope you all brought your walking boots.'

The men grabbed their gear, and the group set off along the Great Western Road. It was only when they reached the top of the ridge where Delaney had discovered the body that the true roughness of the country dawned on the doctors, the senior officers and the civilians.

'It looks like there's a great green blanket covering everything,' Dr Paton commented as he cast his eyes across the vast expanse of eucalypt forests and sandstone plateaus.

'Yes, doctor, you certainly wouldn't want to get lost out there. We'd have one hell of a time trying to find you!' McLean said as he patted the doctor on the back and began the descent down into the valley. The group walked in single file, snaking their way along the narrow track down the side of the cliff until they came to a halt at the top of the rocky outcrop.

McLean moved to the edge. 'The body was found underneath this ledge. I must warn you, it's not pleasant.'

'That's fine, Detective,' Dr Taylor replied. 'We have seen this kind of thing before.'

Each man held on to various trees and shrubs as they descended into the valley, steadying and bracing themselves so they wouldn't topple into the ravine below. After having to duck under the last section of the ledge, the doctors and the others were surprised to find that they were able to stand upright. The doctors paused, but were quickly pushed forward as more and more men arrived, eager to watch as the grisly proceedings unfolded. With everything abuzz, McLean failed to notice the angry looks on the faces of Constables Johnson, Draper and Shelley, who had been sent to guard the gravesite.

'It's about time,' Johnson sniped.

'What?' McLean snapped back.

'I apologise, sir,' Johnson said, his weariness and anger having caused him to forget his place. 'It's just that we thought someone would be sent to relieve us. We've been out here all night, listening to the dingoes howling and scratching around. We've had to fire a few shots to scare them off!'

Encouraged by his colleague's boldness, Draper now joined in. 'And we've had no food or water all night, sir.'

McLean was unsure what to do. On the one hand, he needed to reproach the outspoken constables but on the other, he *had* failed in his duties.

'Constables, I thank you for your vigilance, and I apologise for not relieving you. You can be certain I will make it up to you in the future, but for now, we have more pressing matters at hand,' he said as diplomatically as he could.

Hardly pleased or placated, the constables wanted to push the matter further, but had little choice other than to move to one side to allow the dig to begin.

'You there,' McLean said, pointing towards his subordinates. Several men looked at one another, unsure who McLean was referring to. 'You, with the small shovel,' McLean said by way of clarification. 'Bring it over here and start digging around the outside.'

The constable moved to the grave and started to dig.

'Careful, man!' McLean scolded. 'We don't want everything destroyed before the doctors can get at it!'

Like a chided child, the constable dipped his head and resumed digging, but this time with much more caution and finesse. He'd barely cleared a few inches of dirt before the stench from the decaying body rose and filled the confines of the cave. Scrunching up his face, and momentarily turning his head away, the constable held his breath and then continued. Soon enough, he'd revealed Preston's head and body. The dead man's legs were drawn up towards his torso, and his arms were clasped around his right leg. His head was bent forward and tucked into his chest, his face not yet visible.

With the entire body now exposed to the open air, the nauseating stench intensified, causing several men to reach for their handkerchiefs and quickly place them to their mouths and noses. Two men nearer to the body turned, made their way through the crowd with their hands to their mouths and vomited in the nearby bush.

Satisfied that his job was finished, the constable moved well back from the body before making his way out of the cave to take a deep breath of crisp, clean mountain air. The two doctors and the coroner moved forward and began a preliminary examination. Squatting down beside the body, Dr Taylor looked up and down its length before looking up to McLean. 'Detective, you see the size of the grave and the position of the body within it?'

'Yes,' McLean responded as he moved closer.

'This is clear evidence that the body was put in under tremendous force. If we try to pull it out like this, we risk destroying the body, and we might lose some vital clues. Would you be so kind as to have one of your men dig around the grave, probably about two feet around the outside, and the same in depth.'

McLean nodded. Initially, he looked at the original constable, but upon seeing that the exhumation had clearly taken its toll on the young man, he ordered another officer to retrieve a shovel and oblige the doctor's request. Taking a deep breath, the second constable stepped over to the body as the doctors moved out of the way. By this time, the exhumation had attracted a lot more visitors; not morbid onlookers, but thousands and thousands of flies that had come to feast on the smorgasbord of dead flesh. Buzzing and zipping in every direction, the swarm made it impossible to continue.

'It's no use, sir,' the digging constable said as he spat some of the insects from his mouth and stepped back from the grave. 'I can't see anything with all these bloody flies in the way!'

Without hesitating, McLean said, 'Boys, start a fire, and make sure you green it up plenty. Maybe we can smoke these little bastards out.'

The men quickly constructed a small fire, lit it, and then when it was burning nicely, stacked it with a pile of green branches almost three feet high. As the flames began to draw the moisture from the branches, a thick blanket of white smoke filled the cave, stinging everyone's eyes. After letting the fire burn for some minutes, McLean was finally satisfied that the flies had been driven away, and ordered the fire to be extinguished. The smoke began to clear as soon as he barked his orders. 'Hurry up, Constable!' he shouted. 'Get in there before those blasted flies come back.'

Quickly, but carefully, the constable resumed digging in almost perfect accordance with the doctor's instructions.

Meanwhile, McLean turned his attention to another pair of constables.

'You two, fetch a blanket out of one of those packs and lay it out next to the grave. Grab those sticks over there and carefully place them under the body so you can transfer it onto the blanket.'

The first constable retrieved a blue blanket and carefully laid it out beside the grave, while the second collected four suitable sticks from nearby. Taking great care, the two men manoeuvred the sticks under the body.

'You two,' McLean said to another two constables, 'grab the other side and help them lift the body.'

The two men hurried around to the opposite side, bent down and took hold of the sticks.

'Alright,' McLean said. 'On the count of three. One, two, three.' The four men lifted the body and placed it onto the adjacent blanket. Freed from the confines of the grave, Preston's body now resumed a normal position, allowing them to see the dead man's face. Preston was still clothed in his dark-blue coat, and a black leather belt kept his light-coloured leggings, similar to those that had been found at Glenbrook Lagoon, in place. One of his feet was still enclosed in a boot, but the other was only covered by a blue sock.

'Fellas,' Roche said as he stepped in to examine the body closely, 'have a look around and see if you can find his other boot.'

The officers began poking and prodding in the scrub until one officer, searching a clump of bushes about fifteen yards away from where the body had been buried, cried out, 'Found it, sir!'

Now Roche turned to Fielding and Thompson. 'Mr Fielding, Mr Thompson,' he said. 'I'm sorry to have to ask you to do this, but if you could step forward and give us a positive identification, please.'

Fielding and Thompson stepped forward, their reactions eagerly watched by the assembled police, but before the formal identification could be made, an officer had to clear the congealed dirt and clay from Preston's face.

Fielding closed his eyes, rubbed the bridge of his nose, and then opened his eyes again. He dropped his head and let out a deep sigh before speaking. 'Yes, Detective, his nose may be missing, but that is definitely Arthur Preston.'

'Thank you, Mr Fielding,' Roche said sympathetically. 'Mr Thompson, is this the man whom you saw in your establishment, and then again at Emu Plains?'

'Yes, sir, that is most certainly the man.'

Fielding stepped away from the body and wandered off to a far corner of the cave to be alone with his thoughts. McLean and Roche, having secured a positive identification, now began a more detailed examination. Roche began by searching Preston's pockets, finding a wad of pulped paper in a right-hand-side pocket about halfway down the coat.

'Can you make any of it out?' McLean asked as Roche attempted to unfurl the soggy ball.

'Not much. It looks like promissory notes, but we'll have to wait until it dries out,' he said as he handed it to a nearby officer, who placed it in an evidence bag.

'Hey, John, have a look at this,' McLean said after examining the towel that was knotted around Preston's neck. 'What do you think Butler used this for?'

Roche stood up and looked around the area before pointing to one side of the grave. 'You see the tracks there? Preston was murdered there, and then Butler tied the towel around his neck to drag him into the grave.'

Roche turned and looked in the direction of Fielding, who was still taking intermittent glances at his deceased friend's body. 'C'mon,' he said, to no one in particular. 'Let's get Preston out of here. Let's give him some dignity.'

With these words, two officers set off back up the ridge and soon returned carrying a makeshift wooden coffin. The sticks that had been used to raise the body from the grave were now employed a second time as four officers lifted Preston's body up and carefully lowered it into the coffin. Once they had completed the task, a fifth officer quickly nailed the lid into place. Two men went to the front and two to the rear as they squatted down and lifted the coffin, placing the makeshift planks on their inside shoulders. The carrying party slowly began to make their way out of the cave, but even with four men, it was arduous work. As the coffin passed, several men had to put their hands up to shield their mouths and noses from the foul stench, but it was worst of all for the four pallbearers. The steepness of the slope made for an almost impossible task, and the men continually grasped hold of trees or rocky outcrops with their free hands as they hauled themselves slowly upwards. A hundred feet felt like a hundred miles, and on several occasions, as the men at the front raised themselves up the steep descent, the ones at the rear had trouble maintaining their balance while they held the coffin up and tried to keep it level as it bobbled around between them. The remaining men in the party watched on intently, certain that the coffin was going to slip and they'd have to struggle to catch it before it tumbled down into the gully.

Finally, the pallbearers managed to reach the peak of the hill, and immediately lowered the coffin onto the first piece of flat ground they found. Roche immediately ordered four replacements to take over, but they only lasted a few minutes before the smell became overpowering and they needed respite. Roche quickly organised several carrying parties and, after more than three-quarters of an hour of painstaking upward progress, rotating the coffin amongst several groups of pallbearers, the party eventually reached Linden railway station.

The stationmaster and his assistant had been watching out for them, and at long last, they saw them approaching in the distance. When they set foot on the platform, the stationmaster hurried over to McLean and Roche.

'So, where would you like me to put the poor chap?' he said, before the smell overwhelmed him and he too had to cover his mouth and nose.

'Do you have a spare room? That way, we can contain the smell a little,' Roche said.

The stationmaster nodded. 'This way,' he said, and turned and led them along the platform. When he reached his destination, he stopped, retrieved his keys from his belt, and quickly unlocked the door to the luggage room. As the coffin passed by, he commented to Roche, 'You know, Detective, I do have quite a bit of chlorizone which we can use as a disinfectant, if you think it might help.'

'Yes, sir,' said Roche. 'Please retrieve it. It will be better than nothing.'

The last team of pallbearers carefully lowered the coffin, and then hurried from the room.

'C'mon,' McLean said as the stationmaster returned with the chlorizone. 'Let's get to it.'

After they had removed the nails and lifted the lid, the stench quickly permeated every square inch of the room. The stationmaster worked as quickly as he could, and had soon covered the majority of the body. McLean refastened the lid and the two men left the room, the stationmaster carefully closing and locking the door behind him after they'd emerged onto the platform. Both men gave an audible sigh of relief as the stench subsided.

McLean looked out across the valley on the opposite side of the tracks, seemingly deep in thought about what needed to be done next. Many of the officers stood at various points along the platform, smoking assiduously in an attempt to calm themselves. The stationmaster came up beside the burly detective. 'Detective?' he said.

McLean snapped out of his thoughts and turned to face the stationmaster. 'Yes?'

'The next goods train will be here at about nine o'clock. We can put him on that, if that will be acceptable.'

'Excellent,' McLean replied.

Soon enough, the sound of the goods train could be heard echoing through the valleys, and before long the black locomotive appeared around the sharp bend leading into the straight part of the track adjacent to the station. The stationmaster waved it down, and the engineer gave a brief wave in response as he passed by before bringing the train to a halt.

Four officers retrieved the coffin from the luggage room and slid it into an empty carriage. Once they had fastened it in place, they leant out of the carriage and watched the other officers, the doctors, and Fielding and Thompson move further along the train and board the passenger carriage.

The locomotive wound up again, let out a loud whistle, and pulled out of the station. Gradually picking up speed, it slowly wound its way down through the vertical sandstone cliffs and onto the plains below. After crossing the Nepean River, the train reached Penrith station shortly after 10 am. McLean stuck his head out the window as the train slowed, but quickly pulled it back inside. 'Bloody hell!' he moaned.

'What?' Roche asked.

'News travels fast down those mountains,' McLean said. 'Bloody locals are everywhere.'

As the train approached the platform, the crowd rushed forward, eager to get a glimpse of the dead man. Dozens of people mounted the sides of the train and stared through the windows at the bewildered officers. When the train came to a halt, McLean and the others stepped down from the passenger carriage and made their way to the carriage carrying the coffin. Now realising which carriage contained the body, the crowd surged forward, but McLean was one step ahead of them and hurriedly ordered the dozen or so officers to form a semicircular cordon around the carriage. With some difficulty, the officers managed to restrain the excited crowd as the carriage door was unlocked and opened.

A stifled gasp emanated from the crowd as Preston's coffin was lowered and placed onto a waiting buggy. McLean, the two doctors, Thompson and Fielding joined the driver in the front seats, while the remaining officers followed close behind, attempting to keep the crowd at bay as best they could. The procession made its way down the High Street, into Henry Street and over the railway line. McLean watched Fielding intently as he continually turned his head to look at the box containing the body of his dear friend. Realising that it had not yet been said, he placed his arm around the young man's shoulders. Fielding looked up at him.

'Mr Fielding,' McLean said, 'I am terribly sorry for your loss.'

'Thank you, Detective,' Fielding replied as the tears began to well. 'Arthur was a very good man, and he certainly didn't deserve an end like this.'

'Nobody does, Mr Fielding. Nobody does.'

The buggy eventually arrived at the Nepean Cottage Hospital, the crowd becoming agitated as Preston's body was lowered and taken into the mortuary, followed by McLean, the two doctors, Fielding and Thompson. When they reached the entrance, Doctor Taylor and Doctor Paton stopped, turned and blocked the doorway.

'We think it's best if you wait out here whilst we wash and clean the body,' Paton said, shooting a quick glance in Fielding's direction.

'Of course, Doctor,' McLean said. 'Would you like to join me for a cup of tea, Mr Fielding, Mr Thompson?'

'Yes, Detective, that would be lovely, thank you,' they replied in unison.

McLean ushered the two men through to a small lounge room, where Fielding and Thompson sat and waited until McLean returned a short time later with two cups of tea. The three men exchanged some small talk, mostly about the procedures that would take place between now and the time when Preston could be given a proper funeral.

Meanwhile, Dr Paton conducted the autopsy, and compiled his report.

This is the body of a well-nourished man, about twenty years of age and approximately five feet seven inches tall. There are two plates containing false teeth in the upper and lower jaw. There are a few straggling hairs on the chin and cheek but none on the upper lip. There is a circular wound on the back of the head, and two fractures of the skull; one upward and the other downwards. The wound traces from the base of the skull to the nose. Death occurred as the result of a gunshot wound, the bullet passing forward and then downwards. The weapon has been discharged from a point above the head of the deceased.

Having completed his post-mortem, Dr Paton now reappeared. 'Mr Fielding. I am sorry to have to ask you to do this,' he said apologetically, 'but we need you and Mr Thompson to make another formal identification.'

'Yes, of course,' Fielding replied dejectedly. Putting his cup of tea to one side, he raised himself from his chair, Thompson following suit. Paton stepped to one side, allowing McLean to lead the way, with Fielding and Thompson following close behind.

When they entered the mortuary, they saw Preston's body laid out on a table with Dr Taylor standing on the opposite side. 'We have been very fortunate,' he began, pointing at Preston. 'The ledge of the cave and the type of soil stayed the decomposition process. The body is in remarkably good shape considering the amount of time it has been in the ground, which we estimate to have been about five weeks. I can also confirm that, based on the type of wound to his skull, there is no way that this was self-inflicted.'

Fielding moved over and stood beside his dead friend, taking his left hand and grasping it tightly as he looked over the dead man's countenance.

'Detective McLean,' he said with a sigh as he let go of the hand, 'this is definitely Arthur Thomas Osborne Preston.'

'Thank you, Mr Fielding. Mr Thompson, if you please.'

Thompson moved over to the body and only needed a quick look before he said, 'Yes, Detective McLean, 'this is the young man who met with the man I knew as Frank Clare in my tearooms several weeks ago.'

'Thank you, gentlemen,' McLean said. 'Perhaps you would both like to join me for a drink, something a little stronger than tea after all this unpleasantness perhaps?'

Fielding gave a slight nod, as did Thompson, and the three men walked from the mortuary and made their way to the rear exit from the hospital, keen to avoid the crowd waiting outside the front entrance. Heading back towards the station, they soon arrived at the Red Cow Hotel, where Fielding and Thompson found a vacant table in the beer garden while McLean headed into the bar, returning soon after with a bottle of whisky and three glasses. After pouring a generous amount for each of them, he raised his glass.

'To Arthur Preston.'

'Arthur Preston,' the other two echoed.

16

A Chance Find

6 December 1896

Following the discovery of the body and the subsequent post-mortem, the senior officers returned to Sydney. Arthur Preston was buried at Rookwood cemetery, and after he had been laid to rest, Roche continued to search for the elusive Frank Butler, while McLean returned to Glenbrook to look for Lee Weller, every man in the search parties now possessing renewed enthusiasm as they scoured the gullies and valleys once more. The fervour of the locals also increased after the reward for finding the body was raised to one hundred pounds. It was mid-morning, and McLean had just returned from examining a creek adjacent to Mitchell's Pass, and from doing yet another circuit of the lagoon, when two young constables came rushing up the road.

'Sir! Sir!' the men gasped, both out of breath.

'What is it?'

'We found something!'

'What?'

'We found something!' the officer was about to say more when McLean noticed a young girl riding a horse up the street.

'I think it better that this young lady tell you,' one of the constables said. 'This is Miss Woods.'

'Miss,' McLean said as he doffed his hat.

'Detective McLean,' she began, 'my father and I live down on the opposite side of the railway lines. My father was out searching behind the back of our place with his mate and they've found something. I think it best you come and see.'

McLean, Tate, the other officers and scores of local residents followed as Miss Woods rode down the road, across the railway lines and back to her house. She continued on past the house and into the bush beyond, following a narrow trail. When she came to the end of the ridge she dismounted and walked a short way into the scrub, where two men were standing in front of a large pile of rocks leaning on long shovels.

'This is my father, Mr Woods,' Miss Woods said, indicating a man sporting a long, grey beard.

'Mr Woods,' McLean said as he moved over and shook his hand. 'Can you tell me what you've discovered?'

THE FINDERS OF THE BODY

Woods and Champion, *The Finders of the Body*, *The Nepean Times*.

'Mr Champion and myself decided we'd come down this ridge and have a search around. We were coming down the track just over there when Champo dropped his knife. He was looking for it in the scrub, and while he was doing that I thought I'd have a look around. I went off into the bush, and hadn't gone far when I noticed those logs lying under that small cave there,' Woods said as he pointed to three logs, each one about three feet in length. 'It seemed to me that they weren't placed there by accident, so Champo and I started poking our sticks in the ground. We soon realised it was really soft. We tried a coupla times, but third time's the charm, as they say, and as soon as the stick broke the surface a bloody awful stench came up. We knew we'd found him, and that was when I decided I'd stay here to guard it while I sent Champo to get my daughter to grab you guys.'

McLean nodded as he moved underneath the small sandstone ledge to begin his preliminary examination.

'There,' Woods said as he indicated the spot with his stick. McLean nodded for Tate to send over two local fettlers, who immediately started excavating a small hole. They'd barely begun to dig before the foul stench arose. Turning his head away, McLean looked around and realised that there were nearly a hundred locals looking on, some perched on top of the rocks, while others had climbed trees in an attempt to gain the best view.

'Fill it back in,' McLean ordered. 'We're not going to do the exhumation until we get the government medical officers and the witnesses to identify the body. I'll go back to Glenbrook and telegraph it through to the bosses and await further orders.'

Upon hearing McLean's words, the assembled onlookers let out a communal sigh of disappointment, and then a large man suddenly stepped forward out of the scrub, picked up one of the shovels and started to advance towards the grave. 'Nothing is going to stop me from doing my duty!' he pronounced loudly.

'Stop that man!' ordered McLean sternly.

Several constables leapt forward, and it took half a dozen of them to subdue the man, who protested noisily as they pulled his arms behind his back. Tate moved over and calmly informed the man of the consequences of his actions should he choose to proceed. With that, the man turned, frustrated yet placated, and moved back into the crowd. McLean withdrew his pistol from its sheath and waved it in a repetitive semicircular motion towards the crowd. 'I will only warn you all once. If anyone else advances on the grave, there'll be another dead man lying here,' he said.

McLean then ordered half a dozen of his men to form a circle around the grave. The men remained steadfast after McLean had departed, but there was little they could do to stop the people from beginning their own search in the surrounding scrub. Soon one man emerged from beneath some small shrubs grasping a tiny miner's pick, while another man emerged carrying a magazine. Both men held their discoveries up to the crowd like prize-fighters claiming victory before taking them over to Tate. Examining the pick, he found nothing out of the ordinary, it serving only to confirm that Weller had gone prospecting, but when he looked over the magazine, he realised that it was the *Review of Reviews*, and when he turned it over, he saw the name 'Lee Weller' inscribed on the back cover.

SCENE AT THE GLENBROOK DISINTERMENT.

Scene at the Glenbrook Disinterment, The Nepean Times.

Shortly after 4 pm, the crowd, now almost five hundred strong, watched on as McLean returned at the head of the official party, which included Inspector-General Fosbery, Detective Roche and Constable Michael Conroy. Most importantly, however, Robert Luckham, Mrs

Tresnan and Doctor Paton and Doctor Taylor were with them. With so many people gathered in the vicinity by now, the officers and doctors had some trouble weaving their way through the crowd, and on several occasions they stopped and looked around the scene, shocked that families had opened picnic baskets and were sipping tea and eating sandwiches as they looked on.

'Those two men over there were the ones that found him,' McLean said as he pointed to the two miners.

'Good work, gentlemen,' Fosbery said, acknowledging Woods and Champion. 'Doctors,' he said as he took another look at the large crowd, 'I think it best we begin our examinations as soon as possible.'

Doctor Taylor and Doctor Paton both stepped forward cautiously. The six constables who had been guarding the gravesite were now assigned the arduous task of exhuming the body. They were soon joined not only by the doctors but also by the senior officers and Robert Luckham. They took up their shovels and began to carefully clear away the soil. Before long, the body could be seen in clear view. The hole was little more than three feet in length when the full extent of the body was revealed. It had been crammed into the grave with the head tucked down onto the chest, the knees drawn up to the dead man's torso and the arms pressed up towards the shoulders. The constables manoeuvred a blanket under Weller's body, lifted it up and placed it to one side, the transfer of the body unleashing a stench that permeated every inch of the ridge top. People pushed and jostled, eager to catch a glimpse of the corpse, and when they caught sight of it, there were several screams of horror. Dozens of women fainted, and within minutes, as the stench intensified, the crowd had completely dispersed, leaving the official party to continue their gruesome duties.

Well accustomed to such things, the officers and doctors went about their business, but poor Luckham could only stand and watch on helplessly as McLean and Roche began to unfurl the body and examine it. Roche found the pipe laying in the grave whilst McLean found the knife, both of which they showed to Luckham.

'Do you recognise these, sir?' Roche asked as he handed over the two items. Luckham barely needed to glance at them before replying, 'Yes, of course I do, I gave both of them to Lee as presents.'

'Detectives,' a constable who had been searching the scrub called out, 'I found this.'

Emerging from the scrub, the constable handed over a small revolver cartridge.

'I recognise that too,' Luckham said before the detectives had time to ask. 'It's from a Bulldog revolver that I gave to Lee for his protection.'

'Come on,' Roche said. 'Let's get him out of there.'

As they had done with Arthur Preston's body, four constables retrieved four long sticks, which they manoeuvred under Lee Weller's body and then lifted it and lowered it into a coffin. They then carried the coffin the mile or so back to the station, where it was loaded on board a train to Penrith. When the train arrived in Penrith, the body was taken to the mortuary, where Dr Paton conducted the autopsy and issued his report.

There is a wound on the upper part of the neck. There is a flattened bullet lodged in the sphenoid. The cartridge patterns are the same as those on the one recovered from the gravesite, which clearly indicates that he was shot with a revolver and not a rifle. From the position and shape of the wound, it is evident that as the bullet entered Mr Weller's skull it was travelling in a slightly upwards direction, so it can be safely assumed that the fatal shot was fired whilst Mr Weller was bent down.

When Dr Paton was done, Weller's body was sent back to city to be interred in front of a crowd more than a thousand strong at Waverley Cemetery. The good captain was laid to rest with an eternal view of the ocean to remind him of the happier times of his life.

17

The Taupo

27 November 1896

With two bodies found and the identity of the murderer almost certainly established, the media went into a frenzy. Every paper in the country carried each minute detail for a hungry and eager public. One of the most interested readers was Detective James McHattie, who sat eating his breakfast and sipping his tea as he picked up a copy of the *Newcastle Herald*. The news of the Glenbrook murders was spread across the front page, and staring back at him was the photo of Frank Butler that Mrs Gilham had given to the detectives. Stroking his chin, he looked into the suspected murderer's dark eyes and examined his weathered face. As he looked more closely, he was certain he'd seen this man before, but where? Tracing back through his memories, it soon came to him. He abandoned his breakfast and rushed out the door, paper in hand, towards the Sailor's Home.

'Good morning, Detective McHattie,' Charles Booth said as McHattie entered.

'Mr Booth,' McHattie said through laboured breaths, 'have you read this morning's edition?'

'No, sir, not as yet.'

'I am sure I have seen this man in your company,' McHattie said as he held the paper up for Booth. 'I believe he is a sailor.'

Booth took the paper and examined the photo closely.

'Do you know this man?' McHattie pressed.

'Yes,' Booth said as he handed the paper back. 'His name is Lee Weller.'

'Weller? It says his name is Frank Butler. Are you sure?'

'Positive. Well, at least that is the name he gave me.'

'Do you know where I might find him?'

'Of course I do!' Booth said. 'I got him a berth on the *Swanhilda*. It's sailing for San Francisco as we speak. It left four days ago.'

'San Francisco! Damn! That means they are going to be out of contact for nigh on sixty days!' McHattie exclaimed as he rushed from the Sailor's Home and made his way to the office to telegraph Sydney.

≈

'Detective Roche,' the Sydney telegraphing officer called out as the telegraphing machine began to beep furiously.

'Yes, what is it?' Roche replied as he slowly walked across the office rubbing the bridge of his nose with his thumb and forefinger, the weeks of sifting through the hundreds of reports of Butler's whereabouts beginning to take its toll.

'I'm receiving a telegraph from a Detective McHattie in Newcastle.'

'This better be important,' Roche growled. 'What's he saying?'

'He's saying that he saw Butler in Newcastle, but he is using the name "Lee Weller". He says he saw the photo of Butler in the paper, and that our man is on a ship sailing for San Francisco.'

'Just put it on my desk,' Roche said. 'That must be the hundredth sighting of Butler this week. There's a sighting of him here in the city and another of him down in Ballarat that I have to investigate. I'll get to it shortly.'

6 December 1896

As the *Swanhilda* steamed steadily across the Pacific, a wry smile came over Frank Butler's face as he moved back inside and joined some of the other sailors who were seated in the dining room gambling and drinking. Butler sat to one side, inconspicuous, and watched on.

Involved in the main poker game were two gruff and burly sailors, McCarthy and Simmons, both possessing hefty beards and weatherworn faces from numerous voyages around the world. In between them was a young man, James May, who'd barely entered adulthood, his youthful features in stark contrast to the men seated on either side of him. May, plainly due to his inexperience, was down to the last of his chips, and after several more hands, he was completely broke. Rising from the table, he spied Butler in the corner and moved over to join him. 'Hey, Captain Weller,' May said as he sat down next to Butler and offered him a flask.

'Hello,' Butler said, keeping his eyes on the poker game.

'You don't want to join in?' May asked.

'No, my son, the Lord looks down on gambling and drinking. It's not for me.'

'Oh, sorry, Captain, I didn't realise you were a religious man,' May apologised.

'No, need to apologise. You're only a young man. You have much to learn.'

'Hey, Weller!' McCarthy called out. 'Come over and join us! You're missing out on all the fun!'

Butler simply shook his head.

'Come on, *Captain*,' Simmons added sarcastically. 'What, are you too good to come and have a drink with the average man?'

They both laughed loudly and returned to the game.

'You know you do not have to be like them,' Butler said as he turned to face May. 'There is another way.'

'Mr Weller, I do have to be like them. There is nothing more important to me than being accepted.'

'The only person whose acceptance you need to seek, my son, is the Lord's. If you give yourself over to Him, He will take care of everything else.'

'Are you a preacher, Mr Weller?' May asked.

'No, Mr May, I am merely a man who is here to do God's work; to bring the light of salvation to men who have lost their way.'

'Hey, May!' McCarthy called out. 'When you're done with your boyfriend over there, how 'bout you get over here and get us a new bottle!'

'I'd better go,' May said, and started to rise, but before he could stand upright, Butler grabbed him by the left arm.

'Just remember, Mr May, there is a better way.'

The young man smiled weakly before moving back to the table. Butler rose shortly after, having decided to head back to his cabin. As he passed the poker game, Simmons continued to push. 'Where you going, Weller? To pray for our souls?'

Butler passed by without a word, but the sailors kept calling out to him as he made his way from the room. 'Don't bother praying for us, Weller! We're already going to hell! We'll see you there!'

Butler ignored their jibes, and when he reached his cabin, he retired to his bunk, reading for a while before going to sleep.

The following day, Butler went about his work and then joined the others for supper. Grabbing his plate of salted pork and bread, Butler sat at the main table, noticing that many of the sailors were already sucking on hip flasks and bottles of rum after a hard day's work.

'Fuck! What a day! Hey, Weller,' Simmons said as he and McCarthy both sat down opposite Butler.

'Fuckin' ay,' McCarthy added. 'Hard work trying to get to San Fran so bloody quickly.'

'Can you gentlemen please go easy with the cursing,' Butler asked politely, in between mouthfuls of bread.

'Oh, sorry, *Father*,' Simmons said sarcastically.

'Gentlemen, I know you degrade me and talk behind my back, but I promise that if you pay attention to what I am saying, and read your Bibles every now and then, you will find that there is a better path in this life than the one you have chosen. Boys, there is a hereafter, and you all believe in it. Now what excuse will you have to offer on Judgement Day, when you come to account for all the blasphemy you have uttered tonight?' With that, Butler finisher his meal, left the main cabin and headed for his bunk.

9 December 1896

Over the next few days, Butler went about his business as the *Swanhilda* continued on past New Zealand and the Kermadec Islands. Early one morning, Captain Fraser stood on the bridge gently moving the wheel back and forth. Keeping his eyes on the flat eastern horizon, he watched as the sun slowly began to rise. The seas were calm, almost dead still, and it pleased him to hear the *Swanhilda*'s strong pistons pumping deep in the hull beneath him. Fraser felt relaxed, and given the calmness of the sea, he began to contemplate handing the helm to his first officer so he could take a well-earned break. He was about to turn and give the order when a small silhouette on the horizon caught his eye. Immediately refocusing his attention, he watched carefully and continued to steer the ship as the silhouette gradually grew larger. Before long, the speck became a definitive shape, that of another steamer. Cautiously turning the wheel to the left to ensure that there was no chance of a collision, he expected nothing more than for the other ship to pass without incident, as this was a well-used trade route. The white hull of the other ship glistened in the strengthening morning sun, and Fraser kept a steady course as he readied himself to give a friendly wave to the other skipper.

'Semaphore officer, give our warmest greetings,' he yelled down to the deck. The semaphore officer, arms outstretched with red and yellow flags in hand, began spelling out a friendly 'Hello'. The ship was now closing in, allowing Fraser to see its name, *Taupo*, painted on the bow.

The semaphore officer soon received a response, and relayed the message to his captain. 'They say, "A warm hello to you also, *Swanhilda*. Clear sailing ahead."'

Realising where the *Taupo*'s home port was, Fraser said, 'Tell them that it is also clear sailing all the way to New Zealand.'

The semaphore officer began to move his arms, when suddenly the *Taupo* changed course and headed straight for them. The *Taupo* was the larger ship, and Fraser, his senses now heightened, was certain that his ship would come off second best if there was a collision. Numerous thoughts ran through his mind. 'What's going on?' he called down.

'I don't know, sir. It seems they think we need assistance of some sort.'

'Tell them everything is okay.'

The semaphore officer began to flail his arms wildly, and upon finishing, watched the *Taupo* intently, waiting for a reply, but when there was none forthcoming, he looked back up to Fraser. The *Taupo* was still heading straight for them.

Fraser kept one eye on the open sea to his left and one eye on the *Taupo*, preparing to turn the wheel hard left should the need arise. Suddenly, the *Taupo* changed course again and slowed, coming to rest a few hundred feet short of the *Swanhilda*.

Pulling the levers back, Fraser also slowed, and the *Swanhilda* soon came to rest. Intrigued, Fraser watched the red and yellow flags of the *Taupo's* semaphore officer intently. 'What are they saying?' he called down.

'They want to know if we have any passengers on board.'

'What?' Fraser asked, somewhat perplexed by the question.

'They want to know if we have any passengers on board,' the officer repeated.

'What? Tell them "No".'

By this stage, word of the presence of another ship had circulated through the crew, and the other sailors began to gather on the starboard deck, watching on as the *Taupo* moved slowly past them, coming to a halt once more just beyond the *Swanhilda's* stern.

The *Taupo's* semaphore officer started signalling again as Fraser continued to look down. 'What are they saying now?' he called.

'They say "Heave to – I have something important to communicate."'

Confused, yet equally fascinated, Fraser nodded down to the semaphore officer to tell the *Taupo* that he would comply. After steering the ship in as close to the *Taupo* as he dared, he ordered the anchor to be dropped. The *Swanhilda* came to a halt, and Fraser looked out from his cabin as several crew members from the *Taupo* prepared to lower a rowboat.

By now, word had spread to every part of the *Swanhilda*, and the entire crew now hung across the railings like soldiers waving to their families or sweethearts as they departed for war, including Frank Butler. Ominously, a wind had now sprung up, and the small rowboat rode each crest and trough of the increasing swell as it made its way between the ships. When it reached the *Swanhilda*, the only officer on board the rowboat climbed the rope ladder up to the deck, leaving the other four men bobbing about in the rowboat beneath him.

Fraser descended from the cabin and made his way to the side of the ship, where he greeted the officer from the *Taupo* warmly. 'How do you do, sir?' he said as the officer clambered over the railing. 'Welcome aboard the *Swanhilda*.'

'Thank you, sir,' the officer replied as he steadied himself on the deck and shook Fraser's hand. The latter examined the young officer's face expectantly, waiting for an explanation. The officer looked up at the lines of sailors, all of whom were staring back in the same expectant manner, the most curious of all being Frank Butler.

'Sir,' the officer said, leaning in close and whispering to Fraser, 'do you mind if we discuss our business somewhere a little more discreet?'

'Of course,' Fraser said as he extended his arm in the direction of the cabins.

When they reached Fraser's quarters, Fraser motioned for the officer to enter, then followed him inside and snapped the door shut behind them.

'So,' he said as he poured two glasses of scotch from a crystal decanter. 'What is so important that you feel the need to hold up my ship? We were intending on making a record crossing if possible.'

'Captain, I apologise for the delay, but I must ask if you have read any of the Auckland papers?' the officer said as he gratefully accepted his drink.

'No, young man, I have not,' Fraser laughed as he sipped on his own drink. 'We embarked from Newcastle and, as I said, we are trying to make good time to San Fran.'

'I see,' said the officer, nodding. 'Then you wouldn't be aware that your ship is all over the papers. Indeed, I would venture to say that the *Swanhilda* is one of the world's most famous ships at the present minute.'

The Captain shot the officer a queer look, before voicing his confusion. 'What the hell are you talking about?'

'Sir, if what I have read is correct, there is a man on board your ship who is suspected of murdering several, possibly dozens of people.'

'A murderer?' Fraser exclaimed. 'I think you have the wrong ship, sir!'

The officer, certain in what he'd read, now looked confused.

'Have you not read any newspapers?'

'Sir, we have not pulled into a port since we left Newcastle. As I said, I am trying to make a quick voyage to America, I have no time for news.'

'Captain, do you not have a man on your books by the name of Frank Butler?'

Meticulous in every aspect, Fraser knew the name of each man on his ship.

'Officer, I can absolutely assure you that I do not. I fancy the authorities must be wrong, because I have no man of that name on my articles, and I have an exceptionally good crew, as it happens.'

Shaking his head, the officer replied assuredly, 'I may be mistaken, sir, but every paper in New Zealand and Australia is reporting that the man Butler is on *this* ship. Perhaps you would allow me to lead a search party and take a look around.'

'Certainly not!' Fraser bellowed. 'You have no authority to search my ship. I have no one on board that I would put down as a murderer. My crew have all been well behaved, and I can do nothing further in this matter!'

To emphasise the strength of his convictions, Fraser opened the door and nodded for the young officer to leave. The officer gave a polite nod and bowed as he passed Fraser and began to make his way back up to the deck. Fraser followed him and, just before the officer reboarded the rowboat, said, 'Best of luck to you.'

'Thank you, sir,' the officer said as he climbed down the rope ladder. He had barely set foot in the rowboat before he ordered the other men to toss a stack of newspapers up to Fraser.

'Just read them,' the young officer called out as the rowboat pushed off and headed back to the *Taupo*.

Nodding his assent, Fraser flicked his head to signal for his subordinates to take the papers to his cabin. Remaining on the starboard deck, Fraser watched until the officer reboarded his ship and the sailors hauled the rowboat up onto the deck. The *Swanhilda* lingered on the

Taupo's starboard side until her engines eventually burst into life and she slowly started to move again. The officer saluted Fraser, who donned his cap and turned to go inside. 'First officer, I will be in my cabin presently,' he said. 'We'll get the ship underway shortly.'

After locking the cabin door behind him, Fraser stood and stroked his beard as he stared at the stacks of newspapers. He was deeply intrigued by what had just transpired, but there was one thing bothering him; he prided himself on knowing everything about his ship, and so if this man was indeed on board, he wondered how on earth he'd missed it. Letting out a deep breath, he picked up the first paper from the nearest stack and began to examine the front page. True to the young officer's words, reports of murder were sprawled all over it. Something stood out immediately, repeated again and again: the name Lee Weller.

Fraser picked up several more papers, each of which carried the Glenbrook murder as its lead story. He put the last paper down and sat down in the nearest chair, pouring himself another scotch. Draining the glass, he resolved to study Weller very closely for a few days before he made any snap decisions but before he did that he decided to consult with his first officer.

Fraser left his cabin and began to search the ship, eventually finding his sub-ordinate in the engine room. 'First officer,' he said, somewhat exasperated.

'Yes, sir,' the first officer said as he raised himself from one of the pistons, turned and stood to attention.

'What are you doing?' Fraser asked.

'One of the pistons wasn't running at full capacity, so I thought I'd come down here and have a look.'

'Excellent work, first officer, excellent work. Now, can you please leave that for the time being? I need to see you in my cabin.'

'Yes, sir,' the officer said as he handed a wrench to a nearby petty officer and followed the captain up the stairs and to his cabin.

'What is it, sir? Is there something in those papers?' he asked as he closed the cabin door behind him.

'Pick one up and read the story on the front page, and then tell me if you see anything odd.'

'Any particular paper, sir?'

'No, any one will do.'

The first officer picked up the paper nearest to the decanter and, being as meticulous as Fraser, he only needed to read a few short paragraphs before he picked up the Captain's line of thinking.

'What do you make of all this?' Fraser asked as he sat down and poured two drinks.

'I know the man. I have got him. I will put him in the brig.'

'Wait just a minute,' Fraser said as he handed the first officer a glass of scotch. 'I'm not entirely sure that is the best course of action.'

'What do you suggest?' the first officer asked, after sipping his drink.

'We're still forty or fifty days out from San Francisco. That's a long time for a man to spend in the brig planning how he will implement his escape. If we confront him, he may cause a drama, or he might even throw himself overboard. Besides, if he tries to escape upon reaching San Francisco, we don't know if there will be any Australian policemen there to arrest him. Above all, those papers say that Mr Butler "allegedly" killed Lee Weller. For all we know, he may be innocent.'

'Sir, it seems a bit strange that a man called Lee Weller has been murdered, and we happen to have a man of that name on this ship.'

'I agree, but that's still not proof of his guilt. He may have come across Weller's papers in some other fashion.'

'So what do you suggest we do?'

'You and I are the only ones who have any knowledge of this matter. I think it best if we simply let this Mr Butler go about his business and just keep a silent watch. If the need arises, we'll arrest him just before we dock in San Francisco.'

18
The Hunt Begins

12 December 1896

Roche, Conroy and McHattie milled around outside the Attorney-General's office waiting for their summons.

'I'm glad you eventually decided to follow up on my cable,' McHattie said.

'Me too!' Roche laughed. 'But you know better than anyone that I had to follow up every lead.'

'True, but at least you didn't take too long getting to mine! Let's just hope he hasn't docked in the States yet.'

Roche was about to reply when one of the Attorney-General's assistants appeared.

'Gentlemen, if you would follow me please,' he said, holding the door open. The three officers followed him inside and up the stairs, where they were led into a large boardroom. Men in stiff suits sat around an enormous oak table, each of them with their gaze firmly fixed on the three officers. The two experienced officers were unfazed, but the young probationary constable shifted nervously from foot to foot.

'Ah, Detectives Roche and McHattie, young Mr Conroy, won't you join us please?' said the Attorney-General, John Henry Want QC, as he stood at the head of the table adjusting his suit.

'Thank you, sir,' the three men responded simultaneously as they sat down.

'Gentlemen,' Want began, 'as you know, the premier is currently overseas attending to other affairs, and he has instructed me to make sure that we bring this Butler matter to a head as soon as possible, which is why I have summoned you all here today. Now, contrary to the normal behaviour of politicians, no cabinet minister wants any part of this whole affair, because we're going to have to play hard ball with Whitehall on this one, so expect some resistance. Now, we know Mr Butler is aboard the *Swanhilda*, and by my calculations we have maybe a few weeks before the ship arrives in San Francisco. Given that our men actually manage to make it there in time and that they do arrest Butler, we still have another problem. As I am sure you are all aware, our new colonial secretary, Mr Chamberlain, recently changed the rules regarding extradition proceedings. We are still a colony and, as such and unlike before, we are no longer allowed to make direct legal contact with foreign sovereign nations, meaning we cannot apply directly to the United States government for Butler's extradition. Now we must apply through Whitehall, which is why I am expecting resistance.'

'Sir,' Inspector-General Fosbery began, 'you know what the Foreign Office is like. We could apply for the extradition, but then it will get lost in all the bureaucracy. If my boys don't arrive in time, or if the Americans fail to arrest him, Butler might simply disappear, and then we'll never find him. We can't have that happen; the papers would never let us live it down!'

'That is, of course, our main concern,' Want said calmly, 'and it is something I will not allow to happen. This Butler has sent this colony into an absolute state of frenzy, and I, for my part, have had quite enough. My other concern is that we know Butler has Captain Weller's possessions. If we do not get there soon enough, we run the risk of him destroying these items, leaving us with no evidence with which to prosecute him.'

'So what are you planning?' Fosbery asked.

'I will not have this colony thrown into turmoil because of one maniac's bloodlust! I may be risking my career on this,' Want stated emphatically, every man holding his breath in anticipation of his next words, 'but I do not see that I have any other course of action. If losing my career means we restore some sense of order to this colony, then I am prepared to risk it. I have thought long and hard about this, and it is my decision that our best course of action is to wire the American police directly and ask that they arrest Butler on arrival, detain him and get the extradition proceedings underway. I will inform the Legislative

Council of my decision this afternoon, when I shall give them the following notice.'

Want reached down and retrieved a piece of paper from a leather-bound folder in front of him and began to read. 'I took the liberty of disregarding that portion of Mr Chamberlain's minute with regard to ordering an arrest, and cabled direct to the San Francisco police to effect it.'

A muffled gasp permeated the room as the magnitude of Want's proposal hit home.

The three officers sat quietly, rather pleased with what they'd heard. The colony's extradition laws were familiar to them, and had been bothering them whenever they considered what might happen if, and when, they caught Butler. The last thing they wanted, after all their hard work, was to have Butler escape at the last moment.

'Detective McHattie, Constable Conroy, I have organised for both of you to take the *Miowera* to Vancouver. She's a quick ship and, barring any bad weather, you should be able to round the *Swanhilda* and get to San Francisco before Butler. Here's your paperwork. You'd better hurry if you're going to make it.'

McHattie stood and walked around the table to collect the leather case containing the documents they would need for the voyage. 'Good luck, gentlemen,' said Want.

McHattie paused only to shake Roche's hand and wish him good luck before he and Conroy departed.

'Detective Roche,' Want said.

'Yes, sir?'

'You may be wondering why we have asked you to be present at this meeting.'

'Well, no sir, actually I was expecting you to send me with Detective McHattie.'

'No, I need you to go to London with all the documentation, and present it to the colonial secretary to gain his approval. Then I need you to go to Washington to get the Americans to approve everything as well.'

'Isn't the colonial secretary going to be upset that you disobeyed his order?' Roche asked.

'Yes, I expect he will be,' Want said with a heartening laugh. 'That is why I need you to go. You are one of our most experienced men, and you have put the most effort into this case regarding the paperwork, so you know it better than anyone. Who better to convince Mr Chamberlain of the necessity of taking the course of action we have embarked upon.'

'Yes, sir, thank you, sir.'

'Good luck, Mr Roche.'

Taking his cue to leave, Roche placed his arms stiffly at his side, bowed and moved towards the door.

'Ah, Detective,' Want said with a slight smirk on his face.

'Yes, sir?' Roche replied as he turned.

'Are you forgetting something?'

'Sir?'

Want produced a light-brown leather case and a large package wrapped in brown paper. 'Everything you need is in the case, and this package contains Arthur Preston's coat, should you need it.'

After retrieving the case and package, Roche made his way from the government offices and back to police headquarters. He quickly filled another case with every piece of evidence he could find, bumping into several desks in his haste.

'You'll never get to London at this rate!' McLean laughed from his desk on the other side of the office.

'I'll get there in time, by hook or by crook,' Roche retorted.

'I'm sure you will, John, I'm sure you will!' McLean said more seriously.

As he walked past another row of desks, Roche tripped again, paper and files flying in all directions. McLean leapt up from his desk and helped Roche to gather everything up, and when it was all in order, he patted Roche firmly on the back.

'Make sure you get him, John. Make sure you get him.'

'I will absolutely do everything in my power to make sure we do; the rest is in God's hands.'

With that, Roche rushed home, only taking time to pack the bare essentials before he was back out the door and hurrying towards Redfern station. To the hundreds of other passengers either waiting for or boarding trains, John Roche would have seemed like any other man, perhaps on his way to see his family, off for a holiday, or off to new employment, so the other citizens of Sydney paid little attention to the man making his way down the platform carrying two cases and a large package. Little did they know that the suitcase in his right hand carried almost every detail about the case that was on the tips of all of their tongues. Little did they know that the man charged with one of the most important tasks in capturing and prosecuting the notorious Frank Butler was walking past them as they discussed the front pages of the papers.

Roche slowed his pace just before boarding the Melbourne-bound train, and passed an old man sitting on a bench with the daily paper held out in front of him. Tilting his head to the left, he could clearly make out the sketches of Frank Butler on the front page. Passing more and more passengers, it dawned on him just how much the case had captured the imagination of the entire nation, which in turn reminded him of the magnitude of the task he'd been assigned. Continuing on, he found his carriage, and before boarding, he purchased a copy of *The Sydney Morning Herald* from a nearby vendor. Stepping onto the foot ladder, he slid his cases into the carriage.

'Can I take these for you, sir?' a porter said, as he started to pick up Roche's luggage.

'Ah, no, no,' Roche said quickly. 'I'm fine. I need to keep my cases and this package with me at all times. Thank you.'

'As you wish, sir,' the porter replied, shooting Roche an odd look before putting the cases down and continuing on to help other passengers. Roche jumped up into the carriage and slid the two cases down the narrow corridor until he found his sleeper. Hurriedly snapping the door shut behind him, he stacked the cases in the overhead luggage compartment and placed the package on the seat next to him. Slumping down into the seat, he began to examine the front page of *The Herald*.

Peering into Butler's eyes, Roche began to wonder what kind of man he truly was. Yes, he had investigated every detail of this case, seen all the evidence, spoken to all the witnesses, and throughout it all he'd kept one thing at the forefront of his mind: what motivated a man like

Butler? He'd traced every possibility through his mind, but there was simply no way he could comprehend what had happened. What made a man shoot another man in the back of the head for nothing more than a few measly possessions?

A loud toot interrupted his thinking, and he lurched forward as the train pulled out from the station. Putting the paper down beside him, he stared out the window as the terrace housing of Sydney's southern suburbs flitted by. In between dozing off and staring out at the countryside, the same thing kept replaying over and over in his mind; would he get to London? Would he get permission for the extradition? If so, would he get to Washington in time and, more importantly, would McHattie and Conroy make Vancouver and then San Francisco in time?

As the train moved into Victoria, Roche became increasingly impatient. The one consolation was picturing McHattie and Conroy aboard the *Miowera* as it steamed past Butler. Leaning back in his seat and closing his eyes, he envisaged the moment when they would arrest Butler, and the triumphant day when they brought him back to Sydney.

Finally, the train pulled into the outskirts of Melbourne. The landscape looked remarkably similar to that of Sydney, and were it not for the fact that he'd just spent hours and hours on a train travelling south, he felt as though he may well have completed one large circle. The train finally pulled into Flinders Street station, whereupon Roche grabbed his cases and the package and was off the train and running down the platform as quickly as he could manage. He checked his watch. The Adelaide train was due to depart shortly, so he hurriedly made his way across several platforms, handed his ticket to the conductor, boarded the train, found his sleeper and stowed his luggage before making his way to the dining carriage.

The next day, he arrived in Adelaide, and made his way as quickly as he could from the station to the port, where he boarded the *Austral*, bound for London, Washington, and then, hopefully, San Francisco.

20 December 1897

As Roche traversed the globe in one direction and McHattie and Conroy the other, Inspector Fosbery was sitting in his office seeing to some paperwork when the telegraphing officer knocked on his door.

'Yes, what is it? Is it something from Roche or McHattie perhaps?'

'No, sir, it's from a Constable Smith at Waroo.'

'Waroo?'

'Yes, sir.'

'What does he say?'

'It says: *Have just unearthed body of a man in Black Ranges in a small hole covered in about two feet. Had trousers and boots on. Answers description of missing man.*'

The missing man was, of course, Burgess. People like Lawrence whom Butler had met in the dining rooms at Parkes, had given their descriptions when they had read the papers and the police were on the hunt for a third body.

Burgess' grave had been discovered when James Mulhall and his young fifteen-year-old son had left their station early that morning hoping to take home a brace of conies for supper. Upon pitching camp the boy had decided he wanted to satisfy his sweet tooth and would find a bee hive. Moving down towards the creek bed he noticed some darker soil.

'Father!' he called out.

'Yes, son,' Mulhall replied as he moved to the creek's bank. 'What is it?'

'Somebody's been prospecting here.'

Mulhall joined the boy and scratched away the soil with a stick and pushed aside some stones.

'Ewwwww! Father, what's that smell?'

'That smell can only mean one thing, boy.'

'What's that, Father?'

'A dead body, we'd better let the authorities know. Get back to the station and send someone to Waroo.'

Mulhall waited until Constable Smith, and another policeman, arrived.

'What have you got?' Smith asked as he moved to the creek's bank and stood beside Mulhall.

'My young fella was looking around down here and he found this,' Mulhall said as he pointed to the dark soil. 'I started scratching away with a stick and a foul smell came up. Reckon we might have a body here.'

'Righto, then,' Smith said as he and the other officer began digging. Soon enough, they had exhumed Burgess' body. In the same way that Preston and Weller had been removed, Burgess was placed onto a blanket and his corpse placed in a wooden coffin which was placed in the back of Smith's wagon.

The body was taken to the local mortuary at Parkes where the local doctor, Dr J. O. Henson, conducted the post-mortem. His report read:

There is a bullet wound in the left occipital region, behind the ear. The bullet was embedded in the skull, which was expanded and misshapen, as the result of the bullet forcing its way through the bony structures. The bullet had come from a revolver of .38 calibre, and death must have been instantaneous. In the trousers pockets of the deceased were a box of percussion caps, a white-handled knife and some cut-up tobacco. The deceased also had one tooth stopped with gold.

As had been done with the other bodies, the deceased needed a positive identification was necessary, and this came in the form of the lone traveller who had met them at the creek, George Woodford. Woodford identified Burgess's hat, his gold chain and ring, and his trousers. Butler's third victim had been found.

19

A World Away

6 January 1897

The *Miowera* rode the small waves as it entered Vancouver Harbour.

'I still can't believe it,' McHattie said as he and Conroy leant on the bow railings looking at the tall pines on the coastline and the snow-capped mountains in the distance.

'What can't you believe?' Conroy asked.

'How lucky you are.'

'How do you mean?'

'You *actually* met this Butler character!'

Conroy laughed as he pulled a packet of cigarettes from his coat pocket, tapped it on the railing, withdrew two cigarettes, lit them and handed one to McHattie. 'I think I'd better have a word with my sister when we get back, and get her to reassess her decision-making processes!'

'I thought you would've already had that talk!' McHattie scoffed as he exhaled, the smoke indistinguishable from his steamy breath.

'Strange how life works out,' Conroy said as the *Miowera* turned towards its docking point and several large buildings came into view.

'How so?'

'If it hadn't been for the fact that I actually met him, I wouldn't be here.'

'True,' McHattie agreed as he stubbed his cigarette out on the railing.

'Here we are, one short boat trip to San Fran, and we're about to make one of the biggest arrests in Australian history, and I will be part of it,' Conroy said as he continued to look at the distant mountains. 'Good way to get my career underway; may even get a promotion, too.'

'Don't get too far ahead of yourself, Conroy,' McHattie said as he turned to make his way inside to collect his belongings and the evidence against Butler. 'We haven't got him yet. Come on. If we don't get down to San Fran quickly enough we may miss him altogether.'

The next day, they took the *Oregon Express* for San Francisco, and when they eventually arrived, they were met on the docks by two uniformed American officers who took them to a waiting carriage and then on to the US Marshalls' office. The two officers escorted the Australians inside before saying their goodbyes. Left to wait in the reception area, McHattie and Conroy spotted a well-groomed young lady sitting behind the desk who, were it not for a little too much make-up, would have been rather attractive.

'G'day,' Conroy said as he and McHattie walked up to the desk. Hearing an unfamiliar accent, the woman gave them a strange look before replying with a hesitant 'Hello.'

'Yes, hello,' McHattie said, stepping in front of Conroy. 'We're from Australia. We're here to see Marshall Baldwin.'

The reason for the unusual accent now clear, the woman's disposition immediately became polite. 'Certainly, sir, I will just call for him. It may be a few moments.'

'Of course.'

'You can just wait over there if you'd like,' she said, gesturing as she stood up.

Looking to where she was pointing, the officers noticed two rows of benches sitting at right angles along the opposite wall. McHattie nodded to the receptionist and watched her disappear into the back offices, and then he and Conroy moved over to the benches, where they sat down and waited. The half dozen people waiting in the office, having heard their strange accents, looked at them with curiosity, making them uncomfortable and uncertain as to where to direct their gaze.

Before long, the receptionist returned, followed by three tall men dressed in perfectly pressed uniforms. She pointed to McHattie and Conroy, and the men made their way to where they were seated.

'Good morning, gentlemen,' said the older man, a burly character sporting a trim moustache.

'Marshall Baldwin?'

'Yeah, that's me. Welcome to San Fran. I trust you boys had a safe trip?'

'Not too bad. Got some bad weather when we were not too far out of Hawaii, but apart from that, we made good time. I just hope we're not too late.'

'That would not be my main concern, Detective. I'd be more worried about whether we'll actually be allowed to arrest him. The American legal system is a little different to yours,' Baldwin said with a broad smile as he gestured towards his office door and motioned for McHattie and Conroy to follow him.

'By the way, these men are Deputy Bunner from the US Marshalls and Detective Egan from the San Francisco Police Department,' Baldwin said, indicating his colleagues.

McHattie nodded to Bunner and Egan. 'James McHattie. And this is Michael Conroy.'

Baldwin led them to an office door, which he held open as they entered. 'Please have a seat, gentlemen,' he said, closing the door behind them.

'So what *exactly* can we do for you boys?' Baldwin said, as he and Bunner took seats opposite the Australians.

McHattie could tell from the intonation in Baldwin's voice that the question was largely rhetorical. Not about to be outdone, he placed the leather case on the desk in front of him, opened it and said, 'I think I'd like to start by asking what you gentlemen know about why we are here.'

'We understand that you have a man who you want us to arrest as soon as he arrives in San Francisco,' Baldwin said bluntly.

'That is correct,' McHattie said as he unclipped the leather case, lifted the flap and reached inside. 'I have an official warrant here, signed by the Governor of New South Wales, Lord Hampden, authorising the arrest of one Lee Weller.'

Baldwin examined the warrant closely before handing it to Bunner, who examined it equally as closely before handing it to Egan who read it and handed it back.

'Your Consul-General here in San Fran has applied for a provisional warrant for this man,' Baldwin stated. Both McHattie and Conroy's eyes lit up at the news.

'But,' Baldwin continued, 'it is only a provisional warrant. I want to look at all the evidence and hear the details of the case first before we actually grant it.'

McHattie began to remove assorted evidence and other paperwork from the case, handing over the reports of the two murders and the photograph of Frank Butler.

'The picture you have there is of a man who goes by the name Frank Butler, amongst others.'

'Butler?' Bunner said as he looked at the picture. 'But the arrest warrant is for a Lee Weller.'

'Yes, it is, but that is Butler's modus operandi. As you will see when you read the documents in front of you, Butler first lured Arthur Preston to his death with promises of a lucrative gold mining expedition only to have him dig his own grave before he shot him in the back of the head. He then advertised for more partners for a mining expedition, but only Lee Weller seemed to be suitable, and he took him up into the mountains and murdered him in the same way, maybe fifteen miles further down the mountain, and then stole his identity. That is why you have a warrant there for Lee Weller and we have to have the authority to arrest him under that name because that is what he is using, and not Frank Butler.'

'Hmm,' Baldwin agreed as he read. 'Sounds like a right charming character. We have also received numerous requests from London to grant the arrest and extradition. Boy, your two countries must want this boy real bad.'

'Sydney, and all of Australia for that matter, has been in a right state ever since this stuff hit the news. As I am sure you can imagine, it will look rather bad for us if we let him slip through our fingers.'

'You are in America, Mr McHattie! You do not need to remind me of how much a pain in the ass the media can be!' Baldwin laughed as he looked through the last of the documentation. When he was done, he motioned for Bunner and Egan to join him in an adjacent office.

'If you gentlemen would excuse us for a moment, I need to confer with my colleagues here regarding your request, and then I will have to telegraph Washington to get their approval. You can wait outside if you wish. If you want a cup of coffee, you need only ask my receptionist.'

McHattie nodded and watched as the two Americans disappeared into the next room.

'What do you think?' Conroy whispered as they made their way back out to the reception area.

'I'm not sure, but I can't really see how they can refuse our request considering the pressure coming from home and from Whitehall.'

'Yeah, but they are Americans. Like they said, they do things differently here.'

McHattie and Conroy paced up and down the reception area. With every passing minute, their apprehension grew, and when they finally made their way back inside, Conroy said, 'I don't reckon they're gonna grant it.'

'Patience, young Conroy,' McHattie replied. 'They're just delaying it so they can show us who's in charge. Remember, it's their show.'

'Yes, sir, I will try,' Conroy said. He was about to say something else when the receptionist appeared and said, 'Gentlemen, you can go back in now.'

McHattie and Conroy walked back into the office and sat down opposite to Baldwin, Bunner and Egan, both Australians leaning forward in anticipation.

'Gentlemen, we have carefully considered everything you have presented to us,' Baldwin began.

'And?'

'We have agreed to your request. We will arrest this Lee Weller for you.'

'Outstanding!' McHattie said, before turning to Conroy and shaking his hand gleefully.

'Now, unless you boys do things differently on the other side of the world, I think we should celebrate our new arrangement with a drink,' Baldwin said.

Standing up, McHattie took the documents and photographs that Baldwin passed back to him and returned them to the briefcase. 'Do you mind if I leave this here?' he said to Baldwin. 'I would hate for it to go missing.'

'Of course, there's a safe in my office.'

McHattie locked the case and handed it to Baldwin, who disappeared into yet another office, before returning a minute later. 'Right, let's go for a drink.'

The five men made their way through the station and out onto the promenade, strolling along the Embarcadero until they came to a tavern. It was clear to the Australians that this must have been the local policemen's watering hole, as Baldwin, Bunner and Egan were greeted warmly by the waiter and immediately taken to an outside table. Shortly after, a bottle of whisky appeared, along with five glasses, which were quickly filled and placed in front of each man.

'To a successful arrest!' Baldwin said as he raised his glass.

'To a successful arrest,' the others repeated as they raised their own in response.

They downed their drinks, and then McHattie looked pensively out over the bay towards Treasure Island. Picking up on the Australian's mood, Baldwin poured another drink for each of them. 'I've already received numerous cables from Sydney, London and Washington, and I was aware of the ship that this Mr Butler is on before your arrival. It's called the *Swanhilda*, if I am not mistaken.'

'That is correct,' McHattie confirmed, slightly annoyed that they'd had to wait so long for confirmation of the arrest when the Americans plainly already knew so much about the case.

'I checked the port manifests, and I'm sure you'll be glad to know, the ship is not due in for some time yet.'

McHattie and Conroy breathed an audible sigh of relief.

'So, what's the best way to go about arresting him then?' McHattie said, scanning the bay and docks.

'I have been thinking about that,' Baldwin said. 'You see down there,' he said, pointing to his right, 'that's where the ship will dock, and I think it's best if we arrest him on board the ship. I don't want to wait until he comes ashore.'

'Why is that?' Conroy asked.

JAMES McHATTIE. **M. A. CONROY.**

James McHattie is the experienced Newcastle detective who is anxiously awaiting the arrival of the Swanhilda and Butler. Conroy is the young Sydney officer who narrowly escaped being one of Butler's victims, but who is now his pursuer.

Detective James McHattie and Constable Michael Conroy in court,
The San Francisco Call, 9 January 1897.

Baldwin could see that the younger of the two Australians was still raw in the ways of policing, but sensing the genuine enthusiasm in the young man's question, he was happy to oblige. 'If he sets foot on American soil, it presents too many chances for him to try to escape or to create a scene. If he gets far enough into the docks, we will have lost him forever.'

Being an experienced detective, McHattie felt compelled to add his two bob's worth. 'Mike, if we arrest him on the ship, it seriously limits his options. All that is left for him is to try to create a scene or try to jump overboard.'

'I have been considering that,' Baldwin said, 'and I think our best course of action is to board the ship and arrest Butler before he knows what's going on. We'll do it under the guise of a medical inspection.'

'I agree,' Bunner added. 'I think we should also put a watchman up in the tower of the Merchant's Exchange. We can't be certain of the exact time the ship will arrive, so we need someone watching around the clock.'

'Sounds good,' McHattie agreed. 'My colleague, Detective Roche, should be here shortly. He will be in charge of our team.'

'Yes, I have heard his name mentioned. Your compatriot telegraphed our Washington offices from London. He is crossing the Atlantic as we speak and I am sure it will comfort you to know that, as far as I can tell, he gained all he needed from England. He will, as you say, be here shortly.'

'Then, all we can do is wait,' McHattie said as he sipped deeply on his whisky.

20

Black Hat

26 January 1897

With little else to do but to wait for Roche and for Butler, McHattie and Conroy spent their time taking in the sights of San Francisco and checking in at the police station with Baldwin and the others. Roche telegraphed ahead on a regular basis and they knew he would be arriving today or tomorrow and that they were to meet him at the station.

They walked into the station late in the afternoon.

'Is he here yet?' he asked Baldwin.

'You asked that this morning!' Baldwin mocked.

'I know. I know, but we need him here before Butler arrives. I hope he doesn't get held up.'

'Today must be your lucky day then!' Baldwin said with a smile.

'What?'

'Detective Roche arrived just after lunch. Come on, the other boys are taking him through how we are going to arrest Butler.'

McHattie and Conroy followed Baldwin into the office. As soon as Roche saw them he rose from his seat and warmly greeted them.

'James! Michael! So glad to see you!' he said excitedly.

'John!' McHattie replied. 'We were starting to wonder if you were ever going to get here.'

'I got here as quick as I could, I'll tell you that much. To be honest, there were times when I wondered if I was ever going to get here.'

'I don't know about y'all,' Baldwin laughed. 'But I reckon this calls for a drink!'

The group of men headed from the station and made for the same tavern to which Baldwin had taken McHattie and Conroy.

Baldwin and Bunner ordered a bottle of whiskey and returned to the table.

'Detective Roche,' Baldwin said as he poured a glass for the new arrival. 'You see that dock down there?'

'Yes.'

'That is where the *Swanhilda* will dock. As we said to you before, we don't want him to land so we'll arrest him on the ship and out in the bay.'

'Sounds good to me,' Roche said as he sipped. 'Let's just hope he's still onboard.'

'So, John, from my reckoning it's taken you less than fifty days to get here,' McHattie said. 'Is that about right?'

'Yes, that sounds about right.'

'Care to tell us about your trip then?'

'Sure.'

Roche then explained to his eager audience how his trip had taken him from Adelaide to Ceylon, where he had arrived two days before Christmas. From there he made his way through the Suez at the beginning of January then onto Naples, Paris, Calais, Dover and then onto London.

'Wow, John! You can now call yourself a true world traveller! You must have some amazing stories to tell!' Conroy exclaimed.

'I don't know about being a world traveller!' Roche laughed. 'I barely had time to look around before I was on the next boat or train. The more delays I had the more anxious I became that I wouldn't make it in time.'

'So, where did you go after London?' Conroy eagerly asked.

'I left London on 13 January and went by train to Liverpool where I got a boat to Dublin.'

'Aren't your parents from Ireland?' McHattie queried.

'They most certainly are.'

'Did you drop by to see them?'

'Are you kidding? I knew the *Swanhilda* was going to make San Francisco in around sixty days and there was no way I was not going to get here on time! Anyway, from Ireland I took a boat across the Atlantic to New York and arrived there on the 20th and I have taken God knows how many trains to get here.'

'Has Fosbery been able to telegraph you at all?' McHattie asked. 'Was he able to tell you that they found another one, Burgess, out near Parkes?'

'Yeah, I got the message when I arrived in London. It's a shame, though, I don't have any briefs or evidence on that one. Would come in handy when we try to get his extradition through.'

'Well, we have what we have,' McHattie said ruefully. 'Let's just hope that is enough.'

'A third one?' Baldwin said incredulously.

'It would seem so,' Roche said as he sipped his drink. 'Once a serial killer, always a serial killer.'

1 February 1897

Captain Fraser was checking the manifests spread across his table to ensure that everything was in order for their arrival in San Francisco when a knock came at the door. 'Enter,' he called. The door opened, and he looked up to see his first officer. 'Yes, what is it?'

'Ah, Captain, Mr Weller is seeking a private audience with you.'

'I'm not the bloody queen, man. Send him in.'

The first officer disappeared, and a moment later Frank Butler stepped into the cabin.

'Captain Weller,' Fraser said cordially, making sure that he did not slip and call the man 'Butler'. 'Take a seat. Would you like a drink?'

'Yes, sir, a drink would be lovely, sir.'

'Whisky okay?' Fraser asked as he rose from his chair and moved to the decanter set.

'Yes, sir, perfect, sir.'

After pouring two glasses, Fraser placed one in front of Butler before sitting back in his chair. 'So, what is it, Captain?'

'Sir, if it's not too much trouble, I'd like to be able to leave the ship as soon as we dock.'

'I'm sorry?'

'I have some urgent business I must take care of, so with your permission, I would like to be granted my leave as soon as we arrive.'

'There is a lot of work to be done upon our arrival in San Francisco, as I am sure you can understand. I will need every hand.'

Butler drained his glass, placed it firmly back on the desk and rose to leave. 'Captain, wait,' said Fraser, not wanting to alarm Butler, who was already halfway across the room, but now paused and turned on his heels.

'Why do you really want to leave early?' Fraser asked. Regretting the question as soon as he'd asked it, Fraser immediately retracted it. 'Never mind. Your business is your own, not mine.'

Sitting back down and holding his glass out for Fraser to refill, Butler took a large swig and looked long and deep at Fraser. 'Sir, you have been a good captain, so I feel compelled to tell you the truth.'

Unbeknown to Butler, Fraser shifted uncomfortably in his seat. Nevertheless, his curiosity got the better of him and he leaned forward in anticipation of Butler's confession of murder.

'But first you need to promise me that you will not tell anyone of this.'

'Of course.'

'Sir, I think it would be embarrassing for a man with a Master's ticket to be landed as an ordinary seaman. It is beneath my standing. It might be the means of my finding a good situation if I can get ashore without it being known that I am here before the mast.'

The expected confession not having eventuated, Fraser tried his best to hide his disappointment. 'I understand, Captain Weller,' he said with a smile. 'You have been one of the hardest working men on this voyage, and you have tried to bring these men the word of God. I respect both of those things. I think you have earned the right to leave straightaway if you feel you must.'

Butler's expression now changed from a slight scowl to a beaming smile. 'Thank you, sir, that is much appreciated. You're a good captain, sir.'

2 February 1897

Black clouds raced past the face of the glistening moon, the intermittent light casting an eerie glow on the white crests of the waves below. The bow of the *Swanhilda* dipped and bobbed as it broke the swell, ploughing its way through the rough waters outside the heads of San Francisco Bay. As they passed between the huge cliffs, Fraser, confident in his knowledge of the navigation charts, kept a close watch as he carefully steered the ship into the calmer waters of the bay.

When he was confident he was away from the worst the ocean could throw at him, he picked up the telephone handpiece from its cradle on the wall. 'Slow her down,' he called to the engine room.

Down below, his men stopped shovelling coal into the fires and the ship's speed decreased dramatically. Fraser checked his pocket watch. It was nearing 4 am and, much to Fraser's relief, the bay was almost empty. Steering the ship towards the distant shore, he could just make out the rise and fall of the lights on the masts of the docked ships. He ordered his telegraph officer to contact the dock for instructions, and the response came as no great surprise.

Man on your ship to be arrested using alibi "Weller". US Marshalls will board your ship under pretence of conducting medical inspection.

Fraser finished reading the telegraph before looking up towards the docks, searching for any sign of a ship, and quickly spied several lights adorning the mast of a tug that was heading towards him. It slowed as it approached the *Swanhilda*, and Fraser watched his counterpart hurriedly moving the wheel back and forth as he manoeuvred the tug into place alongside the larger vessel, whose first officer and sailors grabbed hold of the ropes thrown by the tug's crew and began tying them off.

Fraser relaxed ever so slightly as he ordered the engines to a complete stop. The thump-thumping of the engines ceased, the ropes tightened, and the tug began to pull away.

Meanwhile, Michael Conroy leant against a lamppost watching a woman of the night head into a dark alley with a drunken sailor. His instincts compelled him to arrest them, but he reminded himself that he was here for a higher purpose, and that he didn't have the authority to arrest people in this country, so he simply watched on as their silhouetted bodies writhed together in the darkness.

He lit a cigarette and set off to pace the docks once again. Reaching the end, he began to make his way along a wharf jutting out into the bay. Weariness was getting the better of him, and he rubbed his tired eyes. After taking another look out into the bay, he resigned himself to the fact that he had no choice but to call it a night.

Tilting his head upwards, he watched the clouds continue to skip past the moon, letting out a sigh as he watched his steamy breath evaporate into the early morning sky. Taking one last look out into the foggy bay, suddenly he saw the stringed lights running from the mast down to the deck of the tug. He had seen numerous ships pulled into dock by tugs by now, and although his hopes rose, there was no way he could be certain that this tug was pulling the *Swanhilda*. Soon, the two ships came into full view. Conroy strained his eyes trying to make out the name of the larger ship, but just when he thought he could make out the name, a huge plume of clouds covered the moon, darkening the entire bay. Along with the early morning fog, this made it almost impossible to see anything.

Conroy looked for the ship, and then up to the sky, as he waited impatiently for the clouds to clear. As if to taunt him, this mass of clouds, unlike its brothers, did not race by, but instead slowed to almost a standstill. It seemed like hours passed before the clouds finally cleared, the last of them lingering as if to toy with him for a few moments longer. The clouds eventually moved on, and the moon illuminated the bay once more. Conroy's eyes made straight for the bow of the larger ship and, as if in apology for the delay, the moon now seemed to brighten and pierce through the fog. There it was, clearly visible; the *Swanhilda*!

Conroy turned and sprinted back along the wharf and the docks, heading for the Taylor Street police station. By the time he burst into the office, he was almost out of breath. Sitting around a table drinking coffee and playing poker were McHattie, Roche, Egan, Bunner and Baldwin.

The Swanhilda, the Pilot-Boat America and the Tug Active Inside the Farallones. The Ship Is In Irons Waiting for the Pilot From the America and the Tug Is Lying Close Awaiting a Chance to Tow the Big Four-Master Into Port. The Above Picture Is Made From a Sketch Furnished by Captain Harry Marshall.

A sketch of the *Swanhilda*, *The San Francisco Call*, 3 February 1897.

'Are you alright, Mr Conroy? Has the *Swanhilda* arrived?' Baldwin asked as he looked up from his cards.

Conroy placed the palms of his hands flat on the table, struggling to regain his breath, and could only manage an affirmative nod of his head.

'Right! Let's go!' Baldwin said as he snatched up his revolver and holster, which he hurriedly strapped around his shoulders and chest as he ran out the door. The others followed, the last one to leave being Conroy, who sucked in a deep breath before rushing out the door again in pursuit of his colleagues.

When they reached the docks, they hurriedly boarded their ship the *Hartley*, which Baldwin had previously arranged to have docked as close to the police station as possible. They were barely on board before Baldwin was screaming, 'Go! Go! Go!' to the *Hartley's* crew.

The men of the *Hartley* had been ordered to stand at the ready, and as soon as the policemen were up the gangway and on board, they began casting off and tossing the ropes onto the dock. The *Hartley* moved away from the wharf and steamed towards the *Swanhilda*, while Baldwin and McHattie hurriedly glued a fake beard to Conroy's face, McHattie barely applying the finishing touches before the *Hartley* drew alongside the *Swanhilda*.

Stationed at the helm, Fraser kept a close eye out for another ship steaming towards his. Eventually, he spotted the *Hartley* in the distance, and called out to his first officer, instructing him to give the order to assemble the men ready for a medical inspection. The *Hartley* soon came up alongside the *Swanhilda*, the ropes were tied and a plank was laid across the railings between the two ships. Baldwin, Bunner and Egan were the first to run across, while the plain-clothes Australian officers waited on board the *Hartley*.

The sailors from the *Swanhilda*, accustomed to medical inspections whenever they entered new ports, casually lined up along the starboard side of the ship and placed their hands, palms down, straight out in front of them.

Fraser descended from the helm and stood waiting near the bow. Deputy Bunner moved in close and whispered into Fraser's ear, confirming his identity. Fraser nodded and motioned for the officers to follow him down the line as they began checking each sailor's hands. After examining the first sailor, they moved on to the second man, who had a black hat pulled down over his face. They checked him, and seeing nothing untoward, continued moving along the line.

'Sir,' the first mate whispered into his captain's ear. 'Black hat.'

Fraser stopped, turned and moved back towards the concealed man. Stepping between him and the next man, he moved behind the man in the black hat, put his hand on his shoulder and said to Baldwin, 'Officer, here's your man.'

'Put your hands up and don't try anything stupid!' Bunner said firmly as he withdrew his pistol and placed it under Butler's chin, causing Butler's hands to shoot skyward. Baldwin then moved behind Butler, grasped his arms, pulled them behind his back and shackled Butler's hands before the two men then manhandled the prisoner towards the hatch and forced him to sit down on the edge. Butler's calm demeanour now evaporated, and he screamed, 'What is all this about? You've got the wrong man! I demand that you tell me what is going on!'

The other sailors now took up every vantage point on the deck, from the stern to the bow and even up the masts, watching on in amazement as the man who had preached the word of God, and whom they had thought was a teetotaller, was placed under arrest. The Australian detectives had boarded the *Swanhilda* as soon as they'd seen Butler being shackled, but the gathered sailors now made it extremely difficult for them to get to him. Pushing and shoving their way through the crowd, they stood behind Baldwin, Bunner and Egan and listened as Baldwin, standing directly in front of Butler, began to speak. 'I have a warrant here authorising your arrest for the murders of Arthur Preston and Lee Mellington Weller. You have the right to remain silent…'

Before Baldwin could finish reading Butler his rights, Butler started yelling again.

'You are making a terrible mistake! I am Lee Weller! I know nothing about it!'

'You are under arrest for murder,' Baldwin continued as he pushed Butler towards the side of the ship.

Roche and McHattie, who had disappeared below deck during the arrest, had now returned, having retrieved Butler's seachest. Baldwin pushed Butler towards them as the sailors, still looking on in awe, stepped aside. Roche and McHattie lowered the chest onto the wooden deck. Baldwin made sure that Butler was standing right in front of the two Australians as they squatted down and unlocked the chest. McHattie opened the lid, and they began to remove the contents.

First, Roche pulled out a small, black, leather-bound book and began flicking through the pages. 'Frank Harwood's diary,' Roche said to no one in particular as he carefully placed it back in the chest and withdrew another piece of paper, 'and Harwood's mining certificates.' McHattie, examining the other side of the chest, pulled out another small book and several photos. He flicked through the pages before looking at Roche. 'Lee Weller's cheque book,' he said as he put the book back into the chest and began to turn the photos over in his hand, 'and these pictures are of Captain Weller's wife.'

The last item they removed was a slightly worn piece of sheet music that bore Lee Weller's signature. '*The Sailor's Grave*,' Roche said. 'How appropriate.' He put the sheet music back in the chest, closed the lid and locked it.

'I think we have all we need here,' McHattie said, looking at Baldwin, who nodded and then indicated for Butler to be taken to an inside cabin.

After being taken to the cabin, Butler was sat down at a table while a small crowd filed into the room, Butler staring defiantly at each man as they entered.

'I have a warrant here authorising your arrest,' Bunner began. 'I am authorised, as a United States Marshall, to make this arrest. You are charged that, on 31 October 1896, at Glenbrook, you did feloniously and maliciously murder Lee Mellington Weller.'

Butler, who was dressed in a heavy white sweater, a black coat and blue jeans, looked at each of the officers' faces but said nothing.

'You won't get away now, will you?' Baldwin said as he removed Butler's shackles.

'What the fuck do I want to get away for?' Butler said in a sudden outburst. 'That old man over there has been reading a pile of rot. It's got nothing to do with me.'

Michael Conroy, who had been standing inconspicuously to the rear of the group, now stepped forward. Conroy removed his disguise, and Butler looked him over.

'Look at me, Butler,' Conroy said. 'Don't you remember me?'

'No! I don't know you, nor do I want to know you!' Butler retorted.

'Although, Frank, I can hardly recognise you. You're as thin as a shadow. I never saw such a falling off in a man in my life.'

Bunner, who was standing in front of Butler, reached inside his coat pocket, withdrew a photograph and held it up so Butler could see it clearly. 'Do you recognise the man in this picture?'

'It looks like me,' was all Butler said.

'We can stay here all day and have you protesting your innocence but we all know you're not. So, why don't you just give us your real name?' Egan interjected.

'*You* say it's Butler,' Butler snapped, 'but the name I shipped by on this ship is my real name. Anyhow, *you* shouldn't be asking me any questions. Mind your own business!'

Roche and Baldwin duly disappeared to check that the arrangements had been made to transfer Butler to the *Hartley*. While they were gone, several minutes of silence passed as the other officers stared at Butler, who glared right back at them. Realising he had no choice or options, he eventually said, 'Can you at least give me a new pair of trousers? Don't drag me ashore in these things; they are not fit to be seen.'

'That's alright, my boy,' McHattie responded. 'You'll get a brand new suit of clothes by and by.'

'I ain't scared a bit!' Butler retorted.

Baldwin and Roche soon returned, along with Captain Fraser, and as soon as Butler saw him he pleaded, 'Here's a great deal of bother to arrest one poor sailor, ain't it, skipper?'

'Well, I guess they wanted to get you safe,' Fraser replied.

'Now, captain, I've been a good sailor on board, ain't I?' Butler pleaded.

'You have been that, my man. I've nothing against you on that score. You've been one of the best sailors aboard my ship.'

Butler looked forlornly at Fraser, seeking some last chance at salvation, and kept his gaze on the captain as he was taken up to the deck.

'Perhaps we'd better rope him off,' Egan suggested.

'Yes!' Butler cried. 'Get a chain around my legs, too, while you're about it. I ain't done nothing that I can't answer for.'

Baldwin smirked at Butler: 'No, Frank, no shackles for you. Wouldn't want you jumping in the bay now would we?'

Baldwin attached one circle of his handcuffs to Butler's right wrist while he locked the other around his own. A rope was tied around Butler's waist and he was led to the plank between the two ships. McHattie and Roche each took a handle of the chest, lifted it and followed close behind. As he was being walked up onto the plank, Butler stopped and looked at Fraser, who was standing with his head slightly bowed.

CAPTAIN DONALD FRASER.

Captain Donald Fraser, *The San Francisco Call*, 3 February 1897.

The sailors from both ships, those from the *Swanhilda* still in a state of shock, watched on as Butler was taken safely on board the *Hartley* and led below deck. With nothing more to see, the sailors from each ship began untying the ropes that had bound the ships together and tossing them to each other. The two ships then went on their respective ways, one ship's crew left to ponder the amazing events that had just transpired, the other to convey their newly gained cargo safely to shore.

Once he was below deck on the *Hartley*, Butler was taken to the brig, chained to a bed and left to his own devices under the watchful eye of McHattie. Butler sat on the bed with his elbows resting on his knees, contemplating just how close he'd come to escaping as the *Hartley* quickly picked up speed, rocking both men from side to side. McHattie took a seat, reached inside his coat, withdrew a pipe and some matches, stuffed the pipe full of tobacco and sparked it before slowly puffing away. For several minutes, he watched Butler, who now had his head buried in his hands, through the smoke haze.

'Do you remember me?' McHattie eventually asked.

Butler took a good look, but he was unable to clearly see McHattie in the dim light and smoke. 'No, sir, I don't believe I do.'

'Haven't you wondered why Mr Conroy and myself are here?'

'No, sir, I have not, as I don't believe I know either of you.'

The smoke poured from McHattie's mouth and nose as he let out a laugh. 'You should have been more careful, Frank! Maybe then you would have got away with it!'

'My name is Lee Weller,' Butler persisted. 'I don't know anything about this "Frank Butler" to whom you keep referring.'

'Yes, yes, sorry, *Captain Weller*. Well, we had to arrest you under that name anyway,' McHattie said sarcastically, 'because the real Captain Weller was found buried in a shallow grave in Glenbrook with the back of his head blown out.'

'That's a real shame. It is certainly unfortunate that such a terrible thing should happen to a man with the same name as me, but I assure you, I had nothing to do with that man's death.'

McHattie laughed again, albeit a little more softly. 'You keep thinking that, Frank. However, do you remember the day in Newcastle when I spoke to a man named Hill from the Sailors' Home?'

'No, I cannot remember. I don't care to say anything more at present.'

McHattie knew he'd struck a raw nerve, and shot Butler a knowing smile before making his way back up onto the deck. Out in the cold night air, he gazed up and down along the length of the ship, and saw his colleagues standing up at the bow looking towards the city lights. He moved along the deck, glancing out towards the horizon where he could see the first rays of the morning sun beginning to spill into the bay. He came to a halt alongside Roche, who handed him a hip flask, from which he took a sip before handing it back.

'Don't suppose he made any admissions, did he?' Roche asked as he took another sip.

'No, he's maintaining that his name is Weller.'

'Hmm, would you expect anything less?'

'No, but he was quite talkative until I mentioned the Sailors' Home, and then he closed up as tight as a clam.'

'All we need to worry about is making sure we get him home safely,' Roche said as he slapped McHattie on the back.

The half dozen men stayed at the bow watching the city coming closer and closer until eventually the *Hartley* slowed, before pulling into the dock shortly after. McHattie, Roche and Baldwin headed below deck, returning a short time later with Butler positioned between them, his hands and feet shackled once more. The *Hartley's* sailors lowered the gangway onto the dock and Roche led the way, while Baldwin walked behind Butler, his pistol drawn and firmly positioned in the small of Butler's back.

'You try and make a run for it,' he said to Butler, 'and I'll shoot you dead.'

Butler said nothing, but shuffled down the gangway. When the remaining police disembarked, they formed a circle around Butler and hurried him into a waiting patrol wagon as numerous sailors and prostitutes watched on with interest.

A quarter of an hour later, they reached the Taylor Street station, where Butler was quickly taken to an interview room and forced to sit down, his shackles now fastened to the table. 'Just so you don't try anything,' Baldwin smirked as he shook the shackles to ensure they were secure as Butler bowed his head and dropped his gaze.

Waiting outside, Roche, McHattie and Conroy eagerly anticipated Baldwin's return so that they could get inside and begin the interview. Baldwin had barely set foot outside the room when Roche was at him. 'Can we go in and interview him now?'

'Detective Roche, you have not been here as long as your fellow countrymen, but I am certain you have realised that we do things very differently here. Butler was arrested on American soil, and therefore he must first be interviewed by an American detective, Detective Egan will do it.'

FRANK BUTLER, THE ALLEGED MURDERER.
[Sketched from life by a "Call" artist.]

Butler after his arrest, *The San Francisco Call*, 3 February 1897.

'You're not serious, are you?' Roche said, exasperated.

'Do not worry, gentlemen,' Egan said sensing the Australians' unease. 'I know what I am doing. I have been reading up on your Mr Butler ever since you arrived.'

Butler lifted his head when Egan entered. 'What now?' he asked cautiously.

'I am Detective Egan of the San Francisco Police Department,' Egan said as he sat opposite Butler. Egan withdrew a folder and a sheet of paper from his briefcase and began. 'Can you tell me your name please?'

MURDERER BUTLER BEHIND THE BARS.

Butler behind bars, *The San Francisco Call*, 3 February 1897.

'Captain Lee Weller.'

'Come now, Mr Butler. We both know this is not true.'

Butler remained silent.

'Okay, so let's get right to it shall we, as I am sure those Australian detectives waiting outside want to get everything over and done with as quickly as possible and have you on your way back home.'

'It is not my home,' Butler said curtly. 'I am an Englishman.'

'Nevertheless, I should think that Australia will be the last country you see.'

'Maybe,' Butler growled. 'We'll see.'

'How about this young man Preston that you roped off out in the country?'

Realising they knew more than he expected, and perhaps due to the unexpectedness of his arrest, Butler let his guard down and mumbled a response. 'I left Arthur Preston at the railway station and never saw him again.'

'So what about Captain Weller, did you rope him away also?'

Bowing his head and staring into his lap, Butler said nothing more.

'I take it you have nothing more to say.'

Butler stayed silent.

Egan nodded, rose and left the room. The Australians were sitting around a single table and leapt from their chairs as soon as they saw him emerge. 'So?' Roche asked eagerly.

'He didn't say a lot, but at least he admitted he knew Preston. He still wouldn't make any admissions about the murders, though. Looks like we're going to have to do this one the hard way.'

The three Australians' shoulders slumped and, seeing their disappointment, Baldwin stepped in to offer some reassurance. 'Don't worry, boys. We'll try and have this one done as soon as possible and get you on your way. You'll have your man.'

'Thanks, Marshall Baldwin. We really appreciate that,' Roche said. 'I think I need a cup of tea.'

'I think we could all use a cup of something,' Baldwin said.

Several hours passed, during which Butler was left to stew in his cell. Around mid-morning, Detective Egan returned. 'Good morning, Mr Butler,' he said as he entered the room. 'Can I get you anything? A cup of tea perhaps?'

'I'm fine.'

Laying a piece of paper flat on the table, Egan proceeded to outline its contents. 'I have a warrant here authorising me to search you. Would you like to read it?'

Butler shook his head. 'No, it's fine. I ain't got nothin' on me anyway.'

'Stand up, please,' Egan said as he moved over to Butler and undid his shackles, 'and put yours arms out.'

Butler complied, and Egan started to pat him down. Finding nothing out of the ordinary, Egan took Butler's coat and began rifling through it.

'See, I told you I didn't have nothin' on me.'

Butler sat down, a self-satisfied grin spreading across his face, but Egan paced backwards and forwards behind him, sensing that Butler was hiding something. Becoming increasingly uneasy now, Butler looked from side to side before removing his hat and starting to fiddle with it. 'Are we done here?' he asked abruptly.

Egan paused. 'Mr Butler, may I see your hat please?'

Reluctantly, Butler handed the hat to Egan, who turned it over and ran his fingers around the inside. At first, he found nothing, and was about to hand it back when he suddenly felt a raised area in the lining. Pulling it to one side, he withdrew a small paper package. Sitting back down opposite Butler, Egan placed the sachet on the table and proceeded to unfold it, revealing a small quantity of white powder. 'Would you care to explain what this is?' Egan said.

'It's my medication.'

'Medication for what?'

'I get these headaches from time to time. It helps calm me down.'

'Medication?' Egan said, unconvinced.

'Yes, can I please have it back?' Butler said, reaching out to grab the sachet.

Egan was a split second faster. 'I don't think so, Mr Butler. I think we will have this analysed. If it is what you say it is, then you can have it back.'

Leaving Butler massaging his forehead with both hands, Egan left the interview room and made his way straight to the police laboratory to get the substance analysed. He returned an hour later to find Frank Butler with his head lolling onto his chest, drifting in and out of sleep. He was soon fully awake after Egan re-entered the room and slammed the door behind him.

'Would you care to explain why you had ten grams of strychnine hidden inside your hat?' said Egan.

'I didn't know that's what it was. I bought it thinking it was toothache medication,' replied Butler.

Egan laughed heartily. 'I thought you said it was for a headache. Either way, it would certainly cure a headache or a toothache! There's enough there to kill five men! Look, Frank…can I call you Frank?'

'No, you may not, because my name's not Frank, its Lee,' Butler quickly responded.

'Frank,' Egan said, 'why don't you save yourself the trouble and just tell us what happened?'

'I had nothing to do with any of this, I keep trying to tell you.'

'Frank, it seems like an extraordinary coincidence that Captain Weller ends up dead, and not only do you try to pass yourself off as that same man, but you are also in possession of all of his belongings. Unless you give me something, I can't help you.'

Butler buried his head in his hands and let out a deep sigh before looking back at Egan.

'Frank, I'm gonna need more than that. C'mon, Frank, the only way to clear this whole mess up is for you to be totally honest with us. I'm gonna have to go out there and tell those Australian detectives something. If you don't help me, Frank, then I can't help you. You know that everyone in Australia is calling for your head, and the only way to avoid that is for you to tell me the truth.'

'Okay, I will tell you what I know. It's not much, but I'll tell you. There were three of us together – Lee Weller, another man, and myself. The other man and Weller went prospecting. I stayed in camp. The other man came back alone and he gave me Weller's property. That's all I know.'

'Frank, there are a few things bothering me. First, why did that other man give you Weller's property, and second, if you, as you say you did, remained at the camp and were an innocent bystander in all of this, why didn't you go to the police? Wouldn't it have made sense to go to them and clear your name right away? Don't that look kind of bad?'

Butler closed his eyes, rubbed them with his thumb and forefinger and rolled his head from side to side, before saying, 'Yes, that does look bad for me.'

'You'll be in court soon, Frank, and if you don't start telling us the truth, it's only going to get a whole lot worse,' Egan said, as he rose and left the room.

The effects captured with Butler aboard the Swanhilda, revealing property such as private papers, books, photographs and jewelry belonging to Captain Weller; also the hat and a package of strychnine hidden beneath the band:

No. 1—The bulldog pistol with the initials "J. R." and "J. K." found in Butler's possession.

No. 2—Some of the jewels and trinkets.

No. 3—Butler's blankets covering the remainder of his apparel.

No. 4—The soft Fedora hat taken off Butler's head when he was arrested by Detective Egan, and in the band of which ten grains of strychnine was found.

No. 5—The package of strychnine.

No. 6—Butler's valise, enclosing the Weller jewels, photographs and papers.

Butler's Tell-Tale Property, *The San Francisco Call*, 3 February 1897.

21

Jumping Through Hoops

3 February 1897

With shackled hands and feet, Frank Butler was led from his cell accompanied by two heavily armed guards. He shuffled his way along the corridor and into the courtroom, shooting a quick glance at Roche, McHattie and Conroy who were seated at the front of the room.

McHattie returned Butler's look before leaning in close to Roche and whispering,

'Things are going crazy back in Sydney. I wish we could just get this over and done with. Did you send word through to the Attorney-General?'

'Yeah, I sent the code word through as soon as we got him.'

'So, why is all of this taking so long?'

'The Americans are just flexing their muscle. You have to remember, they are independent from Britain, and they will, at every opportunity, assert that. We are still a colony. Unfortunately, we have no power in any of this, and we will just have to play by their rules.'

McHattie shook his head before leaning back in his chair and casting his eye over the grey-haired and slightly overweight judge dressed in black robes, wondering what type of man he was as he walked to the bench from the door on the right-hand side of the courtroom through which he had made his entrance.

'All rise for the honourable Commissioner Heacock,' the bailiff said. Everybody, police and assembled media alike, duly rose. Commissioner Heacock sat down, and a silence descended over the court.

'Who are they?' McHattie whispered after Roche pointed to two men seated at the prosecution's table.

'They were appointed by Whitehall. They're two Irish lawyers. The one on the left is Donohue and the other one's name is Cormac.'

'Well, that makes me feel a little better, knowing that we have Irish guys on our side. What about the defence?'

'They're from a firm called Stone, Pidwell and Black.'

'Why did they agree to take him on? They look like pretty flash lawyers. How the hell can Butler afford them?'

'That's something I've been trying to figure out ever since I heard they'd agreed to defend him. I guess this case has been getting that much press, they see it as a good way to enhance their firm's reputation.'

'Bloody lawyers,' McHattie scoffed as the commissioner banged his gavel.

'Mr Frank Butler,' he began. 'You appear in this court today to determine whether there is enough evidence to grant an extradition order to send you back to Australia. Do you have anything to say before we begin?'

Butler remained silent.

Heacock continued. 'You appear in this court today to determine whether you did indeed murder Arthur Preston and Lee Weller on or about 23 and 31 October last year, respectively. Do you have anything to say about this?'

'Your Honour,' Butler said as he rose, 'I don't see how I can be questioned about whether I murdered Lee Weller, as I am that man, and you can plainly see me standing here before you.'

Stone tugged at Butler's jacket and shook his head to indicate for Butler to sit down and remain silent. Butler looked down, and seeing his lawyer's displeasure, sat down and said nothing more. Stone then stood to address the court.

'Your Honour. I would ask that we delay this hearing as my client has had no time to prepare an adequate defence. My client had been on a long voyage, was arrested before he even set foot on American soil and has been incarcerated ever since. My associates and I have had very little time to confer with the defendant, and therefore we do not believe that we have had sufficient chance to represent our client in a fair manner.'

Murderer Butler and His Attorney, Leonard Stone, in Court.

Butler posing for the newspapers, *The San Francisco Call*, 3 February 1897.

'Mr Stone,' Heacock replied, 'I understand what you are saying, but I will hear from witnesses and from the prosecuting lawyers before I give further consideration to your request.' Stone nodded and resumed his seat.

Donohue now rose and gave a slight cough before addressing Heacock. 'Your Honour, you have seen all the evidence that our excellent Australian colleagues have presented to you, and therefore you are aware of the sheer weight of that evidence. We have several witnesses here who will testify to the fact that the accused man presented himself under a different name. I would also remind Mr Stone that this is, in fact, a preliminary hearing to decide whether there is enough evidence to extradite Mr Butler. Should that be the case, then there will be adequate time for the defence to prepare their case, and so there is no need to delay this hearing any further.'

Stone rose immediately, his body language suggesting that he was not going to give any ground. 'Your Honour. I would like to repeat my request for more time to prepare an adequate defence for Mr *Weller*. He is still in a state of shock over all of this, and we are certain that, at this time, he is not mentally ready for the rigours of a trial.'

Heacock pondered the request again, looking from the defence to the prosecution and back again. 'Mr Stone, I will not grant your request for an indefinite delay,' he said firmly, 'but I will give you six days to prepare your defence, and not a second more. Court adjourned.'

Slamming his gavel down, Heacock's annoyance at the delay was evident, and everyone in the court watched him intently as he rose and left the room. Butler was helped to his feet and, with every pair of eyes upon him, kept his head down as he was led out of the courtroom and taken back to his cell.

5 February 1897

Over the next few days, Butler's cell became a hive of activity, with reporters from every newspaper desperately begging for an interview with the notorious 'alleged' murderer, and with each new visitor, Butler began to revel more and more in his rising fame.

'Good morning, Mr Weller,' said one journalist as he entered the cell one morning.

'Good morning,' Butler replied, remaining seated on his bed.

'I am from the *San Francisco Call*, and I was wondering if you would mind doing an interview?'

'Sure,' Butler said as he rose and shook the journalist's hand, 'but it will cost you.'

'Of course, of course,' the journalist said. 'Shall we sit?'

Butler lay back on his bunk as the journalist handed him two dollars and sat down on a chair. He then proceeded to ask Butler a series of questions about his past. While he did so, Butler was looking beyond him at a man who was loitering outside the cell. The journalist was asking Butler a question about his treatment in an American prison when Butler piped up and said, 'Who is that man hanging around out there?'

The journalist turned around before turning back and replying. 'That is Mr Lyon. He is the one of *Call's* sketch artist. We were wondering whether it would be possible to sketch you?' In the midst of asking his question, the journalist handed Butler a cigar.

'Of course!' Butler beamed as he took the cigar, lit it and put it in his mouth. 'How would you like me to pose?' Butler started to arrange himself into all sorts of poses, only stopping when the journalist stood up and Lyon stepped into the cell.

'Actually, Mr Weller,' he said, 'I would like to sketch you sitting on a chair.'

'Okay then,' Butler said, slightly disappointed that a more outlandish pose was not required, and sat down, leant forward and puffed away on the cigar that he held in his left hand while he rested his right elbow on his knee.

'Actually, Mr Weller, I do not think that is an appropriate pose for a man of your fame,' Lyon said as he examined his subject from several angles. 'If you could sit with your legs crossed, with your right knee on top, and your toe facing the wall to your left. Yes, that's it. Now, if you could put your right hand on your waist, and rest your left arm on the back of the chair, and if you could hold the cigar just out in front of your mouth. Yes, that's excellent. Yes, very refined, very refined indeed.'

Hearing the word 'refined', Butler's chest puffed out and he did he best to adopt what he considered to be a 'refined' expression.

Lyon sketched furiously away, and when he was done, he and the journalist thanked Butler and left. They were the first of a steady stream of journalists and autograph hunters who came and went throughout the day, with Butler charging fifty cents per autograph. For the most part, he smiled and put on a show, but he became particularly interested when a man from the Montgomery department store arrived and offered to provide new shoes for him if he would be permitted to display the old ones in his shop front, something to which Butler immediately consented.

And so it continued for the next few days, and the more Frank Butler's celebrity status increased, the more he began to believe that maybe, just maybe, fate would smile on him and he'd escape after all.

8 February 1897

Roche sat with McHattie and Conroy at an outside table in a café adjacent to the courthouse, sipping coffee.

'So what do you think?' he asked his companions.

'About what?' McHattie asked.

'About today? Do you think we'll get what we want?'

'I don't know,' McHattie said mournfully. 'These Americans sure do like to draw things out. Plus, they've split things into two separate hearings, one for Weller and one for Preston. We could be here for months yet.'

'I hope not!' Roche said. 'But those Irish lawyers have done a bloody good job in organising their witnesses. We'll just have to wait and see.'

Almost on cue, Donohue came walking down the street, pausing when he reached them. 'Good morning, gentlemen,' he said. 'I hope you're all suitably prepared for today,' he continued, looking directly at Conroy.

'Ready as we'll ever be,' Roche responded.

'Right, let's get to it then,' Donohue said as he paid for the Australians' coffees and began to make his way towards the courthouse. The Australians followed, and when they turned the last corner, they were immediately swamped by the media. They filled every square inch of the dozens of stairs leading up to the courthouse, and as soon as they saw the prosecution lawyer and some of the star witnesses, they immediately converged on them, forcing the lawyer and police officers to fight their way through the crowd while being bombarded with questions from every direction.

Repeating 'No comment' over and over again, it took them a good five minutes before they reached the large wooden doors and were safely inside. However, the media scrum did not end there, as the foyer and the courtroom itself were also packed with hungry press hounds begging for any scrap to be thrown their way. Much to the Australians' relief, several American officers came to their rescue and escorted them to their seats.

Shortly after, Butler was brought from his cell and led down the hallway and into the courtroom. The journalists lucky enough to be inside the room rushed forward, elbowing and pushing one another as they attempted to get close to him. Taking it all in his stride, Butler waved to them like the celebrity he believed himself to be, the broad smile that was etched across his face as he sat down in the dock soon turning into a self-satisfied grin. Behind him, there was a hubbub amongst the spectators as they loudly discussed every facet of the case, only hushing when Commissioner Heacock entered the courtroom.

'All rise,' the bailiff said, and everyone stood up.

'Be seated,' Heacock said. 'Mr Donohue. You may begin.'

Donohue stood, turned, and paused as he surveyed the assembled crowd, each of whom stared intently back at him. 'Today, ladies and gentlemen, I will set out to prove to you that this man seated here before you,' he began, sweeping his hand in the direction of Butler, 'is, in fact, Frank Butler and not, as he claims, Captain Lee Weller.'

Donohue proceeded to outline the prosecution's version of events, and when he was done, Heacock asked him to call his first witness. 'The prosecution calls Constable Michael Conroy.'

Conroy stood, adjusted his coat jacket, and made his way to the stand. The bailiff stood in front of Conroy and held out a Bible, upon which Conroy placed his palm. 'Do you swear to tell the truth, the whole truth and nothing but the truth, so help you God?'

'I do.'

'Can you state your name and occupation for the court?' Donohue asked.

'Yes, my name is Michael Conroy. I am a constable with the New South Wales police force.'

'Mr Conroy,' Donohue began as he pointed in the direction of Butler, 'have you seen this man before?'

'I have.'

'Can you please identify him?'

'Yes, his name is Frank Butler, but when I first met him he introduced himself as Frank Harwood.'

'Can you please tell the court of the circumstances in which you met this man?'

'I met him through my sister at Gilham's Hotel. The meeting was to discuss a prospecting trip he was planning.'

'And can you tell us more of what happened during and after that meeting?'

'He told me he was planning a trip to Albury, and asked me to look at a map and to mark out some places I thought might be worthwhile for prospecting. He showed me some miner's certificates with the name Frank Harwood on it. After the meeting, I took the map home, but I decided I didn't want to go with him, so I returned to the hotel and left the map at the reception desk.'

'Did you see the defendant again after that?'

'Yes, a few days later.'

'Did you have a conversation at this point?'

'Yes, I told him I was sorry, but other business had prevented me from going on the trip, and he replied, "Yes, it is your bad luck. You see, I always treat a man as he ought to be treated."'

'I said, "Fair enough. Thank you then, I suppose. Good luck with your next venture, sir."'

'Nothing further,' Donohue said as he sat down.

'Your witness, Mr Stone,' Heacock said.

'Mr Conroy, you have told this hearing that you know this man by the name Frank Harwood.'

'Yes, that is correct. That is the name he used. Like a said, he showed me some miner's certificates with that name on it.'

'Did you drink at all during this meeting?'

'Yes.'

'Did you drink a lot?'

'No, I wouldn't say I drank a lot.'

'But you were drinking, and hotels can sometimes be hazy and dark.'

'I guess they can be.'

'So, even though you saw some certificates, there is a possibility that my client is not this Mr Harwood at all, just maybe someone who looks like him. Considering the circumstances, there is no way you could be absolutely certain.'

'No, I am certain of what I saw!' Conroy said adamantly. 'That man there is Frank Harwood.'

Stone continued to try to cast doubt over the quality of Conroy's memories and the young constable continued to refute his suggestions, maintaining the surety of his convictions. Eventually, Stone finished his questioning, and Conroy was allowed to step down.

'Mr Donohue. Your next witness, please,' Heacock said.

Donohue stood and adjusted his robes and walked over to stand adjacent to Butler, then said, 'The prosecution calls Captain McAlister.'

Roche, McHattie and Conroy's gaze was immediately drawn to Butler, the three of them totally absorbed in his reaction. Roche thought he saw some strain in Butler's unflappable façade, but just as quickly his expression returned to one of smugness, that of a man revelling in his notoriety.

Halfway along the benches, a large man dressed in a starched white uniform stood, shuffled his way past the others and made his way to the front of the room and into the witness box. After dispensing with the swearing in, he looked up at Heacock before turning his attention to Donohue.

'Can you please state your name for the court?'

'Yes, my name is Captain McAlister.'

'Can you confirm for the court that you were once the captain of the ship *Langdale*?'

'I was indeed the captain of the *Langdale*.'

'How long ago did you serve on that ship?'

'It must be a few years now.'

'Do you remember most, if not all, of the men who served with you on that ship?'

'Yes, sir, I remember most of them. It was a tight crew.'

'Did you serve on that ship with a man named Lee Mellington Weller?'

'Yes, sir, I did.'

'Could you please tell me if the prisoner you see before you is that same man? Is the prisoner Lee Weller?'

'No, sir, that man is not Lee Weller.'

'Can you repeat that? Is that man Lee Weller?'

'No, sir. He looks no more like him than you do.'

'Objection!' Stone piped in. 'The prosecution is asking the witness to identify my client based on memory, not on fact.'

'Overruled,' Heacock said. 'The witness is answering the question to the best of his knowledge. If we denied every witness's testimony because we questioned their memory, then we would not be able to admit any evidence.'

Donohue continued questioning McAlister about his relationship with Lee Weller, with Stone continually interjecting, only to be overruled by Heacock time and time again. When his turn came to question McAlister, Stone tried to place as much doubt as he could on McAlister's recollection of Weller, saying that many years had passed and his memory could not be trusted. The longer Stone went, the more impressed with his efforts Butler seemed, and he began to relax, leaning back in his chair with his arms folded as he continually looked around the courtroom, being reprimanded by Heacock on several occasions for his lack of attention. When he finished, Stone sat down beside Butler and patted him on the right shoulder, both of them rather pleased with how things had gone over the last few minutes, particularly Stone's discrediting of the witness.

McAlister was dismissed, and Heacock asked the prosecution if they had anymore witnesses to call. Before answering, Donohue shot Stone a knowing look.

'Yes, we do, Your Honour.'

Donohue slowly rose, paused again, and fixed his coat. His body language and slow stride across the courtroom indicated that he was not bothered by the defence's efforts to discredit his witnesses, but rather that he knew that they had dug Butler's grave even deeper.

Roche leant in close to McHattie. 'He doesn't look rattled at all. What's he got up his sleeve?' he said.

'Didn't you read it in the paper?'

'Read what?'

'Some smart reporter discovered that Butler had been in San Fran previously, and he found the names of some of the ships he'd been on. He spoke to a Captain Petrie, and showed him pictures of the "Monster of the Blue Mountains," as they've taken to calling him. The reporter asked him if he recognised the picture, and he said he did. It should be interesting to see what he has to say.'

'Will the Prosecution call their next witness,' Heacock said to Donohue.

'Yes, Your Honour, the prosecution calls Captain Petrie.'

Butler immediately snapped his head around, and upon seeing Captain Petrie rising from his seat and slowly striding down the aisle, his beaming smile suddenly dissipated.

'Who is he?' Stone asked Butler, having seen the effect the appearance of this witness had had on Butler.

'He's a captain from a ship I was once on.'

Stone shot Butler a fierce look and whispered, 'Where the hell did they find this guy?'

'I don't know,' Butler said under his breath. 'More to the point, what are the chances of him being in San Francisco?'

'Pretty high, apparently,' Stone snarled as he grabbed his pad and pen and prepared to write down everything that this unexpected witness had to say.

The bailiff finished swearing in Petrie, and Donohue moved to stand in front of him.

'Can you please state your name for the court?'

'Captain Colin Petrie.'

Roche leant in to McHattie. 'We're bloody lucky Petrie happened to be here. We seem to have ruffled Butler's feathers.'

'Do you see the prisoner, the accused man, seated there?' Donohue continued.

'Yes.'

'Have you seen this man before?'

'Yes.'

'Can you please tell the court this man's name?'

'Certainly. I think that his true name is Richard Ashe.'

A hush descended over the crowded courtroom.

'I'm sorry,' Donohue said sarcastically. 'This man claims to be Lee Weller, and others have told us his name is Harwood and/or Butler. Are you sure that his name is Richard Ashe?'

'I think that is his true name,' Petrie repeated.

'Captain, can you please tell us how you came to be in this courtroom?'

'You came and asked me to testify, as my ship, the *Olive Bank*, pulled into port a few days ago.'

'A reporter came on board your ship and asked you some questions, did he not?'

'Yes, a reporter boarded my ship and asked me what I knew about the "Monster of the Blue Mountains". He showed me a photo and asked me if I knew this man. I said, "That is Richard Ashe. He shipped on board this vessel under that name early in 1893 as an able seaman at Rio de Janeiro for a voyage to Newcastle. I briefly met him again in Newcastle last November, just before the *Olive Bank* sailed for San Francisco.'

'Can you please tell the court about Mr Butler's behaviour whilst on board with you in 1893?'

'He was quite a disagreeable chap really. He was particularly lazy, and for the most part, refused to do any work. He threatened to kill me on several occasions. I think his words were that he was going to "blow my brains out", so when we arrived in Newcastle I had him arrested.'

'No further questions,' Donohue said as he walked back towards his table, smiled at Stone and sat down.

'Mr Stone, your witness,' Heacock said.

Stone set about trying to discredit Petrie's memory, as he had done with both Conroy and McAlister, but Petrie's certainty began to convince everyone in the court that the accused man had indeed used several aliases, and with every new detail that was revealed, dozens of journalists rushed from the court eager to relay the news to their offices.

At the completion of Petrie's testimony, he was dismissed. Heacock, given the commotion that the captain's appearance had created, decided it was time to adjourn for lunch. The crowd filtered outside, but Roche, McHattie and Conroy lingered while they waited for Donohue and Cormac.

'Thanks for that,' Donohue said to McHattie as they walked up to the Australians.

'No problem,' McHattie said with a smile as all five men walked from the courtroom and into the lunch room, each of them grabbing something to eat and sitting down at a nearby table.

'How do you think Petrie went down?' Roche asked as he took the first bite of his sandwich.

'Despite the defence's best attempts to discredit everything he was saying, I think he went down well,' Donohue said. 'Regardless of anything else, everyone in there now knows that Butler has been using numerous aliases. He can keep asserting that he is Lee Weller, but no matter how long this trial lasts, that will always be in question.'

The lunch conversation centred around each man's thoughts as to how the trial was progressing, while the Australians pressed Donohue on how long he thought it would be before they could get Butler on a boat and back home, a conversation that continued as they moved outside to smoke.

'You must understand, Mr Donohue,' Roche said as he put his pipe to his lips, 'we are under a great deal of pressure from all and sundry at home to have Mr Butler brought back there and put on trial. All of Australia is calling for his blood.'

'I am well aware of the pressure you gentlemen are under,' Donohue said purposefully, 'but you need to understand that I can only do what I can do, and I guarantee they will lodge appeals. It may be some months yet. However, this afternoon may change some of that.'

Roche was about to push Donohue further on the technicalities of the American legal system when the bailiff came out to tell them that they were required back in court. As they walked inside, Roche was greeted by a familiar face, the sight of which warmed his heart and gave him hope that this would all soon be over.

'Hello, Mr Warburton!' Roche said as he shook the Consul-General's hand. 'What are you doing here?'

'I am here at the request of the British government of course, and at the request of Mr Donohue here.'

Donohue shot Roche a knowing look before turning and heading into the courtroom. The Australians pressed the Consul-General on his opinion as to how long the proceedings might take, but before he could answer, they were called into the courtroom.

Heacock returned, everyone rose, and then resumed their seats once Heacock had seated himself.

'Welcome back, everyone,' Heacock said politely. 'Mr Donohue, do you have your next witness?'

'Yes, Your Honour, I do. The prosecution calls the British Consul-General, Mr Warburton.'

Warburton, who was seated next to the aisle, rose and walked to the stand.

'Can you state your name and position, please?' Donohue asked.

'Yes, my name is Mr Joseph W. Warburton. I am the British Consul-General.'

'Mr Warburton,' Donohue began. 'I believe you have a telegram in your possession that you wish to tender to the court.'

'That I do,' Warburton said as he reached inside his coat pocket, withdrew a yellow telegram and gave it to the bailiff to pass to Heacock, who read it carefully. When he was done, he handed it back to the bailiff, who took it to the defence team's table so they could also read it.

'Your Honour, the telegram the defence are now reading is from Mr Julian Pauncefoote, the British Ambassador to the United States, and it authorises the beginning of extradition proceedings against Mr Butler.'

Black, who had taken over from Stone, immediately stood. 'Objection! This is hearsay evidence.'

Before Heacock had a chance to answer, Cormac interjected.

'Your Honour, I do not see how this can be considered hearsay evidence when Mr Warburton has the authority to order the beginning of extradition proceedings himself.'

'Mr Black, I agree with Mr Cormac that Mr Warburton has such authority. Does counsel admit that Mr Warburton, the witness, is the British Consul-General?

'No.'

'Either way, I still overrule the objection.'

'Mr Consul-General,' Cormac said, emphasising Warburton's title, 'do you perhaps have something on your person that would prove your identity?'

'Yes, sir, that I do.'

'Would you kindly produce that?'

Warburton reached inside his coat once more, withdrew a slightly worn and discoloured piece of paper and handed it to the bailiff. After it was passed to him, Heacock unfolded the paper and elaborated on its contents for all present.

'Mister Stone and Mister Black,' he said slowly and surely, 'this document is an official commission signed by Queen Victoria herself stating that Mr Warburton is her Consul-General in the United States of America.'

He handed the document back to the bailiff, who took it over to the defence team.

'I trust there are no more objections about the validity of Mr Warburton's identity?' Heacock said as the defence team read the document, and then handed it back to the bailiff, who in turn returned it to Warburton.

'No, Your Honour,' Black conceded.

'Do you have any more questions you would like to ask?' Heacock pushed.

'No, Your Honour.'

'Mister Donohue and Mister Cormac, your next witness, please.'

'The prosecution would like to call Detective John Roche to the stand,' Cormac said.

Roche rose from his seat and made his way to the witness box.

'Can you please state your name and occupation for the court?' Cormac said.

'Yes, my name is John Roche, and I am a detective with the New South Wales police force.'

'Detective Roche, can you please inform the court as to your role in these proceedings?' Cormac continued.

'Yes, I was sent to London on behalf of the New South Wales government to gain extradition orders pertaining to Mr Frank Butler.'

'And when you arrived here in San Francisco, were you present at the arrest of Mr Butler?'

'Yes, I was.'

'Can you describe what you found on Frank Butler's person, or the belongings that he had in his possession?'

'Yes, we recovered Captain Weller's seachest.'

'And did you find anything of interest in that chest?'

'Yes, we found Captain Weller's wedding ring and a brooch belonging to his wife. We also found chequebooks and sheet music belonging to Captain Weller.'

'Had you seen the prisoner before the time when you arrested him?'

'Yes. Well, not in person, but I have seen him before.'

'You say "not in person". Can you tell us in what context you have seen him?'

'I have seen photographs of him that we distributed while we were searching for him.'

'Were you present at the discovery and/or the exhumation of Captain Weller's body?'

'Yes.'

'Were you able to make a positive identification of Captain Weller at that time?'

'No, sir, I was not.'

A slight murmur rippled through the spectators.

'And why is that?'

'Because Captain Weller's face was unrecognisable due to the fact that he had been shot through the head and then buried.'

The murmur turned to hushed astonishment.

'Although you had met Captain Weller before, had you not?'

'Yes.'

'Can you tell the court the circumstances in which you met Captain Weller?'

'I assisted him in retrieving some possessions that had been stolen from him.'

'And you are certain that the prisoner over there is not Captain Weller.'

'Yes, sir, I am certain he is not.'

'Can you please tell the court the name by which you know this man?'

'His name is Frank Butler, as best I know it.'

'Thank you, Detective Roche,' Cormac said as he sat down. 'Your witness.'

Black did his best to discredit Roche, but as the expert on the case, Roche was unflappable and, realising he was getting nowhere, Black soon finished his questioning, Roche was dismissed, but only briefly.

The whole process had to be repeated for the hearing regarding Preston's murder. The same witnesses entered the stand and gave almost the same evidence as they had done previously. Every deposition, every document was read again.

22

The Show Goes On

11 February 1897

More days passed until the last of the witnesses had been called and recalled. At the conclusion of proceedings, Heacock stated that he would grant permission for the extradition proceedings to begin. Almost immediately, Stone and Black lodged an appeal, and the whole process had to be repeated. Every witness had to re-enter the stand and repeat, word for word, what they'd said in the initial hearings.

When Butler wasn't in court there was a growing stream of news reporters clambering over one another in an attempt to get a one-on-one interview with the notorious killer. Butler revelled in his newfound fame and, despite Heacock's initial findings, was certain that he was going to be a free man before long, whereupon he could exploit his celebrity status.

Meanwhile, Detective Roche and the other Australians were entirely disgusted by the handling of the whole affair.

One evening, after several newsmen had left Butler's cell, an older man who had been hovering in the background waiting for the newspapers to finish stepped forward.

'Mr Weller,' the man said politely as he stood at the entrance to the cell.

'No more interviews today,' Butler said forcefully. 'Come back tomorrow. I am too tired,' he said, turning his back on the man and rolling over on his bed.

'Ah. Mr Weller, I am not a journalist. I am a merchant, and I have only come here to see if you needed to buy any new clothes.'

Butler's interest now sparked, he rolled over again and propped himself up on one elbow. Seeing that he had caught Butler's attention, the older man stepped closer and introduced himself. 'My name is Groom,' he said, beginning to unpack his wares from a large bag he was carrying. 'I have some nice suits here, and some fantastic new hats.'

As Groom proceeded to lay the various goods out on the floor, Butler moved forward on his bed to inspect them. 'Well, I quite like the style of that hat there, but not that one in particular. Do you have anything similar to it?' he asked.

'I do, but not here. I have plenty more back at my store. Do you see anything else you like?'

'No, just a new hat will be fine. When you send me my new one, I will be happy to give you my old one, which you can do with as you please.'

Knowing that the possession of something previously owned by a notorious killer was far more valuable than anything he could sell him, Groom hurriedly packed his wares away and said, 'I shall have it to you tomorrow. Thank you, sir.'

'No problem,' Butler said, and then rolled back over and went to sleep.

The next day, one of the guards came to Butler's cell. 'I have a package for you,' he said.

Butler, who was sitting at the desk writing, turned around. 'Just leave it there,' he said, motioning to the bunk.

The guard slid the cell door open, placed the package on the bed, and closed the door again. Butler waited until the guard had gone before retrieving the package, and then sat back at the desk and opened it. Inside was a box containing a brand-new bowler hat. Butler removed the hat and fingered the rim before holding it out at arm's length. He then removed his old hat and put on the new one. Placing the old hat inside the box, he grabbed some paper and wrote a note.

I thank you sincerely for the new hat you sent me, and I herewith send you my old hat. Frank Butler.

Groom, perhaps too enraptured with his prize or not noticing the disparity, failed to mention to the authorities that Butler had signed his name thus and when Butler appeared in court later that day, Roche immediately noticed the new hat. 'I am so tired of this! He seems to be making more money in a day from being a murderer than we do in a month!

After the court proceedings had finished for the day, Roche and the others were walking back to their hotel when Conroy suddenly stopped. 'Hey, boys, take a look at this.'

McHattie and Roche moved alongside Conroy. 'Oh, for God's sake!' Roche exclaimed as he peered through the window of Groom's department store. Frank Butler's old hat sat on a stand surrounded by half a dozen signs stating that this was the hat of a "notorious killer". The three men stood and stared in shock for a minute or so until Roche eventually broke the silence. 'What is wrong with this country?' he said.

'I think you've been away too long if you've forgotten what the situation was like back home before we left,' McHattie offered.

'Yeah, true,' Roche said as the three men simultaneously shook their heads and continued on their way back to their hotel. When they entered the foyer, Roche went up to the reception desk. 'Are there any messages for me?'

'As a matter of fact, one came in this afternoon,' the concierge said as he reached behind him and passed Roche an envelope.

'I don't know about you fellas, but I could use a drink.'

'The bar will be open for some hours yet, detective,' the concierge said. 'Anything you have, just add it to your tab.'

'Thank you,' Roche said as he and the others headed into the bar. They'd barely sat down before the waiter arrived.

'Bottle of scotch and three glasses,' Roche said. The waiter nodded and left to get the drinks. The waiter returned and placed the bottle and glasses down on the table. Roche quickly filled his glass and drained it before the other two had a chance to fill their glasses. He was halfway through his second glass before he remembered the envelope that he had placed on the table. He reached out and picked it up, then slid his finger under the flap and opened it. Inside was a note, which Roche unfolded and read. He immediately slammed his fist down on the table, causing the bottle and glasses to rattle. 'Fuck me! This is getting beyond a joke!' he said as he drained the remainder of his glass.

'What?' McHattie asked, sipping his scotch.

'Read this,' Roche growled as he handed the letter to McHattie, who read it silently, and then read it out loud for Conroy's benefit.

To the Australian Detectives,

I will donate to you or any Australian charitable institution the sum of one thousand dollars for the services of Lee Weller for the period of one week. The object is to exhibit him in public for pay.

Thomas H. Shaw

'Can you believe that?' Roche snapped as he drained his third glass and slammed it down on the table. Neither Conroy nor McHattie said a word, both just shaking their heads in disbelief.

'I didn't think I was going to need Preston's coat. I thought we'd get the extradition order without it, but I think the time has come for us to tender it to the court, and see if we can't get this all over and done with.'

The three men continued drinking until late in the evening, each trying to raise the others' spirits by reaffirming that this would all soon be over and they'd be on a ship back to Australia.

23

The Truth?

7 March 1897

Early the next morning, Stone and Black visited Butler, who was already awake and reading his Bible.

'Good morning, Lee,' Stone said.

'Morning, sirs,' he said as he rose and grasped hold of the cell bars.

'Lee, we'd like to have a chat with you,' Black said, sitting down on a chair opposite the cell.

'Yes?'

'As you can understand, our services do not come gratis. You have continually insisted that you would pay us, but we have yet to see a penny. We are, as I am sure you can imagine, considerably out of pocket.'

Without skipping a beat, Butler immediately said, 'You can cable a bank in Sydney for one hundred pounds. I have also signed a contract with a publisher to write my autobiography, and I will get forty per cent of the profits, so I will be able to pay you anything else I owe then.'

'Lee,' Stone said with more enthusiasm in his voice, 'we've been doing our best to argue that you are Lee Weller but even the papers say your name is Butler. Be honest with us, what *is* your real name?'

'Okay, I will level with you both, it is, as they say, Frank Butler.'

'Alright, Frank, we can continue to push the argument that you are Lee Weller, but despite having some success with it yesterday, we don't think it's working. We had a think about it last night. Heacock isn't buying what we're trying to sell him, we're sure of it. He has already found against you once and, Mr Stone and I don't think he will change his mind. We need something else. Our last shot is to submit a writ of *habeas corpus*.'

'What's that?' Butler said curiously.

'It basically means that they have to have the right person under arrest in court. If we can prove your name is something else then we can ask for a mistrial.'

'Alright, alright, I'll level with you. My name is Frank Butler.'

'We will try by using that first but it may not work,' Stone said as he stroked his chin.

'Why won't it work?'

'Because they have evidence that says you have used that name. Have you ever gone under any other names?'

'Well, Frank Butler is not my real name, nor is Frank Harwood, my actual name is John Newman.'

'What?' Stone said with some shock.

'It's Newman.'

'Okay, *Frank, John*, whatever you want to call yourself. We'll start by trying Butler and then, if that doesn't work, we'll try Newman. See you in court later this morning.'

When the hearing resumed later that morning, Stone was the first to speak. 'Your Honour,' he said, addressing a seemingly disinterested Heacock. 'We would like to inform the court that my client would now like to be referred to as Frank Butler, not Lee Weller, and that he would like to take the stand to make a statement in his own defence.'

Heacock immediately sat bolt upright. 'Excuse me?'

The crowd gasped. It wasn't only Heacock who was now on the edge of their seat.

'My client would like to be referred to as Frank Butler from this point on, and he would like to make a statement,' Stone repeated.

'If that is what you wish,' Heacock said. 'Mr *Butler*, if you please.'

Butler stood and walked to the stand, where he seated himself and took an extended look around the court before taking a deep breath and beginning.

'My name *is* Frank Butler. I have maintained that my name was Lee Weller because I was concerned that, with all the media attention, the hearings against me would not be fair or impartial. I apologise for any undue delays or problems I have caused, but I have taken the stand today to set the record straight so that we may be able to put all of this behind us. I was with Lee Weller at Glenbrook Lagoon. There were three of us camped there. We did go prospecting on that ridge, but Mr Weller was very depressed about the loss of his wife, and the whole time we were together he was drinking very heavily. He kept saying that he could not live without her, and that his life was not worth living anymore. When we went out prospecting, he kept saying this, and not long after we started digging, he picked up his gun and shot himself in the head. I stood there shocked for several minutes, but I have seen men die before, so when I regained my composure, I buried Weller's body, in accordance with camp custom in Australia, and that is all there is to it.' Butler then bowed his head solemnly before stepping down and returning to sit with his defence team.

'Does either the prosecution or the defence have any other witnesses you wish to call or evidence you wish to submit?' Heacock asked.

'No, Your Honour,' Cormac said, echoed immediately by Stone. Heacock nodded and took a look around the courtroom, seemingly waiting for some other surprise twist in this bizarre case, before he presented his findings.

'Having considered all the evidence and all the witnesses' statements, I have no choice but to find against Mr Butler. I find that there is sufficient evidence that Mr Butler was indeed responsible for the death of Arthur Preston. Furthermore, I reiterate that there is sufficient evidence to find that he was also responsible for the death of Captain Lee Weller. If there was ever a case that could possibly have imagined wherein one should, "steal the livery of the court of Heaven to serve the Devil in it," it is the case of Lee Weller. I find that extradition proceedings against Mr Butler can now begin.'

Slamming his gavel down to make his findings official, Heacock rose from his seat and left the room. Butler bowed his head, and there was a noticeable change in his disposition as his shoulders slumped. Behind him, the Australians were shaking each other's hands, and then those of the prosecution lawyers.

Butler was led from the court with his head still bowed, and as he passed the prosecution team, Roche felt compelled to comment, 'Not long now.' Butler refused to look up, continuing to stare at the ground until he disappeared from view.

As he entered the cell block, Butler was met by the chief of police. 'Mr Butler, I hope you have enjoyed receiving all your visitors, because from this moment on, you will not be receiving any. This is Deputy Clarke. He will be keeping a very close watch on you, so don't try anything silly.'

Butler nodded meekly, and when he was placed in his cell and the shackles were removed, he slumped onto the bed and turned his back on his jailers, who left him to ponder how he would now find salvation.

24

The Last Roll of the Dice

9 March 1897

Roche and the others sat sipping their morning coffee in the hotel tearooms, Roche reading the papers just as he'd done every morning for the duration of the trial.

'Why do you keep reading those American papers?' McHattie asked him through a mouthful of toast. 'They just get you riled up.'

'Part of being a good detective, young McHattie. It pays to read the papers, you know. That, after all, is how you spotted Butler in the first place. Occasionally you will get a good journo who will unearth something you may have missed. But then again, you get stuff like this where they haven't done their research at all!'

'Why? What is it?'

'James, listen to this description of the Mountains. "There are kangaroos there in armies – long-distance reachers that leap moderate-sized gullies which would make a human vaulter pale."'

'Don't think I've ever seen a roo leap an entire gully! Sure they can jump, but c'mon.'

'Oh, wait,' said Roche. 'It gets better. "The native bear is to be seen at almost every gnarled tree trunk."'

McHattie dribbled tea from his mouth as he tried to stop himself from laughing.

'I don't know about you boys, but I haven't seen too many native bears, let alone one on every tree,' McHattie chuckled. 'Come on, let's go and get this over and done with.'

The three men finished their breakfast, and then headed towards the court with a renewed sense of hope that today would be the day when the papers would be officially signed, and they could finally get Butler on a boat back to Australia.

They entered the courtroom right on 9 am to find that proceedings were about to begin. Heacock entered and hurriedly sat down. Roche took an extended look at Butler, noting the complete change in his demeanour. He sat fidgeting, looking down at the ground before looking up and around the room, and then up at the roof. His confident body language had totally evaporated, replaced by nervousness and anxiety.

'Gentlemen,' Heacock began, 'I will make this very brief. I have an extradition order, signed by Secretary of State Mr Sherman, copies of which I will give to both the prosecution and the defence.'

'Your Honour,' Black said, 'we understand that the court has issued an extradition order for Frank Butler, but we would like to inform the court that we have issued a writ of *habeas corpus*.'

Heacock's eyes opened wide as he leant forward. 'You what?'

'We have issued a writ of *habeas corpus*.'

'On what grounds?'

'Contrary to what we have previously argued, our client's name is John Newman, and we are issuing the writ based on this.'

Heacock rolled his eyes. 'Fine.' With that, he rose and exited the courtroom, returning shortly after with a fellow judge, who took Heacock's place on the bench while the latter sat to one side.

'Mr Black, it is my understanding that you have issued a writ of *habeas corpus* given that the name of the defendant is John Newman.'

'That is correct, Judge Morrow,' Stone said as he moved forward and handed the writ over.

Morrow read it. 'Okay, let's begin. Judge Heacock, if you would be so kind as to take the stand.'

Heacock moved to the witness stand and was quickly sworn in.

'Judge Heacock, are you aware that the prisoner has claimed the name, John Newman?' Morrow asked as he pointed to Butler.

'He does this morning, I understand. That is the first time I have heard of it.'

'Thank you, Judge Heacock,' Morrow said. 'That is all I need from you.'

Despite Morrow seemingly having made his decision already, the fact that the writ had been lodged meant that the whole process had to be repeated yet again. Two days later Morrow eventually found the same as Heacock had done twice previously, and once again, Frank Butler was ordered to be extradited back to Australia.

As he was removed from the court for the last time, Butler shuffled along dejectedly, his face now forlorn, gaunt and withdrawn. Roche watched him as he passed, knowing that Butler could feel the weight of his stare. He waited, his gaze fixed, for the moment when they would make eye contact, for the moment of victory, but Butler was in no mood to oblige.

Back in his cell, Butler went straight to his bunk and lay down facing the wall. The order prohibiting visitors had been revoked and, with the case now concluded, scores of journalists began to gather outside, all eager to get the first interview with the convicted killer, and to get his reaction.

'Frank?' said a Deputy Johnson who had been assigned to guard him.

Butler said nothing.

'Frank?'

'What!'

'How's your supplies going? Do you need some more stuff?'

'Fine! It's all fine! Everything's fine!'

'C'mon, Frank, take it easy,' said the other deputy, Cartwright, 'we're just asking after you. There's loads of journalists outside, and we thought you might want to make a quick buck or two, or top up your tobacco supplies.'

'Tell them to go away!' Butler snapped.

'You sure, Frank?' Cartwright asked.

'Tell them to go away!' he bellowed.

Cartwright obliged, and the journalists were asked to leave. When the last of them had departed, the chief of police arrived. Cartwright and Johnson immediately stood to attention.

'At ease, boys,' he said. The two deputies stood uneasily as he walked over to Butler's cell and took a look around. 'Boys, I want you to come over here, please.'

Cartwright and Johnson were at his side in an instant.

'Do you see anything wrong with what Mr Butler is wearing?'

They looked the prisoner up and down, and Johnson said, 'No, sir.'

'Well, I do!' the police chief said irately. 'He is still wearing his belt, and his shoes still have the laces in them. You two know better than to leave a prisoner in the cells with these items still present!'

'Sorry, sir,' Cartwright apologised.

'Apology accepted, but I want you to see to it that there are no more mistakes. You see that chair there? I want it removed. The desk, too. I want you to go through that cell and remove anything you can find that you consider the prisoner might try to harm himself with, and I mean absolutely anything. I don't need to remind you that we are under a great deal of pressure from the Australians about this one. They're pretty unhappy that it's taken this long. If anything else was to happen and they couldn't get the prisoner home, it would be very bad for relationships between the two countries. So, if anything happens to him, it's on your heads, understand?'

'Yes, sir,' the two deputies said simultaneously as they hurriedly unlocked the cell and began removing the pieces of furniture, now seriously concerned for their careers. When every scrap of furniture had been placed outside the cell, they went back inside to search Butler, who was still lying on his bed facing the wall.

'Come on, Frank, get up,' Cartwright said as he tapped Butler on the shoulder. Butler didn't move.

'Come on, Frank, don't make it any more difficult than it has to be.' Butler still didn't move.

Cartwright and Johnson shook their heads. Cartwright grabbed Butler by the shoulders, Johnson took him by the legs, and they stood him up. Butler stared blankly into the distance as the two deputies patted him down, checked his pockets and removed his belt and shoelaces before laying him back down, leaving him to stare at the wall.

PART III

25

The Mariposa

2 April 1897

Cartwright and Johnson sat at a table outside Butler's cell playing cards. Johnson was pondering his next move when he casually said, 'How's he doing?'

Cartwright took a quick look and, seeing Butler wrapped up in his blanket and fast asleep, replied, 'Yeah. He's alright, now hurry up would you.'

'Well, after tomorrow, we won't have to worry about him,' Johnson said as he placed a card on the table.

'Good,' Cartwright said as he played his next card. 'I've just about had enough of this.'

They continued on with their game for another twenty minutes, when Cartwright rose from his chair. 'Do you want a coffee?'

'Yeah. I'd better have one, I'm falling asleep here.'

Cartwright moved over to the stove, picked up the kettle and poured two cups before turning back to his companion. He was about halfway across the room when he took a quick glance into Butler's cell. He paused, unsure of whether he was seeing what he thought he was seeing or whether his eyes were just playing tricks on him.

'Oh, shit!' he cried, dropping both cups, which smashed when they hit the floor.

'What?' Johnson cried as he leapt up from his seat.

'Look!' Butler's body could be seen writhing beneath the blanket that covered him. Cartwright fumbled with his keys as he tried desperately to unclip them from his belt.

'Hurry up!' Johnson urged.

'Shit, give me a chance!'

Eventually, he freed the keys, unlocked the cell and threw the door open. They rushed inside and ripped the blanket away from Butler, who was lying in the foetal position, his right hand working furiously at his left wrist, a long fingernail gouging the skin in search of a vein. Blood was already trickling from his right wrist, and also from his right temple, forming a small pool on the mattress beneath him. As soon as he saw the blood, Cartwright cried out, 'Quick! Get a doctor!'

Johnson dashed from the cell, yelling for the doctor as he ran. Meanwhile, Cartwright fought with Butler as he tried to grab his arms and separate them. Butler, despite his blood loss, struggled with all his might, and it was only when Cartwright drove his knee into Butler's chest that Butler was finally subdued.

Moments later Johnson rushed back into the cell, along with another officer and the doctor. While the deputies and the other officer kept Butler under control, the doctor reached inside his bag, pulled out two bandages and proceeded to bandage both of Butler's wrists before taping a gauze pad to Butler's temple.

'Doc, we can't have him doing this again,' Cartwright said, pressing down on Butler's chest.

'I know,' the doctor said, removing a vial from his bag and clamping it between his teeth. Pulling a needle from his bag, he filled it from the vial, found a vein in Butler's arm and administered the injection.

'What's that, doc?' Johnson asked as he watched on.

'It's a sedative. That should keep him out until tomorrow morning, but I think it's best you move your chairs in here and keep a close watch, just in case. I could give him a larger dose, but even though he is quite a big man, I don't want to take the risk. If I give him more, it might be too much for him, in which case he'll get his wish, and then all hell will break loose.'

'Thanks, doc,' Cartwright said as he felt Butler's body relaxing beneath him. 'We will do what you suggest.'

After tidying up his bag, the doctor left the cell, pausing at the door before he departed. 'Just give me a call if you need anything.'

'Will do, doc,' Cartwright said, as he and the other two men set about moving their chairs into the cell.

'Alright,' said Johnson. 'We'll take it in turns. One of us can sleep for a few hours while the other two keep watch. I'm happy to take the first watch if one of you two wants to take the first sleep.'

'You two have been doing the longest watches,' the third deputy, Fisher, said. 'One of you have the first sleep.'

And so it went for the rest of the night; two deputies played cards in Butler's cell while the other slept, and every couple of hours they rotated until the sun's first rays began filtering through the cell window. Butler began to stir, and the three deputies kept a close watch until Roche, McHattie, Conroy, Baldwin, Bunner and another half dozen officers arrived.

'How is he?' Baldwin asked as the party stepped inside the cell.

'He's alright,' Cartwright replied. 'He was a little bit out of it, but he should be right now.'

'Good,' Baldwin said as he pulled out his handcuffs. 'Get him on his feet and let's get this show underway.'

The deputies took hold of Butler and stood him upright. Despite swaying a little on his feet, he appeared to have all his wits about him. He kept his gaze on the floor while his arms were drawn behind his back and the cuffs were applied. Butler then lifted his head and his eyes met those of Roche, who smiled. Butler responded with a scowl, and Roche momentarily contemplated making a comment, but decided against it; nothing more needed to be said.

Baldwin grabbed Butler by the right arm and led him from the cell while the other officers formed a semicircle around them. No sooner had they stepped outside the station than they were swamped by a swarm of journalists who had been eagerly awaiting their appearance. They surged forward, all asking questions that were unintelligible in the hubbub, and it took all the strength that the Australian and American policemen could muster to keep them at bay. Quickening their pace, and leaving many of the journalists trailing behind them, they soon reached the docks, where they made their way down the first wharf to a waiting ship.

With the focus now back on him, Butler's countenance changed completely. He was suddenly brighter, smiling and waving, basking in the attention. As they reached the gangway, he heard a loud voice that clearly stood out from the rest.

'Mr Butler! Mr Butler!'

Butler turned, and although he didn't catch the journalist's name, he did hear him say, 'from *The San Francisco Examiner*.'

'Yes?' Butler responded.

'What do you think will happen when you get back to Australia to face trial? Do you think there will be any mercy shown?'

'There will be no plea for mercy, no sympathy asked for. I have faced death before in the trenches of Tel-El-Kebir, and in the varied occupations of a wanderer's life, and if it comes to the worst, I shall meet it without qualm or fear. I have been an outcast and a wanderer all my life, and it is but the closing scene of a wasted life.'

Butler being taken aboard the *Mariposa*, *The San Francisco Call*, 4 April 1897.

Upon hearing this, even Roche had to shake his head at the honesty of the response, but he wasn't going to allow Butler to have his moment in the sun. Whilst Butler was taken aboard the ship, Roche took a glance at the bow and noticed its name, the *Mariposa*. Once the entire party was on board, they were greeted by the ships' captain, a man named Hayward, and his chief officer, Mr Hart.

'Captain Hayward,' Baldwin said as they shook hands.

'Marshall Baldwin.'

'Can you lead us to the brig please, Captain?'

Hayward nodded to Hart, who retrieved his keys and said, 'Follow me.'

Descending below deck, Hart weaved his way through the ship's narrow confines until he stopped at the end of a small corridor and opened a door.

'In here,' he said. 'By the way,' he continued, looking at the Australians, 'you have a cabin right next door.'

'Excellent,' Roche said as he stepped past Hart and into the brig. The room had a row of bars running across the middle of it, on the far side of which was the cell that would hold the prisoner. Roche examined the specially prepared cell as he walked towards the far wall, and pulled on two chains that were attached to two steel rings bolted to the wall. Below the chains was a chair that was bolted to the floor. Roche kicked it several times before grabbing the leather straps that were attached to the chair and giving them a hard pull. Satisfied that everything was as it should be, he nodded to his colleagues. Butler was bundled inside and shoved forcibly into the chair. He tried to resist, but it was nothing more than a token gesture as his handcuffs were removed and his arms were immediately shackled with the chains and his hands covered in mittens. Roche and Baldwin wrapped the leather straps across his chest, midsection and legs, and gave them one last tug before stepping back.

Hart then left the cell, only to return shortly afterwards carrying something that resembled a large canvas bag. He stood in front of Butler and looked at the Americans and the Australians. Seeing the slightly perplexed expressions on their faces, he unfurled the canvas, revealing a crudely constructed straitjacket, which he fastened around

Butler before kneeling down behind him and tying it off. 'I was thinking it's better to be safe than sorry,' he said as he looked up at Baldwin and Roche.

'Of course,' Roche said with a smile.

'We'll be setting off shortly,' said Hayward, who had now joined them. 'Mr Hart will show you to your quarters.'

'I'll take first watch,' Roche said as he pulled up a chair and placed it beside Butler.

'Right. Looks like our work here is done,' said Baldwin as he began to shake each of the Australians' hands in turn. 'Been a pleasure working with you boys.'

'And you,' Roche said. 'Thank you for all your assistance.'

'It's the least we could do,' Baldwin said with a broad grin as he made his way towards the door. 'Hope you boys have a safe journey. It would be a shame to go through all of this malarkey and not get your *hanging*.'

Emphasising his last word, Baldwin's smile became just a little broader as he shifted his gaze to Butler, who looked up briefly before staring back down at the floor.

'We'll get there,' Roche said confidently. 'Mr Butler here will see his day of justice, don't you worry about that.'

With that, Baldwin and the other Americans departed, leaving Conroy, Roche and McHattie to begin their guard duties while awaiting departure.

Once the American police were off the ship and the ropes had been cast off, the *Mariposa* pulled away from the dock and made its way out of San Francisco Bay. Passing the islands and running through the heads, Roche could feel the steamer picking up speed as the vessel began to creak and groan.

McHattie appeared at the door of the brig. 'We've just pulled out of the bay and into open water,' he informed Roche.

Satisfied that, even if he somehow managed to escape, there was nowhere for Butler to go, Roche began to undo the straitjacket and the mittens, and had soon removed all of Butler's constraints except for one leg iron. Butler immediately started shouting and cursing, and it took every bit of McHattie and Conroy's combined strength to subdue him and refasten his bonds.

Butler was kept in constraints as the days passed and the *Mariposa* continued to steam towards Australia. Eventually, Butler calmed down slightly, and as a consequence the detectives decided to allow him some time free from his bonds. On some days he'd repeat his violent outbursts and would have to be shackled again, but these were interspersed with other days when he'd barely move from his bunk. On several occasions, they tried to engage Butler in conversation, but he was having none of it.

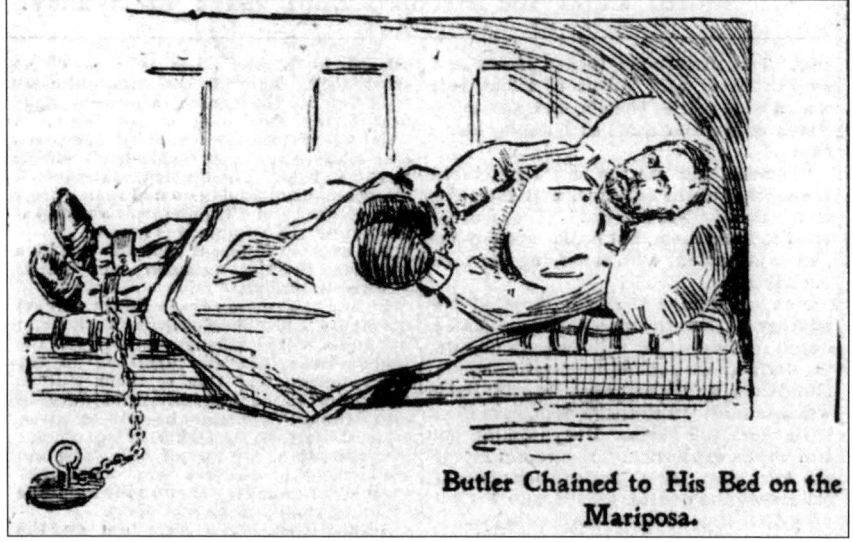

Butler Chained to His Bed on the Mariposa.

Butler in shackles and mittens, *The San Francisco Call*, 4 April 1897.

One night, Roche was on watch when one of the crew brought in Butler's supper. Roche rose from his chair and carefully examined every item.

'Detective, I assure you everything has been prepared according to your instructions,' the crewman said, clearly offended at the suggestion that he may not have done his job properly.

Looking up from the tray, Roche's stare was icy. 'Sir, this man has already tried to commit suicide once, and I am not about to take any chances, especially when we are so close to achieving our objective.'

Tapping the tin plate and checking everything once more, Roche was finally satisfied, and handed Butler his meal, which he ate slowly and silently. McHattie and Conroy entered the brig just as Butler finished his last bite.

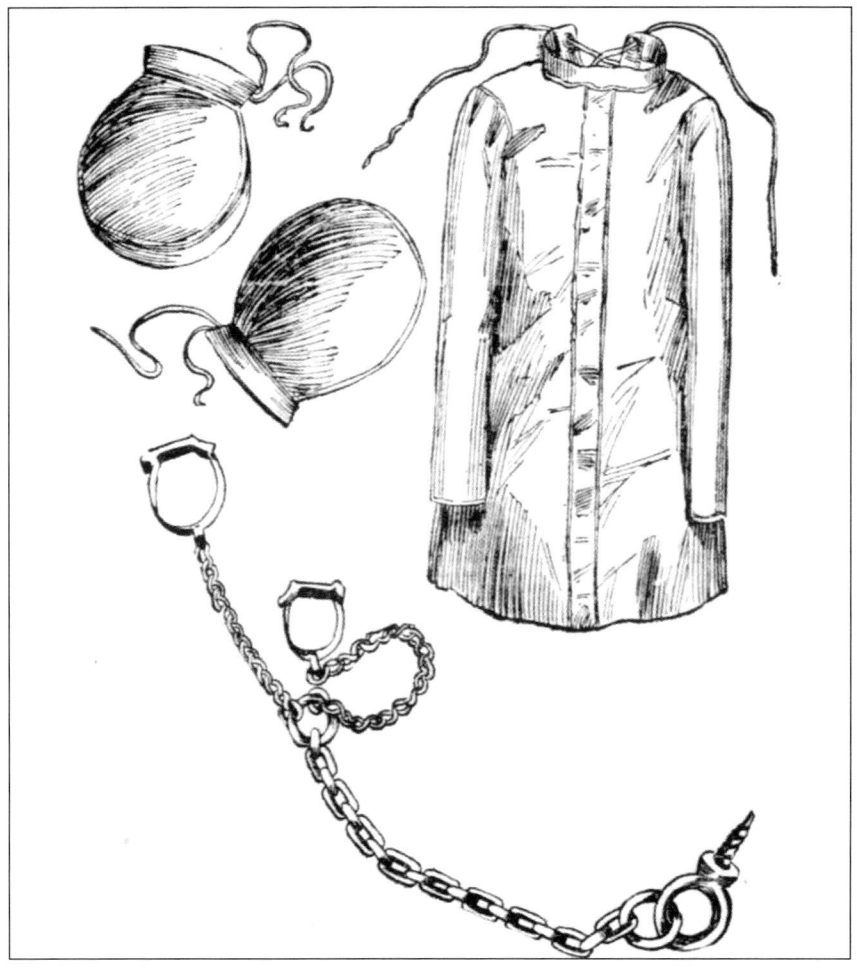

Butler's constraints, *The San Francisco Call*, 4 June 1897.

'So how's he doing?' McHattie asked as he pulled up a chair and sat beside Roche.

'He's fine.'

'Has he said anything?' Conroy asked as he too sat down.

'Apart from his swearing and cursing, he's not said a word, have ya' Frankie boy,' Roche said as he tapped the bars of Butler's cell.

'Alright, John, we'll take over from here. Go and get yourself something to eat,' McHattie said.

'And some sleep too,' Conroy added as he looked at Roche's reddened eyes.

'No, it's alright. I'll get something to eat and then come straight back.'

'John,' McHattie said softly. 'Ever since we left the States you've barely slept a wink. We can take if from here.'

'No,' Roche protested. 'I'm alright.'

'John,' McHattie said more forcefully now. 'There will be two of us here. You know better than anyone, a tired officer Is a bad officer.'

Unable to argue with McHattie's logic, Roche dipped his head and departed. McHattie and Conroy pulled up a table and began to play cards, taking extended looks at Butler in between each hand. Unbeknown to the two officers, Butler was lifting his head when they were focused on their cards and watching them closely, but as soon as one of the officers glanced at him, Butler dropped his gaze again. When he was certain they weren't looking, he would stare at them, paying particular attention to Conroy.

'Michael, I am just going out for a smoke. Back in a minute.'

McHattie departed and headed up onto the deck.

'So, Frank,' Conroy said. 'Are you going to just save us the trouble and confess to everything?'

With McHattie gone Butler suddenly became vocal. 'No! They might have found against me in America but I have a few tricks up my sleeve! They won't get me in Australia!'

'But you went with Captain Weller into the mountains?'

'Yes.'

'So, if you didn't kill him, what happened to him?'

'He killed himself, as best as I know. He went off with the other guy that was with us in the camp. That's all I know. Besides, Lee Weller was a very nice little man, but not adapted to go into the country in Australia.'

'So, why did you take him with you then? Wait, I know, it was the same as it was with me; you wanted to take him out there and kill him. You know, Frank, you're going to hang for this.'

'I'm not a bit frightened,' Butler responded adamantly. 'I knew Lee Weller. He committed suicide. There were four of us in the camp. Two of them were out at the time. I will call one that was with me when the case comes on. I'm not a bit afraid to face the trial.'

'I thought you said to Detective Egan that there was only three of you?'

'No, now that I think on it, there was four.'

'Frank,' Conroy said with a hearty laugh. 'If you were as good a killer as you are storyteller then there's no doubt, you wouldn't be chained up!'

As Butler was about to retort McHattie returned.

'Did I miss anything?' he said to Conroy.

'No, Frank was just about to tell us how he killed Weller, weren't you, Frank?'

Butler glared at Conroy before sulking as he turned his head away.

Conroy and McHattie returned to their card game as Butler stole more furtive glances, particularly in Conroy's direction.

'Detective?' he finally said.

Shocked and surprised that Butler actually spoke, it took McHattie a few moments to respond. 'Yes, Frank, what is it?' he said.

'I wonder if you could do something for me?'

'That depends on what you want.'

'Could you get rid of that officer?'

'What?'

'That officer there, Conroy, Could you please remove him?'

'Why do you want him removed, Frank?"

'That man is the only thorn in my side.'

Taking pleasure in the fact that he was seemingly getting under Butler's skin Conroy stood up and moved over to the cell bars. 'I'm not going anywhere, Frankie boy! I'm afraid you're stuck with me.'

Butler looked calmly past Conroy and said, 'I will continue to make your lives as difficult as I possibly can if you don't grant me my request.'

'Like I said, Frankie boy, I'm not going anywhere,' Conroy mocked as paced up and down in front of the cell.

Suddenly, Butler began to scream at the tops of his lungs, picking up anything he could find and throwing it before violently shaking his leg irons and his bunk. Finally, he started beating his head against the wall.

'Mike, take a break for a bit,' McHattie said hurriedly. 'He may be a murderer, but we want to make sure he gets home in one piece.'

241

'Yeah, I think you might be right,' Conroy said, shocked by the intensity and ferocity of Butler's outburst.

Just then, the door of the brig burst open and Roche rushed in. 'What the hell is going on?'

'Mr Butler here has decided he doesn't want Officer Conroy looking at him.'

'What?' Roche said as he unlatched the cell door and entered. Moving over to Butler and standing in front of him, he said, 'What's up, Frank?'

Butler looked Roche square in the eye. 'It's that man over there. He's the only thorn in my side.'

'Frank, I want to make sure that you're not too unhappy, but you need to understand that Constable Conroy has to take his turn watching you. How about we let you have a little whisky in return for you agreeing to behave. What do you think?'

Butler's countenance immediately changed. Eagerness and excitement were now etched all over his face, giving Roche his answer without need of a verbal response. With Butler enthusiastically nodding his head, McHattie took his cue and left the brig, returning shortly after with a bottle of whisky. Butler hurriedly grabbed his tin pannikin and held it up like a child waiting for milk. McHattie half-filled the mug.

'Aw, c'mon, boss. Just a little bit more,' Butler pleaded.

'Alright, Frank, but you promise you'll be a good boy from now on?'

'Yes, Detective, I promise,' he said as he held the mug higher. McHattie filled the mug another quarter of the way. Butler took a large swig and let out a contented sigh as he wiped his mouth with his sleeve.

'Now, Frank, I need to get some sleep. We're not going to hear any more racket from you, are we?' Roche asked.

'No, sir, I'm rather content now.'

'Excellent. I'll see you fellas in a few hours. Night, Frank.' With that, Roche departed and the other two officers returned to their cards, leaving Butler to slowly sip on his prize.

As the days passed, Butler's mood continued to lift as he was given whisky every morning and night. One evening, Roche was sitting reading over the case files when Butler decided that the time had come to make conversation. 'So, Detective Roche,' he said.

'What is it, Frank?' Roche replied as he put his notes down and looked at him.

'What made you want to be a policeman?'

Roche stood up, turned his chair so that its back was facing the cell and then straddled it, leaning forward with his forearms resting on the back. 'I come from good Irish stock, Frank. Lots of my relatives joined the force, so I just kept going in the family tradition.'

'Is that it? Is that the only reason? Do you enjoy it?'

'Of course I enjoy it. It's good honest work, and I like to think I make a difference. What about you, Frank, what's your story?'

The whisky had loosened Butler's tongue, and once he'd begun, he rattled on and on, retracing his life up until the time he'd come to Australia. 'You know, Detective,' Butler finally said, his speech beginning to slur as the whisky took effect. 'There's really no point taking me home for a trial.'

'Why's that?' Roche asked.

'Because I'm guilty as hell!' Butler began to sing, but no sooner had he begun than Roche stopped him.

'Frank, I know you're a little drunk right now, but I have to warn you that you don't need to say anything, because anything you do say may come up in court and be used against you.'

'Nah, it's okay, Mr Roche!' he said jovially. 'I don't think it'll make much difference anyway!'

Roche, having done his duty, was not about to let an admission slip, so he let Butler prattle on.

'Yep, I've killed a lot of men in my time, yes, sir. Started in Egypt when I was in the navy. I guess that might be where I got my bloodlust from.'

Roche was not going to push, but at the same time, he wasn't going to stop Butler either. 'So, who was the first one you did in Australia?' he asked.

'Well, I can't really tell you that now, can I?'

'C'mon, Frank, you've already started, why stop now?'

'I think I have said enough, Mr Roche. Time to go to bed, I think.'

With that, Butler rolled over and was instantly asleep, leaving John Roche to ponder just what else Butler would tell him before they arrived in Australia.

BACKING OUT.

Oceanic Steamship Company's Mariposa, With Murderer Butler on Board, Gathered Sternway at 9:30 P. M. Yesterday, While the Swanhilda That Brought Butler Here, Was Under Full Sail in the Offing at Daybreak. Extraordinary Precautions Have Been Taken to Land the Accused Man Alive in Sydney.

The Mariposa leaving San Francisco, *The San Francisco Call*, 4 April 1897.

26

Discussions with the Devil

23 April 1897

As the *Mariposa* steamed on across the Pacific, the conversations between Roche and Butler became more and more frequent. Roche started writing notes, with Butler's permission, and became strangely intrigued by this particular criminal's stories. The detective sat with him for most of the day, and when evening came and Butler's supper was brought in, he hurriedly swallowed it down so he could enjoy his whisky. One night, after putting his plate to one side, Butler started rubbing his left leg and began to groan. Roche initially ignored him, so Butler groaned loudly several more times. 'You alright, Frank?' Roche finally said.

'Detective, this leg iron is quite heavy. I don't suppose you'd allow me to take it off for a few moments?'

'Come now, Frank, you know better than to ask me things like that. Of course the answer is "No".'

'That's what I thought you'd say,' Butler said as he readjusted his position on his bunk and rested his leg on his pillow. 'You know, it's probably a good idea that you don't let me walk around. In fact, I'm damned sorry now that I came with you. I intended to hit one of those deputies on the head with a chair. Then they would have tried me for attempted murder, and I would have got five years at least. I'll tell you another thing. After the *Taupo* intercepted the *Swanhilda* and spoke to the captain, I suspected something, but I wasn't sure. If I had known, I would have run the ship ashore on some island. As it was, I intended swimming ashore, but I saw the tide was running too strong for me, and I am not a very good swimmer. If I had known you were coming to arrest me, I would have shot five or six of you and then shot myself. But as you know, I was taken before I knew anything about it.'

Roche laughed loudly. 'Then it's a good thing none of that came to transpire! I think that just means we will have to keep an even closer eye on you.'

While his words were spoken in jest, their seriousness was still evident. Roche, thinking that Butler was getting a little too bold, decided to give him more whisky. 'Frank, we're not far from Auckland now. Then a week or so more, and we'll be back home. I think it is only fair that I allow you to have a little more drink.'

Roche reached over, grabbed the bottle, rose from his chair and moved into the cell to stand in front of Butler, who had his cup held high and carried an eager smile. Roche half-filled the mug and Butler started to sip, but he soon realised that Roche hadn't moved, so he hurriedly consumed all the whisky and held up his mug for more.

Having drunk more than he'd had in months, the alcohol quickly took effect. Butler's speech became increasingly slurred, and with the notion that his demise was imminent occupying his thoughts, he became quite pensive. 'You know, Detective, I have never been a good man. I tried to be, but I guess the good Lord just decided that I was meant to be a crook. I suppose I will just have to be content with the fact that I have played my part in the whole big picture.'

'What do you think that part is, Frank?'

'It takes all kinds to make up this world. If we didn't have the bad, then we would never appreciate the good. I do what I do so that people can remember the good things in life.'

Roche quickly rebutted Butler's sanctimony. 'Frank, I'm sure there are easier ways to remind people of the good things in life than murdering some of them.'

Butler was in no mood to be stopped or swayed now that he'd begun. 'I beg to differ, Detective. It is only the worst things that make us think of the best. If this wasn't the way, then why would God allow it? I am, as I said, part of His grand plan.'

'Then I guess you will get to discuss that with Him very shortly.'

Butler laughed loudly. 'I don't think I shall have that chance! Soon enough, I will be discussing my life with the Devil himself! You have got me for Preston and Weller, but I have been a travelling man all my life, and there are many more boys that will never be found.'

'More?'

'Oh, yes, many more,' Butler smirked as he finished his whisky and held his cup up for more. Roche quickly refilled Butler's mug, and the latter sipped deeply as he leant against the wall.

In the back of his mind, Roche knew Butler's penchant for boasting, nevertheless he was still curious, so he pressed on. 'How many are we talking here, Frank?'

'Come now, Mr Roche,' Butler said, his words increasingly slurred, 'I can't risk telling you that.'

'What's it gonna hurt?' Roche pushed. 'You only need to be convicted of killing one man to find your way to the gallows.'

'Ah, yes, but I haven't been convicted of anything yet.'

'You will be, Frank, I assure you of that.'

'Yeah, I suppose you're right. Hmm, let me see,' he said as he started counting on his fingers. 'One, two, three…I have sent fourteen to an early grave.'

Realising he had him on a role Roche decided to keep Butler's loose tongue talking.

'You know we found Burgess. Did you kill him too?' Roche asked.

'Oh, yeah, I forgot about Burgess. I shot Burgess because he gave me a bad cheque. He paid me for a pair of horses with a bad cheque. I came to Sydney and presented the cheque, and when the bank people told me it was no good, I went to the country and shot him.'

Still mindful of Butler's boasting, Roche couldn't help but believe that his tally was more than the three of which they were certain. Butler continued to offer Roche some inkling of the magnitude of his deeds, only to withhold the most vital of information, until eventually the whisky overtook him and he passed out.

Early the next morning, the *Mariposa* slowly rose and dove in the swell as it ploughed its way through the entrance to Auckland Harbour. McHattie and Conroy stood at the bow smoking as they took in the distant mountains that lay beyond the green meadows and cliffs flanking either side of the harbour. The *Mariposa* continued on until the wooden wharves and docks eventually appeared, with dozens of tall ships moored at every vantage point, their white masts standing out starkly against the grey, overcast skies. Hundreds of smaller boats bobbed in between them, and McHattie and Conroy momentarily wondered if there would be enough space for the *Mariposa* to dock as it slowed and swung to port. McHattie and Conroy were soon under no illusions as to which one was the *Mariposa's* assigned dock as, even from hundreds of metres away, they could see the media swarm, scores of them scouring the horizon eager to be the first to spot the ship they knew would soon be arriving. When the *Mariposa* was within one hundred metres of the dock, the first journalists spied the ship and began jostling for the best positions. When the remaining newsmen realised the ship had arrived, they rushed towards the end of the wharf. The *Mariposa* slowed to a crawl as it sidled up next to the wharf, the newsmen scanning the decks for any sign of the murderer as they followed its path. From the bow, McHattie and Conroy watched on, not surprised by the presence of the media, but truly amazed by the immensity of their numbers.

'I think we'd better go tell John,' McHattie said as he tapped Conroy on the arm.

'Yeah, I reckon you might be right.'

The two men descended below deck and headed to the brig. Roche was hunched over a desk, once again going over the case files.

'Ah, John, can we have a quiet word?' McHattie whispered.

Roche looked up from his notes. 'What is it?'

'I think you'd better come and have a look at something.'

'What?'

'You know how we expected some media attention?'

'Yeah?'

'Well, 'some' seems to be an understatement.'

By this time, Butler's ears, despite his clouded head, had pricked, and he began to listen intently to the discussion.

'Alright,' Roche said as he rose and stepped towards the door of the brig.

No sooner had he done so than Butler piped up. 'Good, my audience is ready. I shall do my best to make myself look presentable for them.'

Ignoring Butler's comment, Roche moved to the mirror to check his face and hair before heading up to the deck. The *Mariposa* had almost reached its mooring, and as Roche emerged onto the deck, all he could say was, 'Bugger me!'

He quickly said to the others, 'Let me handle this. If they ask you anything, just tell them, "No comment", or "I am unable to say anything about that."'

'Yes, sir,' McHattie and Conroy said simultaneously. Roche put his hat back on as he started to mentally prepare for the inevitable barrage of questions. The *Mariposa* finally docked, and the gangway was lowered. It had barely touched Kiwi soil before the media began to swarm at its base. Roche descended amidst a flurry of questions, and when he stepped ashore, he had to yell several times before there was silence.

'Has Mr Butler arrived safely?' one journalist asked.

'Were there any dramas? Did he try to commit suicide again?' another said. Realising it was better if he addressed them from a loftier perch, Roche went halfway back up the gangway, and with the hundreds of journalists poised and ready, pencils in one hand and notebooks in the other, he began. 'Gentlemen, I will tell you everything you wish to know in good time. But for now, all I will tell you is that Mr Butler has arrived safely, and there were no dramas on the voyage. Mr Butler has been very well behaved.'

All of the journalists began scribbling madly.

'And you will all be allowed to pay him a visit in due course but, and I cannot stress this enough, it will be done in an orderly and sensible fashion.'

Roche then turned on his heels and ascended the gangway, and it took the journalists several moments before they realised they wouldn't be getting anything further. The flurry of questions resumed, but Roche did his best to ignore them as he made his way onto the ship. As he passed McHattie, he said, 'Bring them in separately; only one on board at a time, and make sure you let the Australian journalists on first.'

'Yes, sir.'

Leaving McHattie to organise the throng, Roche descended to the brig. When he entered, Butler sat up, but slumped back down just as quickly, plainly disappointed that Roche was alone.

'Where are they?' he asked, standing and moving from side to side as he tried to look past Roche to the door of the brig.

'Don't worry, Frank, your adoring masses are outside,' Roche said sarcastically. 'I will bring the first of them in shortly, but I want you to promise me you'll be good, or I'll revoke your whisky privileges.'

'I promise,' Butler replied quickly. 'Now bring them in.'

Almost on cue, McHattie appeared at the door of the brig with the first of the journalists in tow. The journalist asked Butler several stock-standard questions, all under the watchful eyes of Roche and McHattie, before he was led out and the next journalist was led in. Half a dozen more came and went, each of them offering Butler the same deals as the Americans journalists. Roche and McHattie listened in, and overheard Butler telling one newsman that journalists here were much more respectable than their American counterparts, and how the American pressmen were nothing more than thieves and ruffians, promising all sorts of things but never delivering.

Later that day, McHattie went to fetch yet another journalist. He led him into the cell, and noticed that, despite having been interviewed for most of the day, Butler's enthusiasm had not waned. 'Hello, sir,' he said chirpily. 'And which paper are you from?'

'I am from *The Argus*,' the journalist replied.

'Have a seat,' Butler said as he sat back on his bunk.

The journalist did as asked, and took out a pencil and notebook. 'Mr Butler,' he began, 'can you please tell me about the papers in the States publishing your so-called "admissions"?'

'Not a single statement was ever authorised by me. That is, in writing. They were published by the reporters on their own account, and are false.'

'But you saw the reporters?'

'Oh, yes, I saw them every day. The reporters there are simply thieves and liars, and the only way to get rid of them was to tell them something. But I made no confession. What the San Francisco papers published was a load of rot.'

'You seem to have been a special favourite of the ladies also.'

'That goes without saying. I have been claimed in marriage, and had offers of marriage. One lady claimed me as her husband, and others offered to marry me, but,' he said with a laugh, 'I wasn't taking any.'

'Were you ever married?'

'Yes. No, I should not have told you that; but never mind, that was too far back.'

'Have you any family?'

'That's also too far back!'

'Can you tell me how you came to have Captain Weller's papers?'

At the mention of Weller, Butler shot the journalist a look to indicate that it was a question he shouldn't have asked, and so he changed his line of questioning.

'Do you remember the *Taupo* intercepting the *Swanhilda*?'

'Yes, I remember it well, but I had no idea what the nature of the communication between the two ships was, nor why one of their officers came on board. If I had known, there would have been no *Swanhilda* by now.'

'Did you suspect anything?'

'No.'

'Was your arrest in San Francisco a surprise to you?'

'Completely; I never dreamt of it.'

'What would you have done if you had been prepared?'

'There would have been some shooting, that's all. The police were on me before I even knew they were on board. I was below deck, and all hands were ordered up, as I thought, for a medical inspection. I was taken by complete surprise, and did not bring my revolver up with me.'

At this point, Butler started tapping his mug, and Roche quickly entered the cell and filled it. As Butler sipped away, the journalist sensed that Butler's demeanour had calmed, so he decided to push his luck.

'Okay then, Mr Butler. That seems to be all I need. However, I do have one more question, so I will just come straight out with it. Are you guilty of killing Arthur Preston and Captain Weller?'

'Am I guilty?' Butler said. 'Of course not.'

'That's what I thought you would say,' the journalist chuckled.

'That's not what you told me,' Roche chimed in. 'You told me you killed fourteen.'

The journalist turned in his chair and looked at Roche. 'Fourteen?' he said.

'Alright,' Butler said. 'I will tell you the truth, but it will come at a cost.'

'At a cost?'

'You want a good story, right? I can say whatever you want me to for the right price.'

'Can you please elaborate?'

'For fifty pounds, instead of saying I killed fourteen men, I will say I killed fifty. That ought to make the price better.'

The journalist laughed. 'I will have to come back tomorrow after I have cleared that with my editor, as I do not have permission to authorise such a deal. So, you say you killed fourteen. Who else might we know about?'

'Tell him about Burgess. Tell them what you confessed to me,' Roche said.

'Burgess got what he deserved!' Butler snarled.

The journalist finished his interview with several more cursory questions, thanked Butler for his time, and said he would return the following day with the fifty pounds should his editor approve the transaction.

The train of journalists continued to proceed in and out of the cell, and the more drunk Butler became, the more admissions flowed. Late in the evening, Butler eventually informed Roche that he was tired, so the detective ushered the last journalist out of the cell. As soon as Butler's head hit the pillow he was out like a light.

The following day, the next group of journalists paced up and down the dock as they anxiously awaited being called on board, all of them eager to get their interviews and then wire their stories to their various papers. The first of them entered the cell at 10 am, and as they came and went throughout the morning, Butler told each of them the same thing over and over, with only a few minor variations. Midday was approaching when a journalist and a sketch artist arrived and were led down to the brig.

'Frank,' McHattie said. 'These gentlemen are from *The Sydney Mail.*'

'Yes.'

'Mr Hardy here wants to draw a sketch of you; is that okay?'

'No, I believe I have had enough for today.'

Having done his research, the journalist was well aware of Butler's tastes and weaknesses, and promptly produced a bottle of whisky. 'Perhaps this may sway your decision,' he said, proffering the bottle.

Butler simply nodded. With the intensity of the questioning over the last day and a half, he'd become noticeably surly, his joviality waning as he slumped back on his bunk. Unlike his celebrity days in San Francisco, where he'd happily acquiesced, even asking the artist how he wanted him to pose, he simply slid his pillow in behind his back and manoeuvred it into the corner where the two walls met. He propped himself up, with his knees drawn slightly up towards his chest while holding his pipe in his left hand, which he rested on his right knee. Hatless now, his hair had become scraggly and his features craggy, and he'd been unable to shave during the voyage due to Roche's specific orders not to allow a razor anywhere near him. As a consequence, his previously trim moustache had given way to an increasingly thick and unruly beard. His eyes had become murky and withdrawn, and he kept a close eye on the sketch artist as he began to draw.

'Do you mind if I ask you a few questions?' the journalist said as McHattie took the bottle into the cell and poured some whisky into Butler's mug.

'Sure.'

The journalist went through the same obligatory questions, and as Butler repeated the same answers, it was plain that the alcohol was lifting his mood. 'So can you tell me about the first time you found yourself in trouble with the law?'

'I wasn't always in trouble with the law, in fact I was once on the right side of it.'

'How do you mean?'

'I used to be a copper back in England, both in Warwickshire and Staffordshire.'

McHattie and Conroy both let out loud and derisory laughs. 'Sure you did, Frank! Sure you did!' Conroy scoffed, causing Butler to shift his gaze away from the sketch artist to glare angrily at Conroy.

'You know nothing about me!' he retorted. 'And were it not for a lucky twist of fate, you would be six feet under right now, not thinking about how great your career will be because you had the good fortune of meeting me. Besides, I know what I've done. I was a better policeman than you will ever be. Just remember, if it wasn't for the fact that you met me, you would only ever be a second-rate copper.'

The journalist, realising that Butler's nerves were frayed and he was more likely to open up about things he may have wanted kept secret, pushed on. 'So, when you came to Australia, did you always want to be in mining, or did you do any police work?'

'I was in the coppers in Western Australia for a bit, but the pay was no good, so I gave it away.'

At this point, Roche appeared, having finished his supper, and asked McHattie who the visitors were and how the interview was going.

'They're from *The Sydney Mail*,' McHattie sniggered.

Roche shot McHattie a strange look. 'What's so funny?'

'Oh, nothing. It's just that Frank's trying to convince them that he was once a copper!'

'You're not serious?'

'Oh, quite.'

'This I've got to hear,' Roche said as he moved closer to Butler's cell. Butler was still espousing his police exploits when he noticed Roche, and promptly closed up. 'Why don't you tell him about all the people you have killed, Frank,' Roche said.

'How many have you killed?' the journalist asked, realising the crux of the story had just presented itself. Butler said nothing, simply turning his head to the side.

'He told me he had killed fourteen,' Roche continued. 'But I guess the one you told me about the other day, out at Cootamundra, would make fifteen. Are there any more you want to lay claim to, Frank?'

Butler remained silent.

'So, Detective, is there anything else Mr Butler may have said that our readers might be interested in?'

'Too much for the time you have,' Roche said, smiling. 'But I will tell you one interesting thing Frank has said.'

The journalist leant forward, pen poised in anticipation.

'A few days ago, he told me he was going to plead insanity when he arrived in Sydney. He said, "I may not defend the case, but tell the judge he is a son of a bitch, and that he can go to hell. I am going mad when I get to Sydney. Then they will have to put me in Parramatta Lunatic Asylum."'

'Is that right, Frank?' the journalist asked.

'I never said that,' Butler replied, glaring at Roche. 'But some people may say I am a lunatic.'

'Thank you, Frank,' the journalist said, and then rose and departed.

The journalists continued to come and go, and the interviews continued right up until the last moment before the *Mariposa* left its mooring and set sail for Australia.

27

Back Home

26 April 1897

Evening was settling in as the sun cast a foreboding orange glow over the distant western horizon. John Roche stood on the deck smoking his pipe and watching the clouds streak across the sky as he contemplated the scene that lay beyond. Over that horizon lay Sydney. It was now that it dawned on him how close they were to getting Butler home. A few more miles and the most famous arrest in Australian history would be complete.

McHattie joined him. 'What's going through your mind?' he asked, seeing Roche's pensive posture as he leant on the ship's railing and stared into the distance.

'I'm just wondering what's going to happen tomorrow when we arrive.'

'And?'

'I was just wondering if it may be a low-key affair.'

'You don't seem to think so?'

'No, not when you consider all the media coverage he's had in San Fran, and then in Auckland. I knew we'd get some newsmen in New Zealand, but that was absolutely insane.'

'Well, on the plus side, once we unload him, our job's done.'

'Don't get too far ahead of yourself, young McHattie. We're not there yet. C'mon, I'd better go and give Frank his supper,' Roche said as he turned and headed back towards the bridge. McHattie followed close behind as the two men descended below deck and made their way to the galley, and then to Butler's cell.

Butler was lying flat on his back, but when he heard the two detectives enter he sat bolt upright, grabbed his mug, held it up and began tapping it with his spoon.

'Gees, Frank, give me a sec,' Roche said as he retrieved the whisky bottle and quickly filled the mug. McHattie put Butler's supper on the bed beside him, and then the two detectives took up chairs outside the cell. Butler gnawed on a slice of bread, but was plainly more interested in guzzling his whisky.

'Can I have some more, boss?' he pleaded.

'You should have sipped it, Frank, made it last,' Roche retorted.

'Aw, please, boss, you know it is my last night on this ship. Tomorrow, I might not be allowed to have any more, and in a few weeks I'll probably be dead.'

Roche pondered the request, smiled, and headed back into the cell to refill the mug.

'You can have the rest of the bottle,' Roche said, holding it up to show Butler that it was still three-quarters full, 'but you know the rules. I can't leave the bottle in here.'

'I know the rules,' Butler said as he leant back against the wall and slowly sipped. 'Thanks, boss, I really appreciate you finding some compassion for a condemned man.'

'You seem to be taking all of this quite well,' Roche said as he returned to his chair and sat down.

'I don't see how else I can take it,' Butler replied. 'Besides, I have a few more tricks up my sleeve yet.'

'Have you thought about what you might like for your last meal?'

'I haven't been found guilty yet, Mr Roche,' Butler said through a smile.

'True, but you will be, Frank. It might be something you need to start considering.'

'Well, *if* it comes to that, then I think I would like a nice lamb roast. I've always been a little partial to lamb.'

27 April 1897

The *Mariposa*, seemingly knowing the importance of the cargo it carried, picked up speed as it made its way through the heads and into Sydney Harbour. The three Australian policemen stood at the bow, leaning on the railings as they watched the bushland and sandstone cliffs pass on either side. The *Mariposa* bobbed and dipped as it rose and dove through the white-crested waves. Conroy turned to his colleagues. 'Do you know, some days, especially when we were in San Fran, I wondered if we'd ever get him back to Australia,' he said.

'I know what you mean,' McHattie agreed. 'What about you, John, did you feel the same?'

'I'd be lying if I didn't say that I had my doubts,' Roche said as he steadied his feet and grabbed hold of the ship's railings. 'But it seems we have made it.'

The *Mariposa's* captain eventually cut the engines, and the ship slowed. The policemen watched as one sailor let the anchor ropes out, and after the anchor had embedded itself into the sea floor, the ship quickly came to a complete halt. Out in the harbour, dozens of ships were steaming out of the port, while others were arriving and searching for their mooring. Roche eventually spied the ship he'd been anticipating, a steamer bellowing thick white plumes of smoke into the morning sky as it steadily chugged its way towards them. The *Carrington* slowed as it sidled up beside the *Mariposa*, and several sailors threw lines across, tying the two ships together before they slid a long, thin wooden plank from deck to deck. Superintendent Camphin leapt from the *Carrington* and hurried across the plank and onto the *Mariposa's* deck.

Roche and the others were waiting for him, and Camphin's relief at their success was evident in the fervour of his handshake. 'Glad to see you made it!' he said enthusiastically. 'Any problems?'

'No, he's been kept under strict guard for the whole trip. After everything that has transpired, there was no way we were going to let him get away.'

'Righto then, let's get this over and done with as quickly as we can.'

The officers descended below deck and proceeded to the brig, where Camphin paused at the entrance to the cell. Butler sat bolt upright.

'Hello, Frank,' Camphin said. 'Glad you made it.'

'Who are you?' Butler said with a suspicious glare.

'I am Superintendent Camphin. I've come to take you ashore,' Camphin said, ignoring Butler's stare as he paced up and down the cell's length, his hand stroking his chin.

'How do you want to do this?' Roche asked as he watched Camphin, relieved that his responsibilities were all but finished.

Camphin took several more steps. 'We'll put him in that straitjacket. Who made that?'

'I did,' said Hart.

Camphin stepped inside the cell, picked up the jacket and examined it closely. Turning towards Hart, he smiled and said, 'Excellent work!'

Hart smiled, his face slightly reddened by the compliment.

'Yep, we'll put him in the jacket,' Camphin continued, 'and we'll keep the leg shackles on. Attach a safety line around him, just in case Mr Butler here was having any thoughts of jumping into the harbour. That should do the trick.'

With Camphin's instructions complete, the other officers set about preparing all the required equipment. Butler, however, was not going to comply readily, and lay down on his bed and refused to move. When the officers attempted to roll him over, he began to flail his arms and legs about wildly. Roche and McHattie struggled to get him into the jacket, but try as they might, they needed several burly sailors from the *Mariposa* to step in and clasp him in a bear hug before he could be slid into the jacket. Now unable to move his upper body, Butler's remonstrations dwindled, and he watched on helplessly as his legs were shackled.

Butler was hauled to his feet and led out of his cell, up the staircase and out onto the deck. When they reached the plank, the safety line was tossed from the *Carrington* and Camphin carefully attached it around Butler's waist. After tying several loops and knots, Camphin gave the line a sharp tug. He nodded to several of his underlings, who leant back to tighten the line. Butler was then slowly escorted across the plank and onto the *Carrington's* deck.

Roche, McHattie and Conroy then returned to the *Mariposa* to collect their luggage and all the evidence against Butler, which was carefully passed across from ship to ship. The three officers said their final farewells to Captain Hayward and Chief Officer Hart and made their way off the *Mariposa*. The tie lines were retrieved and the two ships separated, the *Mariposa* moving on to its mooring point.

Seeing the *Carrington* turning away from the direction of Circular Quay, the inexperienced Conroy asked, 'Where are we going?'

'Elizabeth Bay wharf,' Camphin responded. 'There are thousands of people at the Quay. You should see it, it's madness.'

'I bet it's nothing like what we saw in San Fran or in Auckland,' Conroy commented.

'Even though I wasn't there, I assure you the Quay is far worse,' Camphin responded. 'Better we do things this way.'

Shortly after, the *Carrington* docked at Elizabeth Bay, the gangway was lowered, and Butler once again set foot on Australian soil. The officers formed a circle around him as they looked around, expecting a surge of journalists, but there were none, and Butler was hurried into a waiting carriage and driven to the rear of Darlinghurst Court, where he was taken inside to be placed into a cell while he waited to face a preliminary hearing. Once he was in his cell Butler was released from his confines, stretching his arms when the straitjacket was removed, before he was shackled to the bunk. Above him, the court was jam-packed with journalists and various onlookers, all of whom waited for the proceedings with great interest and anticipation.

Coroner Lethbridge was seated at the judge's bench, watching and waiting. Butler was brought up from his cell below. A hush came over the court as he was chained to the dock. He looked around the court, the stern expression on his face indicating to all present that he wanted proceedings squared away as quickly and with as little fuss as possible. When Butler was secure, Lethbridge began, after having to bang his gavel several times to obtain silence. When he was finally satisfied, he quickly came to the point.

'Frank Butler, come Harwood, come Richard Ashe, you appear in this court extradited from the United States to face justice here in Australia. Do you understand that charges of murder will be laid against you?'

Butler nodded tamely.

'Then, Frank Butler, I formally charge you with wilful murder and formally commit you to stand trial at the NSW Criminal Court within the month.'

Lethbridge slammed his gavel down once more and departed. Butler was unshackled. A barrage of questions ensued from the journalists, each of them clambering over one another as they rushed towards the front of the court. Butler said nothing, keeping his head bowed as he was led back down to his cell.

28

One More Trial

28 April 1897

While the *Mariposa* was en route from San Francisco to Australia, there had been much discussion in the Attorney-General's office about the makeup of the prosecution team. Various politicians put in their two bob's worth, but in Jack Want's mind, the answer to the question was simple; he would lead it. Now, both he and the defence lawyer, Walter Edmunds QC, stood as Judges Darley and Stephens entered the court. Off to one side of the room, a constable opened the doors leading to the cells and disappeared into the depths below. A few minutes later, he and another officer returned with Butler, who was dressed in a dark-blue suit. The crowd's quiet chatter now hushed as Butler glanced nervously at each and every eye that was firmly fixed upon him. He sat down, shifting his gaze towards the judge's bench.

'Frank Butler,' the bailiff began, 'you are charged that, on 31 October 1896, at Glenbrook, that you did feloniously and maliciously murder Lee Mellington Weller. How do you plead?'

Butler rose to his feet, his hands resting on the rail in front of him, and slowly and deliberately replied, 'Not guilty.' Butler let his words resonate through the court, and scanned the gallery again before sitting back down.

Edmunds rose and immediately asked for special consideration. 'I would like to make an application to the Court with respect to the position of the jury. Certain proceedings, as the court will remember, have been taken with regard to certain publications, and I would ask the Court to consider the removal from the jury of any gentleman connected with the management of any newspaper, or the writer of any article, as it seems to the defence counsel that such persons ought not to serve on the jury.'

Darley turned to the jury. 'If any gentleman of the jury has hostile feelings, or any feelings of ill will towards the prisoner, he will announce it. More than that I cannot say. With reference to the other matter, I do not think that is a disqualification.'

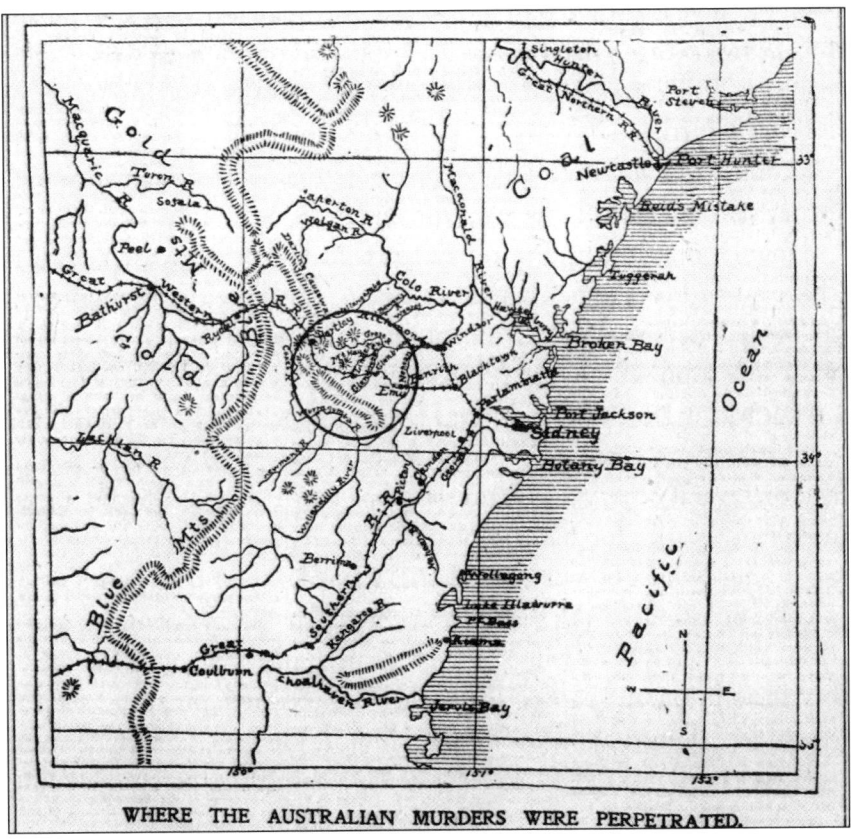

WHERE THE AUSTRALIAN MURDERS WERE PERPETRATED.

Where the Australian murders were perpetrated, *The San Francisco Call*, 4 February 1897.

Edmunds clarified himself. 'I only mean any gentleman who may be connected with the management of any newspaper, or is himself the writer of any such article.'

'Even if that were so,' Darley responded, 'and there was no ill will or personal hostility, it would not be a disqualification. If any gentleman is in such a position, for the satisfaction of his own conscience he should say so, but I think it is improbable.'

Edmunds was persistent. 'Your Honour, as I am sure you are well aware, this case has created a tremendous amount of media interest.'

'Yes, of course I am aware of that,' Darley said irately. 'Continue.'

'Your Honour, considering this media interest, I am asking the court to adjourn the case for six months. Mr Butler is quoted in *The Daily Telegraph* as being a "self-confessed" murderer, but it is pertinent to point out here that this confession was made to Detective Roche aboard the *Mariposa*. Given that this has been splashed throughout more papers than just *The Telegraph*, I do not believe it is possible for Mr Butler to receive a fair trial.'

'I think you will need to give me more than that to convince me,' Darley said forcefully as he leant forward.

'Your Honour, the papers are having a field day with this case, and what I have quoted you is merely the beginning. Mr Butler is also quoted as saying to Detective Roche, "I've got fourteen murders to tell you about, but it's too soon yet. I'm not going to show my hand until I see what the Crown will do in Sydney." Now, Detective Roche has freely admitted that, in order to keep the prisoner calm, he was plied with whisky. In fact, on several occasions aboard the *Mariposa*, Detective Roche traded my client whisky for his compliance. Given that my client has said such things whilst he was intoxicated, the validity of these admissions must be questioned. The media has printed Mr Butler's comments as a truth, and therefore he will be subject to undue bias against him due to this. In addition, the papers have continually printed mistruths, such as Mr Butler killing a child and stuffing him inside a log, for which there has never been a shred of evidence to support this as being the truth. It is clear that it will be impossible for my client to receive a fair trial. Therefore, I ask for a six-month adjournment.'

'Mr Want, do you have anything you wish to add?' Darley asked.

'Yes. I most certainly do! The Crown must argue against any continued delays. I understand the defence's position in wishing to protect their client against undue outside influences, and therefore I am willing to shift this trial to the bottom of the trial list in the next sitting, but to defer it for six months would be far too long, and the media interest would only intensify. May I also remind the Court that all the papers have done is to quote comments that Mr Butler has made on numerous occasions. The defence is arguing that these comments were made whilst Mr Butler was intoxicated, but he made the same comments to the papers in San Francisco and in Auckland when there was no question as to his sobriety.'

Judge Stephens, who had thus far remained silent, came straight to the point. 'Seeing as the Crown has offered it, the Court will defer the trial until the end of the next sitting, but as far as deferring it for six months I concur that it will make no difference. I cannot see that if we were to grant a postponement for six months, the jurymen would be more fitted to trying the case then than in the next sitting.'

14 June 1897

A huge crowd had gathered outside Darlinghurst Court, and despite the pouring rain, they pushed and jostled one another as they tried to get to the prime positions near the entrance. Those holding specially printed tickets held on to them as if they were passes to heaven, and several dozen had to fight to keep hold of theirs. Half a dozen bailiffs peered out from the lobby with trepidation as the crowd began to surge forward.

'We're going to need more men,' one said to the other as he helped him brace the door. One bailiff hurried off to find reinforcements, who duly arrived in numbers, the lead man being one Sheriff Maybury.

He ordered the bailiffs to force the doors, and then stepped outside. Seeing a man of authority, and realising that the time to enter had come, the crowd stepped back. Maybury waited several moments for the din to die down, but the crowd would not be silenced.

'People! People!' he shouted. 'Unless you have a special ticket or a press pass, you will not be granted entry to this courtroom today. I have already organised separate desks and chairs for the newspapers. An officer will direct those journalists to their assigned places. I am sorry, but if you are not with one of the appropriate papers, you will not be granted entry.'

The crowd were momentarily silent, but as the ushers started to check the first of the ticketholders, the clamour started once more, and reached a crescendo as everyone shouted their reasons why they should be allowed entry. Ticketholders and journalists began to file into the court, but Maybury kept a close watch on the crowd. They remained orderly, but when the ones closest to the doors realised that they would be refused entry, they began to shout and curse, claiming to be reporters who had lost their passes. Maybury ordered his officers to close the doors, but as he did so, the crowd surged forward once more, and it took everything the officers had to slowly inch the doors closed until they were finally able to snap them shut. 'Guard this door,' Maybury ordered his men. 'If anyone else gets in, it'll be your jobs.'

The lucky few to gain entry filed into the courtroom, but still jostled with one another as they sought the premium positions. After much clamour, Maybury finally had them all seated, and he then took up a position at the top of the stairs, keeping a watchful eye over an audience whose steady murmur became louder and louder as each of them offered their opinion on what had gone before, and what was yet to come. When Want, Crown Prosecutor Gregory Wade and the rest of the prosecution team entered the room, the buzz began to subside. When Edmunds and the defence team entered, the crowd quietened even further, but it wasn't until Sir Frederick Darley appeared and sat down at the Judge's bench that the crowd fell silent.

When the clock struck 10 am, a constable entered the dock and descended below and returned shortly afterwards with Butler, once again dressed in a dark-blue suit, complemented by a bright shirt and neat scarf, his legs shackled. Butler glanced from side to side, his countenance nervous and uncertain. The chatter of the crowd returned, their conversations revolving around the healthy appearance of the prisoner in comparison to the pictures they'd seen in the papers shortly after his arrival home from America. Butler's unruly beard was now gone, and only a trim and tidy moustache remained. He was helped to his seat, and when he sat down he turned and directed his stare across every face in the gallery, each person present certain that the accused killer was staring straight into their soul.

He held a few of their gazes, offering a sinister smile, before settling back into his chair and looking up to the judge. To the left stood a bailiff who held a piece of paper in his hand as he turned to face Butler. The audience looked on eagerly, their mouths wide open. The bailiff took a brief glance around the court before reading out the charges. 'Frank Butler, you are charged that you did, on 31 October in the year of our Lord 1896, at Glenbrook, in the colony of New South Wales, feloniously and maliciously murder Lee Mellington Weller. How say you, guilty or not guilty?'

Butler half stood, to the extent that the shackles would allow, and cried out confidently, 'Not guilty!'

The selection process for the jury now began. Sixty potential jurors who had been preselected by the Crown as a safeguard against the Defence's right to challenge were assigned special seats at the front of the gallery. They listened intently as twelve names were called out in turn. Each of the twelve men stood and walked from the gallery to the jury box. As they did so, Butler stood as best he could and eyed off each one of them. When the twelve men had entered the jury box, the name of the first man was called again, and Butler immediately called out, 'Challenge!' whereupon the man returned to his seat in the gallery. Indeed, Butler and his Defence team challenged the remaining eleven men. Twelve more men were summoned. Butler challenged several of them. More were called, more challenges were made, but eventually, the jury was formed.

Darley now addressed the jury. 'You will hear arguments from the Crown first, and then from the defence, followed by the Crown presenting their evidence. Your obligation as members of the jury is to determine the facts of this case as they are presented to you, and it remains my role to determine all matters of law. There will be a lot of media interest in this case, but I will remind you that, as far as you are concerned, you are instructed not to speak about matters relating to this case outside this courtroom. Now, the Crown will make their opening remarks. Mr Want.'

Want rose slowly, pulled his long, black robe up over his shoulders, moved to a point directly in front of the jury and proceeded to address them. 'At all times, there is a heavy responsibility that falls upon a juror who is summoned to a criminal court, but when the case you have to deal with is a capital one, and involves the life and death of another creature, that responsibility is greatly increased. In this present case, unfortunately, there has been a great deal of excitement, and a large amount of notoriety surrounding it, and it is my duty to point out how necessary it is that the jury discard all that you have heard or read. In the commencement of this case, you should start with the supposition that the prisoner is, at the moment, innocent of the crime of which he stands charged. Let you not form an opinion from anything you have heard or read or seen outside of this court. You must try to see the case according to the evidence brought before you. Curiosity, as I have stated, has been aroused about the doings and sayings of this man who is now charged with a murder that has been commented upon in the public press, which is undesirable. If any of the jury have read reports, comments, or various correspondence, then I ask that you wash away from your thoughts all that you have read, to leave your minds blank, and unless the Crown can bring before you such evidence as will enable you to go from the jury box with a free conscience, unless the evidence brings you to the conclusion that the prisoner is the one who has committed the crime of which he is charged, then you are bound to give him the benefit of the doubt. On the other hand, if the evidence brings conviction home to you, and you are forced to the conclusion that the prisoner was the one who committed the murder, it is then your duty not to shirk the responsibility that is cast upon you. You must, by your verdict, let the prisoner and others know that no matter what width of water or stretch of land they put between themselves and the scene of the crimes, the long arm of the law will eventually overtake them, and they will have to pay the penalty for their crimes. The Crown asserts that the prisoner before us, and no other man, committed the murder of Captain Lee Weller. I will put the evidence before you and I will comment upon it. You, the members of the jury, are not bound to think as I am asking you, and you may, of course, form an entirely different view to the one I will present. It is for you and you alone to come to your own conclusions.'

At a time when all eyes should have been on the Attorney-General, few were. Most eyes were focused on Butler, who sat leaning on one elbow as he gazed casually around the courtroom. Realising this, Want turned and took a quick look at Butler before returning his attention to the jury and moving closer to them.

'However,' Want continued with more conviction, 'the Crown has the responsibility to prove to you beyond a doubt that this man is indeed guilty of a crime of great cruelty. Captain Weller's Master's ticket was found in the seachest that Mr Butler's had stolen from Captain Weller, in fact Mr Butler used that same ticket to procure his place on the *Swanhilda*. Mr Butler was also found with numerous other possessions of the murdered man on his person, including much jewellery belonging to the dead man's wife. You will be presented with the advertisements asking for a mate to go prospecting written in the accused's handwriting. You will hear evidence that the two men went to the lagoon at Glenbrook together, and that Mr Butler was seen on his own the next day, alone, in the village of Emu Plains. He then went on to Newcastle where he secured his berth on the *Swanhilda* using Captain Weller's identity documents. Mr Butler has fled Sydney, and then Australia. Now, do these seem like the actions of a man who has nothing to hide or nothing to fear? I think not. These are the actions of a man who has something to hide, and wants to be away from the long arms of the law as soon as is humanly possible. The defence will argue that Captain Lee Weller shot himself, but you will have medical evidence shown to you. The skull will be produced, and you will be shown that Captain Weller was shot by a left-handed man while he himself was right-handed. Therefore, all the medical evidence will demonstrate to you that it was utterly impossible for this man to have shot himself.'

The revelation that Captain's Weller's skull would be submitted as evidence caused the crowd to erupt, and several ladies stood and started to march from the court in disgust, but Darley was having none of it. 'The ladies in the court will be seated! People in the gallery will show some control and silence themselves. I will not have this trial turned into a circus!'

Darley was well known for his calm demeanour, and his uncharacteristic outburst had the desired effect, shocking the crowd into submission.

Want let the silence linger momentarily before finishing his opening remarks. 'I will call witnesses that knew Lee Weller. They will identify the murdered man and also his property. As such, we will prove to you that the prisoner killed Captain Weller, and stole not only his possessions but also his identity. In this case, I can quote the words of Shakespeare, in his play *Hamlet*, "For murder, though it have no tongue, will speak with most miraculous organ."'

Want then sat down, and Edmunds rose to deliver the defence's opening remarks, which refuted each of the Crown's arguments and reiterated that Captain Weller had not, as claimed, been murdered, but had taken his own life.

'Mr Want, will you please call your first witness,' Darley said when Edmunds had finished his statement.

'Certainly, Your Honour. The Prosecution calls Robert Luckham.'

The crowd, all too aware of Luckham's connection with the murdered man, leant further forward in their seats. Luckham was sworn in and took a slow, deep breath as Want asked his first question. 'Can you please tell the court your name and profession?'

'My name is Robert A. Luckham. I am a journalist for *The Bulletin.*'

'Can you tell the court how you came to be acquainted with Captain Weller?'

'I have known him since February 1896, when he came to live with me up at Manly, where he stayed until shortly before he went away. Mrs Weller died in July or August. In late October, I gave him Mrs Tresnan's name, and he moved into her lodging house in Phillip Street.'

Want showed Luckham the items that had been recovered from the seachest and from Moss Woolf, each of which the witness confirmed as belonging to Captain Weller. Luckham also confirmed that the jewellery that Want showed him was Mrs Weller's. Want then shifted his questioning to the proposed prospecting trip, and what Luckham had known of it.

'Did Captain Weller tell you about the prospecting trip that he set out for on 29 October?'

'Yes, I saw that he was in a bad state after the death of Mrs Weller, so I suggested he find a new venture. He saw an advertisement in the newspaper seeking a prospecting partner, and decided that it would fit the bill. I saw him just before he set out.'

'And did you give Captain Weller a revolver before he left on this expedition?'

'Yes, even though I had told him to try something new, I had my doubts about his choice. I think people are too trusting these days as it is, so I gave him a Bulldog revolver for his protection.'

'Did you give him anything else?'

'Yes, I gave him a present, a bag that had my initials, R.A.L., sewn onto one side.'

Want produced the bag and showed it to Luckham. 'Is this the bag?' he said, moving it so Luckham could see it clearly.

'Yes, that is the bag.'

'Was there anything else you gave Captain Weller?' Want asked as he produced what remained of the burnt notebook that McLean had recovered at the lagoon. 'Do you recognise this notebook, or what remains of it?'

Luckham took the notebook and turned it over in his fingers a few times. 'Yes, this once belonged to me. I asked Lee to write to me every few weeks, so I gave this to him as a present.'

Want proceeded to produce Weller's hat and trousers, as well as numerous items that had belonged to Mrs Weller, which were also positively identified by Luckham.

'So, you have stated that you last saw Captain Weller on 29 October when you helped him pack for his trip. When did you next see him?'

'It was on 6 December, when the police asked me to come to Glenbrook with them. I was taken to a gully about a mile away from the train station. They took me underneath a rocky overhang. I saw a grave about twelve feet away from a bush track, and I saw the body being exhumed.'

'Did you recognise the body in the grave?'

'Yes, it was my friend, Lee Weller.'

'Can you describe what else you saw?'

'Yes, the body was in a kneeling position. There was a hat in the grave, which I recognised as Lee's. His coat was lying loose in the grave, and the trousers you showed me were also on the body.'

'I believe you were the first person to communicate with the police about this matter?' Want asked.

'I object!' Edmunds said.

Want rephrased his question. 'Did you see the police in connection with Lee Weller, and on what day?'

'In November, about the third week.'

'And why did you see the police?'

'I had not heard from Lee and I was concerned, so I wrote to the police to express my fears and to ask them to look for him.'

'So you held grave fears for your friend's safety?'

'Yes, it was not like Lee not to write to me.'

Want finished, satisfied that presenting Weller's possessions to the jury and listening to the dead man's best friend had had the desired effect.

Edmunds was equally as experienced as Want, and immediately began his main line of questioning. 'After the death of Mrs Weller,' he said as he faced the jury, 'Lee Weller was depressed in spirits, melancholy. Mrs Weller's death affected her husband very much, and about that time he took to more drink than was good for him. He, at times, took a considerable quantity of liquor.' Edmunds then turned towards Luckham. 'When Mr Weller came to stay with you, what was his disposition like?'

'He was upset because of what had happened to his wife.'

'And did he take the occasional drink to alleviate this sadness?'

'Yes, the occasional drink.'

'Was it only an occasional drink, as you have said, or more than that?'

'He was starting to drink more and more.'

'Can you please tell the court why you decided it was time for Captain Weller to move out from living with you and to move into Sydney?'

Luckham shifted in his seat and looked away, plainly reluctant to answer.

'Mr Luckham?'

'He was drinking too much. I was worried about him. I thought it best he tried somewhere and something new.'

'So, you admit he was drinking excessively due to his depressed state.'

'Yes.'

'No further questions.'

'You may step down, Mr Luckham,' Darley said. 'Your next witness please, Mr Want.'

Want called Elizabeth Tresnan, and as she made her way from the gallery she glanced from side to side, painfully aware that everyone was staring at her. She was sworn in, and sat down.

'Can you tell the court how you came to know Captain Weller?' Want asked.

'Yes, he came to lodge with me for about ten or twelve days. He left me on 28 of October. I saw him leave with a large seachest, an overcoat and a small bag. The bag was marked 'R.A.L.' on each side. He left at about seven in the evening, I think it was, and he paid me before he left, but I remember that he had a roll of bank notes on him and some gold and silver coins. I never saw him alive again. The next time I saw him was on 6 December when I went to the Blue Mountains with a policeman who took me to a gully, on the left-hand side of the railway, and that is where I saw the body of Captain Lee Weller.'

'Can you tell the court about Captain Weller's disposition while he stayed with you? Had you seen him drinking a lot?' Want asked, as he tried to diffuse the defence's line of argument.

'No, sir, I never saw him under the influence of liquor in any way, and as far as I am aware, the whole time he lived at my house he was never low-spirited or out of sorts, even though he told me his wife had died some months earlier.'

'Thank you, Mrs Tresnan. Your witness.'

Edmunds forced Mrs Tresnan to admit that it was impossible for her to watch Weller twenty-four hours a day, and therefore could not make comment about the extent of his drinking.

Want then called James Woods to the stand, and Woods described how he had found the body and everything that had happened up until the time Detective McLean had arrived. McLean was the next witness called to present his testimony.

'Detective,' Want began. 'Can you tell the Court your occupation?'

'Yes, I am a detective in the police force of New South Wales.'

'Can you describe what you did when you went to the grave that Mr Woods had discovered?'

'Yes, I was in Glenbrook last November coordinating the search for Lee Weller. I went to a place near the railway station, in very rough country, to a spot pointed out by Mr Woods. We dug the soil away to a depth of around eighteen inches, and discovered the body of a man. I left the body in the position in which I had found it. The head was bent downwards, and the knees were doubled up towards it.'

Darley interjected, intrigued by McLean's descriptions. 'Detective, will you show the jury the position in which you found the body?'

McLean stepped down from the witness box and lay down on the floor, whereupon he bent his head down and brought his knees up to his chest.

'Thank you, Detective,' Darley said. McLean lifted himself up off the floor and returned to the witness box, where Want continued to question him.

'Did you subsequently place Constable Tate in the hole in a position similar to that in which you discovered the body?'

'Yes.'

'And you took photographs of this?'

'Yes.'

'With your permission, Your Honour, I would like to tender these photographs to the court so that the jury may see them.'

Darley nodded, and Want produced a black-and-white photograph showing Tate curled up in the grave, which he handed to McLean. 'Does that show the rock, the hole, the locality, and the position in which the body was found?'

'Yes.'

Want retrieved the photo from McLean and handed it to the jury, who passed it around amongst themselves while he continued. 'Detective, can you please tell the court as to your thinking in taking such photographs?'

'Yes, we decided that Constable Tate was roughly the same height as Captain Weller, so we thought it prudent to illustrate how callous Captain Weller's killer had been with his treatment of the body.'

Darley interjected again, this time addressing the jury. 'You **must** remember, gentlemen, that the body you can see in the photograph is not the body that was found in the hole, but that of a police constable who, the witness states, is lying in a *similar* position.'

McLean continued to describe facets of the search, as well as the possessions found on Weller's body or in or near the grave, including Weller's cap and clothing, a sheath knife, the pipe, the pick, the magazine, and other articles belonging to Weller.

When Edmunds' turn came to cross-examine McLean, he proceeded to question him about the procedures he had undertaken, trying to undermine the quality of McLean's detective work, but the veteran policeman was unflappable, and repeated everything, almost word for word, that he had told Want. Realising that he was not going to discredit McLean's testimony, Edmunds finished.

In the minds of the jury, and those present in the crowded courtroom, the odds were slightly against Butler, but the Crown hadn't yet really presented anything totally convincing as to Butler's guilt. Want, however, was unconcerned. He still had several trump cards to play, mainly in the form of numerous witnesses confirming Butler's identity, the most important of which was Mrs O'Connell.

'Mrs O'Connell,' Want began. 'Can you please tell the court your occupation?'

'Yes, I am the innkeeper at the Metropolitan Hotel in Pitt Street.'

'And in the course of your business, you would meet many lodgers?'

'Oh, yes, many.'

'Would you say you have difficulty in remembering all of the faces of said lodgers?'

'No, I never forget a face. It pays to make sure that you don't.'

'Why is that?'

'I always remember faces so I know the ones who don't pay, so that I can turn them away the next time.'

'Mrs O'Connell,' he asked as he pointed to Butler, 'can you identify the man sitting over there?'

'Yes, that man is Frank Butler.'

'Did he stay at your establishment?'

'Yes, he came to stay with me on 23 October.'

Want walked to his desk, picked up a portrait of Weller and handed it to Mrs O'Connell, who took a prolonged look at it.

'Mrs O'Connell, do you recognised the man in that portrait?'

'Yes, that is the gentleman who came to my hotel to see Mr Butler. I twice saw that man and Mr Butler conversing.'

'When was the second time?'

'When they had breakfast in my hotel and left on the morning of 29 October.'

'Mrs O'Connell, on the day you saw the two men leave, did Mr Butler say anything to you?'

'Yes, he said he was going prospecting in the country and he was going to take the other man with him.'

'No further questions,' Want said as he sat down.

Edmunds rose and attempted to illustrate that, due to the number of people going through the hotel, it would be impossible for Mrs O'Connell to remember every face, but she maintained her stance as to her ability to recall faces, and was eventually allowed to step down.

Want seized on the fact that Mrs O'Connell had referred to the fact that the two men had mentioned that they were going to the 'country', and called Joseph McMiles to the stand.

'Can you please tell the court your name and profession?'

'My name is Joseph McMiles and I am an employee of the Railway Department.'

'And can you tell me if you have ever seen this man before?' Want asked as he pointed to Butler.

'Yes, I have seen him on two occasions. First, when I sat with him and his friend on the way out west, and then I saw him again on my way back to Sydney, at Blacktown.'

'What was the day and time of the first occasion that you saw him?'

'It was 29 October, and I was on the 10.15 am train going along the western line.'

'Is this the other man you saw?' Want asked as he handed the portrait of Weller to McMiles.

'Yes, that is the man.'

'Did they have any bags or possessions with them?'

'They each had a bag, and Mr Butler had a rifle.'

'How far did you travel on the train that day?'

'I went all the way up the mountains.'

'And you saw both men get off the train at Glenbrook?'

'Yes.'

'And did you see anyone else get off the train with them?'

'No, there were only the two of them travelling together as far as I could see.'

'And when did you see Mr Butler again?'

'It was near Penrith on Saturday 31 October. He boarded the train and sat in the same compartment as me.'

'Was Mr Butler alone on this occasion?'

'Yes, he was.'

'Did Mr Butler have any possessions with him?'

'Yes, he still had the rifle, and the same bag.'

'And when you saw Mr Butler what did he do?'

'I said "Hello" to him and he said it back. I asked him where his friend was.'

'And what did he say when you asked him this?'

'He said, "Oh, he decided to continue on out west. I have some urgent business I must attend to in Sydney, so I had to leave him.'

'And what did you say to this?'

'I said: "That's a shame. Well, all the best to you."'

'And what did Mr Butler do then?'

'He got off the train at Blacktown, I think it was.'

'No further questions,' Want said as he handed over to Edmunds. Edmunds did the same as he had with the others, focusing on the point that McMiles had not met these two men previously, and therefore could not be certain of their identities. He made a distinct point of saying to the jury that, 'The mere fact that Mr McMiles had seen Butler on his own was no indication of him being guilty of murder. In fact, he had explicitedly stated that "his companion had continued on out west."'

Want called several more witnesses, all of whom stated that they had seen the two men together, as well as Peter Farrell, who gave his account of his chance meeting with, and the possessions given to him by, Butler. Farrell also detailed how, when he arrived at the lagoon, he found nothing more than a discarded shirt and a few candle halves. Edmunds did his best to rebuke every witness and to call into question their recollection of events.

'The Crown will call their next witness, if you please,' Darley said.

Want could sense that the jury were beginning to be swayed. The time had come for him to pull out one of his star witnesses. 'The Crown calls Dr Paton.'

A chorus of excited whispers ran through the court as the thin frame of Paton made his way from his seat in the gallery, a piece of paper in hand, and entered the stand. The bailiff repeated the process of swearing in the witness before Want began. 'Dr Paton, can you please state your full occupation for the court?'

'Yes, I am the Chief Government Medical Officer.'

'And were you present at the exhumation of the body of Captain Weller?'

'Yes, I was.'

'Can you please tell the court what you found?'

Paton started to speak, but Want interrupted him. 'Sorry, Doctor, but can you just wait a moment please?' Want signalled with a wave of his hand, and an associate brought Captain Weller's bleached skull into the courtroom. The sight of the dead man's skull brought a collective gasp from the gallery. Want took the skull, and strategically placed it directly in front of Paton, in between the doctor and the jury. Taking a brief glance at the jury, the troubled looks on their faces told him that submitting the skull as evidence was having the desired effect. 'Now, Doctor, if you could tell us what you wrote in your report.'

Paton began to read from the sheet of paper he had brought with him. 'There is a wound on the upper part of the neck. There is a flattened bullet lodged in the sphenoid. The cartridge patterns are the same as those on the one recovered from the gravesite, which clearly indicates that he was shot with a revolver and not a rifle. From the position and shape of the wound, it is evident that as the bullet entered Mr Weller's skull it was travelling in a slightly upwards direction, so it can be safely assumed that the fatal shot was fired whilst Mr Weller was bent down.'

'So, am I correct in saying that, in your opinion, there is no way that Captain Weller could have shot himself?'

'Yes, that is correct,' Paton replied, picking up the skull and using it to demonstrate his point. Paton placed his finger near a hole about two inches in diameter at the back of the skull. 'You can see here, right behind the left ear, that the ear has been smashed by the bullet. In my medical examination of the body, I found that the bullet then proceeded to smash the spinal cord at the top of the neck.'

'If a man was working in a hole and someone fired at him from behind, would it be possible to inflict the injury you have described?'

'Yes.'

'Was the wound self-inflicted?'

'As far as I am able to judge, it was not self-inflicted.'

'How do you form that opinion?'

'From the position of the external wound, it could only have been self-inflicted from an extremely contorted position.'

'Could it be done by a person holding a revolver in his right hand?'

'No, I don't think so.'

'Could a man do it to himself with his left hand?'

'If a man held the pistol in his left hand, turned it upside down, and pulled the trigger with his thumb, he could place the point of the pistol against the external wound; but there was no evidence of the revolver being held close to the head of the deceased. There was no burning or laceration of the wound.'

'Dr Paton, the defence will argue that this was a self-inflicted wound, but something has just occurred to me. From the nature of the wound, would you imagine that a man who had been shot like that would be able to bury himself?'

'Such a wound as Captain Weller had would cause instant death.'

'No further questions, Your Honour,' Want said as he sat down.

'Your witness,' Darley said to Edmunds.

Despite Want's successes, Edmunds was not about to back down.

'Now, what is not in question here,' he said as he turned to face the jury, 'is that a bullet was responsible for killing Captain Weller, but as we all must know, there are many ways a man can die from a gunshot wound; shot by another or, more likely, by his own hand. We have heard the testimony of Captain Weller's good friend, Mr Luckham, who told this court that Captain Weller's disposition was that of a broken man, of a man who had lost his wife and who had taken to drinking. So, I put it to you that this sounds like a man who would be very likely to take his own life. Doctor Paton,' Edmunds continued as he picked up the skull, 'you have described that the bullet that killed Captain Weller entered the skull here and exited here, just below the left ear.'

'Yes, that is correct.'

'Now, if a man was to hold a gun like this,' Edmunds said as he formed the shape of a gun with his fingers and held it up to the skull, 'to his own head…is it not entirely plausible that this gunshot wound was self-inflicted?'

'No, the path of the bullet means that suicide would be impossible here,' Paton said, as he shot Edmunds a look of disdain in response to Edmunds daring to question the validity of his medical opinion.

'In my opinion,' he continued, 'there is no way that this was a case of suicide, nor could it have happened in the course of a struggle. The only way Captain Weller could have shot himself, in any manner, is through an unnatural contortion of the left arm.'

'Dr Paton,' Edmunds said as he paced back and forth in front of the witness box, 'you have just told this court that there is no way that this was a self-inflicted wound, but then you also just said that it would be possible through a contortion of the left arm, however unnatural. So, it would seem that your opinion is somewhat contradictory in nature.'

'I stand by the opinion that this man was not killed by a self-inflicted wound,' Paton responded firmly.

'Nevertheless, it would be possible, especially in the event of a struggle,' Edmunds pushed.

'Only with a very unnatural contortion,' Paton retorted.

'But, in a struggle, it would be possible for such an unnatural contortion of the left arm to occur?'

'Yes,' Paton conceded. 'If his arm was twisted up and back in the course of a struggle, it may have been possible, but it would be very unlikely.'

'Nevertheless, it is still possible,' Edmunds said as he turned towards the jury.

'Yes.'

'Dr Paton, could you yourself get into the right position with a revolver to cause a self-inflicted wound?' Edmunds said as he began to contort his body by way of illustration.

'Yes, with practise I dare say I could,' Paton replied wearily, plainly tiring of Edmunds' continual questioning.

'But without practise?'

Paton smiled. 'Yes, but who would pull the trigger?'

With that, Edmunds said that he had no further questions, and proceedings ceased for the day. Butler was led from the court and escorted to his cell, where he was immediately met by Governor Herbert. who ordered the guards accompanying Butler to remove their firearms. The guards looked at Herbert quizzically.

'Mr Butler has already tried to commit suicide once. I will not have him doing so on my watch. Stand him in the middle of the cell.'

The guards removed their belts and weapons and moved into the cell.

'Mr Butler, can you please stand with your arms outstretched,' Herbert said as he stood in front of him. Herbert then withdrew a pair of scissors from his pocket and began to remove every metal button from Butler's clothing, before finally snipping his braces. When he had finished, he left the cell, the metal door clanging loudly as it closed behind him.

'Remember, if he asks for a pen, he is not to have one, only a pencil, and the light will remain on at all times. And at least two of you are to watch him at all times.'

Butler had barely laid down on his bunk before he was summoned by one of the guards. 'Frank, two women have brought you some tobacco.' Butler rose from his bunk and moved to the cell bars. He took the tin, opened it, sniffed the contents and handed it back. 'You don't want it?' the guard said.

'I am a man on trial for my life. I think I can ask for the things I like. If they want to bring me tobacco, then by all means they can do so, but I would prefer William's Light Mixture.'

'Alright, I'll tell them,' the guard said, and left to pass on Butler's message. The two women, slightly disappointed, nevertheless promised to return with the desired brand. Meanwhile, back in the cell, Butler smoked the last of the tobacco he had before drifting into an uncomfortable sleep as he replayed the first day of the trial over and over in his head.

29

The Trial Continues

15 June 1897

The following morning, the crowd milled around outside the courtroom, bumping and jostling one another. Those who had been refused entry the previous day tried everything they could to reverse their fortunes, but Maybury was astutely aware of who he had and had not admitted the previous day. He stood in front of the entrance with his arms folded and announced that no one else would be permitted to enter, not today, not tomorrow, and not on any other day while he was on watch. He had just turned to move inside and seal the doors behind him when he heard a woman shouting.

'Sheriff! Sherriff!' she screamed. Maybury ignored her at first, but when she started to yell that she was Butler's wife, he stopped and turned to see a middle-aged lady, short and plump, dragging a pretty teenage girl behind her as she angrily pushed her way through the crowd.

'Yes?' Maybury said guardedly.

'I am Mrs Butler.'

Unconvinced, he looked her up and down.

'And this is his daughter! We must be allowed in!' she demanded.

He thought on it for a moment, and decided to let them in, much to the annoyance of those who had been denied entry. In response to their protestations, he stated firmly, 'If this lady is who she says she is, then what kind of man would I be if I refused her entry?'

Dozens of ladies now began to shout their claims that they too were Mrs Butler, but the first lady and her daughter followed Maybury into the courtroom and took the only remaining vacant seats.

'There you are Mrs Butler,' he said as he showed them to their seat. The nearby reporters heard Maybury refer to her as such, and were instantly all over her. Clearly revelling in the attention, she blushed in embarrassment as they asked her about their relationship.

'Oh, I haven't seen him in a long time! He left me and my daughter some time ago, and I wanted to check out the man on trial to see if it is my long-lost husband. He ran through several of our fortunes in America and England, and has left me with nothing.'

The reporters scribbled her story down madly, but their interest in her soon waned as Butler was led into the courtroom, followed by Darley. 'Good morning, everyone,' Darley began. 'Mr Want, do you have your first witness ready?'

'Yes, Your Honour, the prosecution calls Moss Woolf.'

Woolf rose from a front-row seat, took his place on the stand and was sworn in.

'Mr Woolf, can you please state your profession for the court?' Want began.

'Yes, I am a second-hand goods dealer.'

'Can you tell me if you have ever seen the prisoner before?'

'Yes, I have.'

'In what context?'

'He came into my store carrying a seachest. He pulled out the contents and showed them to me.'

Woolf went on to describe the chest's contents. 'I offered him two pounds for the lot. He then showed me a rifle, so I added an extra five shillings. After that, he insisted I had swindled him, and so we went for a drink; my shout of course.'

'No further questions,' Want said as he sat down.

Edmunds rose and immediately set about trying to discredit the witness in the same fashion as he had done with the previous witnesses.

'Can you tell the court why it took you so long to come forward?'

'Well, I knew from what I read in the papers that the police were looking for someone but I didn't put two and two together. I must say I am embarrassed that it did take me so long. It was only when one of the New South Wales detectives, I forget his name, was making routine checks of all the second-hand goods dealers that I came forward.'

'So what would you say your memory is like? Is it possible you may be getting things confused?'

'I have not got an extraordinarily good memory. I have a wife and ten children to support.'

'Does that affect your memory?' Edmunds asked with a slight chuckle, which was mimicked by the crowd. Woolf, somewhat oblivious to the laughter, replied, 'It does occasionally. I get very tired, because I work long hours.'

'Thank you, Mr Woolf. That will be all.' Edmunds sat down and Woolf stepped down.

Want then called Charles Booth to the stand and queried him as to his encounters with Butler and, most importantly, had him confirm that Butler had passed himself off as Captain Weller. Edmunds then did his best to discredit Booth, but the tide was certainly beginning to turn against his client.

Want then decided it was time to call one of his star witnesses, but he left it to the Crown Prosecutor, Greg Wade, to do the questioning. It was well known that the Attorney-General and the next witness had a close working relationship, so by leaving things to Wade he would ensure that there was no stain on the witness's testimony.

'The Crown calls Detective John Roche,' Wade said.

Hearing Roche's name, the subdued murmur of the crowd became a boisterous chatter. Roche made his way down to the stand, and after being sworn in he was asked to state his position and rank by Wade, who then asked him to recall his involvement in the case. Roche went through everything, from the time the police had received Luckham's letter, through the search of the mountains, the discovery of the bodies, and his travels to London and then on to America. Roche detailed all the events in San Francisco, from the arrest to the court proceedings to the final extradition order and the voyage back home.

'Detective, can you tell the court more about the arrest aboard the *Swanhilda*?' Wade asked.

'Yes, after we took him off the boat and into custody, we asked him to sign a list of his possessions.'

'And what name did he use to sign that list?'

'He signed his name as Lee Weller.'

'I'm sorry, can you repeat that?'

'Yes, I said he signed his name as Lee Weller.'

'And did you show the prisoner a picture of Mrs Weller?'

'I did. I asked him to identify who she was.'

'And how did he respond?'

'He told me that the picture was of his wife.'

The noise from the gallery now intensified, and it took several sharp raps of Darley's gavel to silence them. 'Continue, Mr Wade,' he said when he was satisfied.

'Thank you, Your Honour. Now, Detective Roche, after you left San Francisco, can you tell the court what happened aboard the *Mariposa*?'

'Yes, we put Mr Butler in a straitjacket because we feared he might make another suicide attempt. Also, because of this, we made sure he was served his meals in tin plates and bowls and only ever given spoons.'

'During the course of the voyage, did you have many conversations with the prisoner?'

'Yes, scores.'

'And can you tell the Court the context of these conversations?'

'Yes, he told me that he had his suspicions that we were onto him when the *Taupo* pulled up alongside the *Swanhilda*. He told me that had he known, he would have tried to run the *Swanhilda* aground, but most of the conversations involved him boasting.'

'Boasting? About what?'

'He boasted that he had killed fourteen people.'

'Fourteen!' Wade exclaimed. 'Are you sure?'

'Yes, he definitely told me he had killed at least fourteen.'

The crowd now started up again, and Darley was forced to exercise his gavel once more. In the meantime, Wade sat down, leaving Edmunds waiting to cross-examine. The crowd eventually quietened, and he was able to begin.

'Detective Roche, first of all, I must make a point of thanking you for your hard work in all of this,' Edmunds said politely.

'Thank you,' Roche responded, unsure as to the sincerity of the statement.

'Detective Roche, I would like to start by asking if anything was said to my client in the way of a caution?'

'No, the Americans did that.'

'I see, and I believe this is not the first time you were derelict in your duties.'

'I am sorry, Mr Edmunds, but I am not entirely sure what you mean.'

'Well, I have a newspaper here,' Edmunds said as he moved to his desk, 'that quotes you as relating what my client supposedly said regarding his boasting. In fact, you gave several of these interviews.'

'I did.'

'So, in giving these interviews, you have, in fact, sullied the validity of your words and, in doing so, made it almost impossible for my client to receive a fair trial.'

'I do not think I have sullied anything but, nevertheless, I stand by my actions. I know what I heard.'

'Ah, yes, now let's get to what you "heard". Correct me if I am wrong, but did you or did you not give my client a lot of whisky?'

'I wouldn't say it was a lot.'

'But you did give my client whisky.'

'Yes.'

'Can you tell us why you did this?'

'He was becoming restless and difficult. We thought it might calm him down a little.'

'So, in return for his cooperation, you gave Mr Butler whisky?'

'Yes.'

'Would you say that, in return for his confession, you offered him more whisky?'

'No. He made those admissions of his own choice.'

'You allowed the accused a favourable time on board?'

'I allowed him everything I could in reason. I had an object in doing so.'

'Was that object to make him talk?'

'No, it was to keep him quiet.'

'Was there a demijohn of whisky in the cabin?'

'There was.'

'Were there not also bottles of whisky?'

'Yes, they were brought in and opened.'

'Was there not champagne introduced for the visitors?'

'None whatsoever. There were very few, if any, occasions where Mr Butler was excessively drunk. Mostly I mixed in a bit of honey, and most of the alcohol was consumed by the cabin steward.'

'Do you expect us to believe that any of what you have told us is true, considering the untruths that you told the newspapers in Auckland? You are an unreliable and biased witness and, I must say, nothing that you say can be considered true!'

'Counsellor!' Darley boomed. 'You are speaking to a member of Her Majesty's constabulary! You will show more respect!'

Edmunds, upon being rebuked, immediately apologised. 'Sorry, Your Honour. I apologise. It will not happen again.'

'See that it doesn't!'

'Mr Edmunds, your personal opinion of me matters little,' Roche said. 'What matters is that Mr Butler also confessed to the murders to the reporters in Auckland whilst on board the *Mariposa*, not only to me.'

Edmunds, whilst he had apologised at Darley's behest, was not about to cease his barrage against Roche. 'Detective Roche, correct me if I am wrong in this, but didn't your own department stage an inquiry into your conduct; conduct unbefitting an officer, if I am not mistaken?'

'Objection!' Want said loudly. 'That is irrelevant.'

'Your Honour, I believe that the detective's reputation as an officer is entirely relevant,' Edmunds added.

'Overruled,' said Darley. 'Continue, Mr Edmunds.'

'Mr Roche, what was the result of that inquiry?' Edmunds pushed.

'It was dismissed. No further action was taken.'

Despite Roche's innocence, the line of questioning had cast doubt over his testimony and, satisfied that he had achieved his aim, Edmunds stated that he had no further questions.

Want called McHattie and, after he had been sworn in and stated his position and rank, McHattie detailed his role in the proceedings.

'Detective, can you please tell the court again exactly why you were sent to America in the first place?' Want asked.

'I was sent because I'd seen Mr Butler briefly while I was stationed in Newcastle. I recognised his picture in the papers and contacted the Sydney detectives to let them know that Butler had boarded a ship for San Francisco and that he was using the name Weller. I was sent so when we made the arrest I could positively say that Mr Butler was not Captain Weller, as he claimed to be.'

'Your witness,' Want said as he sat down.

Edmunds rose and paced up and down in front of the witness box, while McHattie became increasingly apprehensive, recalling the grilling his colleague had received. 'Detective McHattie, can you repeat for the court your role in all of this?' Edmunds began.

'I first saw the prisoner in Newcastle, only very briefly, and when I saw his picture in the papers and that he was wanted for murder, I telegraphed the Sydney offices to tell them that I had seen this man, and that he was going under the name of Weller. When his identity was confirmed, I was sent with Constable Conroy to San Francisco to make a positive identification, and then to assist in the arrest of Mr Butler.'

'And during your time supervising the prisoner on the voyage home, did you have many conversations?'

'Yes, a few.'

'And do you recall Mr Butler saying to you, "Lee Weller was a very nice little man, but not adapted to go into the country in Australia"?'

'Yes.'

'And, in your opinion, would this lead you to believe that perhaps something other than foul play befell Captain Weller.'

'I suppose.'

'No further questions,' Edmunds said as he sat down.

Want then called Conroy. He focused his questions on the first meeting between Conroy and Butler, and on the identification of Butler by Conroy on board the *Swanhilda*.

Edmunds immediately focused on Conroy's conversations with Butler, to which the young constable responded, 'Yes, I had some conversations with the prisoner, but not as many as the detectives.'

'And why was that?'

'Because Mr Butler did not like having me around. He said that I was "the only thorn in his side."'

'But in those conversations, did my client say anything to you about Captain Weller?'

'Yes, he said, "I'm not a bit frightened. I knew Lee Weller. He committed suicide. There were four of us in the camp. Two of them were out at the time. I will call one that was with me when the case comes on. I'm not a bit afraid to face the trial."'

'So, Mr Butler told you, in no uncertain terms, that Captain Weller had committed suicide?'

'Yes, he did.'

'No further questions.'

With that, Darley brought the day's proceedings to a close. All in all, the day had belonged more to the Crown, and an increasingly desolate look began to appear on Butler's face as he was led from the dock and back down to the cells, where Herbert was once again waiting for him. The Governor watched on closely as his subordinates removed anything they considered remotely suspicious before Butler was walked into his cell. The guards left the cell and the door slammed shut behind them.

'Make sure nothing happens to him,' Herbert reiterated as he walked from the cell block. 'And remember, there's to be at least two of you keeping watch on him at all times.'

Two guards duly positioned themselves directly in front of the cell, while two others sat down and began playing cards. Shortly after, the two women from the previous night returned with a tin of Butler's preferred brand of tobacco.

One of the guards handed Butler the tin, which he snatched eagerly and began stuffing his pipe. 'Can I have a light?' he asked.

The guard obliged.

'Thanks,' Butler said as he sat on his bunk smoking and reading his Bible, hoping that somewhere in the good book he would find his salvation.

30

Escaping Justice

16 June 1897

At 8 am the following morning, an associate of Mr Edmunds, Mark Williamson, entered the cell to go over the day's proceedings before court began. 'Have you had any trouble with him?' he asked one of the two guards standing at the cell entrance.

'No, he's been as quiet as a mouse.'

'Good, can you let me in? There are a few things I want to discuss with him before we start today.'

The closest guard retrieved his keys and opened the cell, and the other guard moved inside to rouse Butler. 'Come on, Frank. Time to get up. Mr Williamson is here to see you,' he said.

Butler, who was swathed in his blanket, didn't move.

Williamson then entered the cell and moved over to Butler's bed, tapping him gently on the shoulder. 'Frank! Wake up! Come on. We've got plenty to get through before court begins.'

Butler still didn't move, so Williamson rolled him over. He had barely done so when he suddenly cried out, 'Quick! Get a doctor in here, now!'

The guards quickly pulled Butler's blanket off him to find his throat bleeding and his chest and the blanket and mattress beneath him stained red. 'Shit!' the first guard said. 'Get some bandages!'

'How the hell did he do that?' said another as more guards now rushed into the cell carrying armfuls of bandages, which they hurriedly wrapped around Butler's lacerated throat. The last bandage was just being applied when Dr Paton arrived carrying his leather medical bag.

'What happened?' he said as he reached Butler's bedside.

'We don't know,' said one guard. 'We just found him like this.'

'How did he do it?'

'We're not sure.'

Paton bent down, and was just about to remove the bandages when he suddenly noticed a small piece of metal lying on the mattress. He picked it up and showed it to the guards. 'Where did this come from?' he asked.

The closest guard took the piece of metal and examined it closely before showing it to the other guards. 'Bugger,' one said as he examined it. 'It's off the tobacco tin the women gave to him last night.'

Paton then removed the bandages around Butler's throat and dressed the wound properly. As he was doing so, Herbert turned up. 'What the bloody hell is going on?' he demanded.

The guards looked anywhere but at their boss, for it was clear that he was not in a forgiving mood. 'You lot!' he growled as he pointed to each of them in turn.

'Yes, sir,' they said in unison, their heads bowed in shame.

'What the hell happened?'

'Two ladies brought this tin of tobacco for him last night,' one guard said as he held up the tin. 'He must have broken a piece off it.'

'And you forgot to take it off him! Expect there to be trouble over this, especially if he dies.'

Paton finished applying the bandages, rose from the bedside and turned to face Herbert. 'I don't think that is very likely. The cut is only around one inch long. It's not enough to kill him. He hasn't lost enough blood.'

'Will he be alright to take the stand?' Herbert asked.

'Yes, he'll be fine,' Paton said as he collected his gear and returned it to his bag. 'I believe this is more a delaying tactic than a genuine suicide attempt.'

'Right, Frank, time to go,' Herbert said forcefully, but Butler continued to lie motionless on his bunk, refusing to budge. 'C'mon, Frank, you heard what the doc said. You're good to go. Don't make this any harder than it needs to be,' Herbert said a little more softly. Still Butler did not move. 'Fine,' Herbert sighed. 'You lot, get him on his feet.'

The guards grabbed Butler by the shoulders and lifted him to his feet. Butler kept his body limp, so that the guards had to drag him from the cell and towards the courtroom. When they reached the base of the stairs leading up to the dock, Butler's demeanour immediately changed. He started to fight against the guards, kicking his legs and flailing his arms wildly, while shouting and cursing. 'Bastards! God damn bastards! Let me go, ya' pricks!'

Hearing the commotion, several constables appeared from the dock and raced down the stairs. It took half a dozen men to manhandle Butler to the ground, and when he was finally pinned down, they manacled his hands behind his back and dragged him up the stairs. His protests became louder as he was led into the courtroom. He was forced into his chair in the dock, and two guards stayed with him, one on either side, their hands resting on his shoulders. Realising that he had few options, Butler ceased his remonstrations, and slumped back into his chair.

Fully aware of what had transpired earlier, Darley's first question was more pertinent than it sounded. 'Is the defence ready to begin?'

Edmunds rose from his chair and took a brief look around the crowded courtroom before returning his gaze to Darley. 'Yes, Your Honour, we are. The prisoner would like to make a statement, if that is acceptable to the Court?'

'Yes,' said Darley. 'The Court will permit the prisoner make a statement.'

'As I am sure Your Honour can understand, given the events of last night, it will not be possible for the prisoner to deliver his statement verbally so, given the court's permission, I will be reading the statement on behalf of the prisoner.'

'May I remind you, Mr Edmunds, that under the Acts of Parliament, a prisoner has to speak in his own defence, so what you have proposed is entirely impossible. Any statement Mr Butler wishes to make must be made by Mr Butler.'

'I understand, Your Honour. In that case, the defence requests an adjournment so that our client may receive some medical treatment.'

'Granted,' Darley said as he slammed his gavel down. 'Court is adjourned until 2 pm.'

The appointed hour duly arrived and the crowd rushed inside as soon as Maybury opened the courtroom doors. The room was abuzz as people discussed and formed conjectures about all the wild ways in which Butler had attempted to end his life and escape the justice he deserved. Some even toyed with the possibility that one of the guards had tired of all the commotion and had tried to slit Butler's throat.

Darley re-entered the court with a distinct scowl on his face, plainly disturbed by all the disorder, and after he had taken his seat, it took numerous hefty strikes of his gavel to settle the courtroom. When it was sufficiently quiet, he nodded for Edmunds to begin.

'The defence asks permission for a further adjournment, because whilst my client is capable of speaking, it is barely above a whisper.'

'Mr Edmunds!' Darley said firmly. 'This trial has been delayed for far too long as it stands. There will be no more adjournments!'

Edmunds turned and paced back and forth pensively before turning back to face Darley. 'With Your Honour's permission, would it be acceptable if my client reads his statement to me, and then I relay what he has said to the court?'

Not wanting any further delays, Darley asked the Crown if it would accept such an arrangement. The murmurs of the crowd rose once more as Want and his team considered the proposal. Wanting the trial to finish sooner rather than later, the Crown agreed, and so Darley, while not overly pleased, assented. The anticipation of hearing Butler's words, the highlight of the trial that the crowd had been waiting for, was more effective than any strike of Darley's gavel, and they silently leant forward in their seats, eagerly anticipating what was to come.

Butler stood and started to whisper croakily into Edmunds' ear, the latter nodding several times before repeating what Butler had said.

'My name is Frank Butler,' Edmunds repeated, 'and I stand here accused of a crime I did not commit. I pray that common sense prevails and I am found innocent. I did make a partnership with Captain Weller. I did know him, that much is true, but the picture that has been presented to this court regarding the type of man he was is not entirely accurate. Captain Weller was a drunken widower. He did not take the loss of his wife at all well. You have even heard Mr Luckham testify to this. When we first made our agreement to prospect, he had to pawn his watch just to pay the expenses. As Captain Weller was short of money, he offered to sell me his wife's jewellery, which I bought for fifteen shillings.'

'Mr Butler, can you please tell the Court about your expedition?' Darley said.

Butler, croaked his reply to Edmunds, who duly relayed it to the Court. 'We caught the train from Sydney, and headed for Glenbrook. During the journey, I talked with Captain Weller about his drinking, stating that it was clearly becoming a serious problem for him, and that I thought the country air might do him some good. Besides, if he was drunk all the time, he would be no good to me when it came to prospecting. My plan was to camp near the lagoon at Glenbrook until the good Captain got himself sober. Unfortunately, Captain Weller did not last long without the drink, and the more he thought about the loss of his wife the more he fell into an even worse state. He had got over his drinking, but was very surly and melancholy over the next two days, evidently greatly troubled by his wife's death. He became increasingly depressed, and it was plain that our trip into the mountains was not having the desired effect, so I suggested that we return to Sydney so that he could get some more help. He said, "No, I'm not going back to Sydney." He then pulled out his trouser pocket with his right hand, and said, "Look here, I have no money." I knew he had a revolver with him, the one given to him by Mr Luckham, and I knew that it was loaded. I saw him put his left hand into his pocket and pull out the revolver. I jumped up from where I was sitting and stepped back out of reach, thinking that he might be planning to use it on me. The revolver was resting in the palm of his hand, and he appeared to be studying something. Suddenly, he put the revolver to his head, and when I saw what he was going to do, I immediately grasped his arm and twisted it behind his back, trying to stop him. In the course of this struggle, the revolver went off and Weller fell to the ground, dead.'

Want and his team were furiously making notes, and they immediately asked Butler why, if he was telling the truth, he hadn't immediately informed the police.

Butler croaked his reply to Edmunds, who repeated it.

'As I had been his mate, and had been seen in his company, I was afraid to report it to the police, instead deciding to bury his body where he had fallen. I had no shovel, only a small pick. That is why the hole was so small.'

The Crown lawyers were not about to let Butler off that easily. They asked how Butler had come to be in possession of Weller's belongings, implying that Butler's motive was robbery, pure and simple, to which Butler, through Edmunds, replied, 'The previous day, I'd had an idea that he might do something strange, especially after he had asked me if, should anything happen to him, I could collect all his belongings and forward them to his solicitor in England. That is why I used his Master's certificate to get on the ship, because I was fulfilling Captain Weller's wishes by taking his belongings home.'

Want and the rest of his team implied that while this was all very convenient, Butler could fabricate whatever story he liked, but could not deny the fact that he had made a confession to Roche on board the *Mariposa*. With the mention of his admission, Butler's croak became gravelly and harsh. Edmunds hardly needed to repeat what he said, but did so anyway. 'If there was any statement made to the police while on board the steamer *Mariposa*, it was when I was under the influence of whisky, which I was supplied with all the way from Frisco to Sydney. That is all I have to say.' Butler then sat down and stared down into his lap, and Edmunds returned to his seat.

Butler had given his version of events, the Crown witnesses had been called, and the defence had cross-examined them. 'Do you have any more witnesses, Mr Edmunds?' Darley asked.

The only lingering matter Edmunds needed to deal with was the testimony of Dr Paton. Edmunds knew the strength of Paton's testimony in particular, and he wanted to finish by bringing his own medical examiners to the stand. 'The defence calls Dr Hall, Your Honour.'

Dr Hall was sworn in first, and Edmunds immediately set about convincing the jury that his and Dr Gill's version of events was the more plausible. 'Dr Hall, you and Dr Gill have been conducting experiments to see if Mr Butler's version of events is plausible. Is that correct?'

'Yes, we have.'

'And what did you find? Is it possible that Lee Weller could have died by misadventure?'

'We found that it was entirely possible that, whilst the shot would have been a matter of chance, given that there was a struggle, Captain Weller's death could certainly have been caused by misadventure.'

'Can you please step down to the foot of the jury box and demonstrate how you conducted your experiments?'

Dr Hall duly stepped down from the stand and, after being joined by Dr Gill, the two doctors set about contorting themselves into several positions as they acted out how they believed events had transpired. When they were done, Dr Hall returned to the witness stand.

Darley, interested to hear what he had to say, asked the obvious question before Edmunds could begin. 'Doctor, do you think the wound found on Lee Weller's body was self-inflicted?'

'No, it could not have been self-inflicted,' Hall replied.

'If a second person had assisted in the act, might it have been possible?'

'It would require the second person to hold the hand of the first person in order to inflict such a wound.'

Darley nodded that he was satisfied with the response, and Edmunds continued. 'Suppose a person was struggling with another from behind. Might the wound have been inflicted in that way?'

'It is possible it might have been.'

'No further questions.'

Want stood up and paced back and forth several times in front of the jury before he paused and turned towards Edmunds. 'If a man had killed himself in the manner the defence has suggested, he could not dig his own grave and then cover himself over with earth afterwards.'

There was a slight chuckle from the crowded courtroom, and then Want turned his attention to the doctor, knowing that he was beginning to turn the tide in his favour.

'You and Dr Gill were trying to show how a man could commit suicide,' he said referring to the demonstration they had just given, 'but in this instance Mr Butler maintains he was trying to prevent it. I would like you to show me how you would hold the pistol in order to get the bullet to follow the path it took.'

'I believe we have just demonstrated that to you.'

'I repeat, you were demonstrating how a man could commit suicide. I put it to you that even if Mr Butler was trying to prevent a suicide, he still played a part in Lee Weller's demise. I also put it to you that if Mr Butler played a part in pulling the trigger, he would equally be guilty of murder. Your evidence amounts to this: if a man held a pistol in a certain position, it is possible that he might inflict such a wound upon himself. Despite your experiments, would it be, given the nature of the wounds, your *first* impression that the wound was self-inflicted?'

'No, it would not be my first impression that the wound was self-inflicted.'

'No further questions,' Want said, sitting down with a satisfied smile.

Edmunds, realising that his last chance lay with another doctor being able to ratify Butler's story, now called Dr Gill to the stand.

There was no response.

'Dr Gill?' Darley said as his eyes searched the courtroom.

Still, there was no response.

'Dr Gill?' Darley repeated.

'It seems that Dr Gill has either left the court or does not wish to respond to his name. Does the defence have any more witnesses to call?'

'No, Your Honour,' Edmunds replied, somewhat despondently.

'Then we will hear the closing statements.'

Want now stood and delivered his closing address. 'The Crown is under every obligation to prove Mr Butler's guilt. The defence has continually pushed the line that Captain Weller's death was a result of "misadventure", but they have not presented any sufficiently solid facts to show that this is the case; even their own witnesses have admitted that this scenario is most unlikely. This must lead you, the jury, to the conclusion that Mr Butler is guilty. The truth of the matter is that Mr Butler placed the advertisement in the paper with the specific goal of luring some poor man to his death. Upon finding his victim, he took Captain Weller to the Blue Mountains, where he took him out into the bush and made him dig his own grave. When Captain Weller knelt down in the hole that he had created, Mr Butler callously shot him in the back of the head. There can be no doubt that this was cold-blooded, premeditated murder. Mr Butler then attempted to flee the country in order to escape punishment for his crime. The only reason you have heard this fanciful story was because he got caught. He might have been a success as a murderer, but he was certainly a failure as a liar.' Want sat down, satisfied that he had done his best to send Butler to the gallows, and leant forward on the table as he anticipated how Edmunds would close.

Edmunds duly rose and began to speak. 'It is a point of law that, under the terms of the *Extradition Act*, my client should never have been put on trial in Sydney in the first place. I will also remind the jury that because of this, there has been much sensationalism and excitement surrounding this case. Given this, I put it to you that there is no way my client can possibly receive a fair trial. The conduct of the police in their investigation and handling of this matter has been nothing short of deplorable. The statements said to have been made by the accused might better be termed the ravings of a disordered mind elicited by the provision of copious amounts of liquor by Detective Roche. Added to this, Captain Weller was a drunkard, nothing more. Whilst we must feel incredibly sorry for him that he had become a widower, the fact remains that he did not take this well. My client tried to console him, tried to help free him from the demon drink. My client was nothing more than a good friend who tried his best to save him, and yet Captain Weller, seeing no other alternative, decided to take his own life. Mr Butler tried his best to prevent him from carrying out this act, but in the course of the struggle a very unfortunate accident occurred, and that is all there is to it. It is peculiar that everything we have heard from on board the steamer was said by Mr Butler, but not one word appears to have been said by the police. I will close by reminding the jury of a point of law, which must remain at the forefront of their minds. The Crown must prove Mr Butler's guilt beyond all reasonable doubt, and I am certain that the facts presented in this case should leave them under no illusions that there are many doubts. I will finish by reminding you all that my client is under no obligation to prove his innocence.'

Outside, the sun was setting and darkness was descending over the city like a shroud as Darley began to address the jury. 'The jury has heard both the defence and the Crown present their cases, and before you retire to consider your verdict, there are three questions to which you must pay careful attention. Firstly, you must be satisfied that the body found at Glenbrook was that of Captain Lee Weller. If you are convinced that this be the case, then you must satisfy yourself that he was in fact murdered. Lastly, if Captain Weller was murdered, is Mr Butler guilty of committing that murder? In your deliberations on the first of these questions, you must remember that there were eight witnesses who all testified that the dead man was Captain Weller. Regarding the second point as to whether his demise was a case of murder, you must remember that both Doctor Paton and Doctor Taylor testified to the fact that the bullet hole in Captain Weller's skull could not have been self-inflicted by a right-handed man, and I remind the jury that Captain Weller was right-handed. As to the last point, the defence's version of events must be drawn into question. There were numerous discrepancies in Mr Butler's story. The most important point to remember is that Mr Butler fled to America. A man who has done nothing wrong has no reason to flee, and therefore this must cast serious doubts on his version of events. Mr Edmunds has claimed that the police had not said anything in terms of a warning about making any statement to Mr Butler, but the duty of a police officer when arresting a suspect is to hold his tongue and open his ears. Many police officers have abided by this advice. It is good advice, and the three officers involved in this case, Detectives Roche and McHattie and Constable Conroy, certainly followed this advice. The defence has argued that Mr Butler's confessions were made under the influence of whisky, but none of the prisoner's claims were made under oath. Mr Edmunds has made a great deal of the circumstantial evidence, but the jury must remind themselves that every case where a person is not actually seen committing the crime is one of circumstantial evidence. The jury will now retire to consider their verdict.'

With that, the Crown and the defence teams stood as the jury rose and filed out of the courtroom.

Just over an hour later, the jury returned. Two officers of the court entered the dock and assisted Butler to his feet.

'Has the jury reached its verdict?' Darley asked.

The foreman rose to his feet. 'We have, Your Honour. We find the defendant guilty.'

Butler immediately slumped down into his seat, a dazed and confused look etched across his face. The crowd gasped, and fevered discussion began as dozens of journalists ran from the room, eager to pass the news on to their respective papers, ready for the stories in the morning editions.

Darley smashed his gavel down again and again, finally obtaining silence before he addressed the court. His voice was thick with emotion as Butler was helped to his feet by the guards. 'Frank Butler,' Darley began. 'After a most patient trial, during which you have been defended by able counsel, the jury, after consideration, have found you guilty. On most convincing evidence, they have found that you did commit a most cruel and atrocious murder. You have outraged the laws of this country, and you cannot expect any mercy from your fellow man, but there is one to whom you can appeal for mercy. I beseech you to appeal to the Almighty, who will grant you mercy and, no matter what your sins are, will forgive you. I adjure you to do this, for you can have no hope on Earth. Given that you have been found guilty of murder, I have no choice but to sentence you to death by hanging. May God have mercy on your soul.'

Butler, now recovered from his initial shock, stood up without assistance and shouted back at Darley, 'And may God have mercy on *your* soul!'

The now-convicted murderer, unlike when he had entered the court that morning, left quietly, his hands and legs still manacled, accompanied by a guard on either side. After descending from the dock, they entered the cell block. One of the guards unlocked Butler's cell, and as he stepped inside and the door was closed and locked behind him, Butler said, 'I suppose I have run my head up against a stone wall.'

'That you have, Frank,' said the guard. 'That you have.'

Butler sat down, stuffed his pipe, lit it, picked up his Bible and began to read. Governor Herbert turned up soon after, a group of several men trailing behind him. 'Unlock the cell,' he ordered.

'Yes, sir,' one of the guards said as he leapt from his chair to comply. Herbert entered the cell.

'Up you get, Frank,' he said as he stepped to one side and allowed one of the men behind him to take his place. In his arms, the officer held a specially constructed straitjacket. Expecting Butler to create a fuss, the remaining men now stepped into position to ensure that, should Butler become agitated, he could be placed into the restraints, but he extended his arms meekly, and once the jacket had been placed around him and fastened, he sat back down and simply stared at Herbert.

'Make sure that there are no utensils in here that he can use to inflict anymore self-harm. No knives, no forks, nothing sharp, and make sure you have removed that blasted tobacco tin. Whoever is on watch will feed him from a tin cup.'

'What about my readin' the Bible, Boss?' Butler asked.

'What sort of person would I be if I refused a condemned man the right to read the words of the Lord? If you wish to read, one of the guards on duty will read to you.'

Herbert and his entourage then left the cell. As they reached the exit, he turned to the guards. 'Make sure there are always two of you on duty. He is to be watched twenty-four hours a day, do you understand?'

'Yes, sir,' the guards said in unison.

'I want to make sure he swings from the gallows. The public want their blood, and we must give it to them.' With that, he turned and departed, leaving the guards to do their jobs and Butler to contemplate his demise.

31

Let Her Go!

17 April 1897

The following day, Edmunds was in Darley's office early. 'Good morning, Your Honour,' he said politely as he entered.

'Mr Edmunds,' Darley replied with a hint of irritation. 'What can I do for you?'

'I have come to request that my client's trial be pronounced null and void. I refer you to the *Extradition Act* once more. Everything was handled very poorly, and the trial should never have taken place in Sydney.'

'Mr Edmunds,' Darley said, his voice softening a little, 'you are a good lawyer, and a good man, and I understand that you are only trying to do the best by your client. I respect that, but, in my opinion, and according to the letter of the law, nothing wrong was done. Besides, do you honestly believe that my superiors and the politicians would allow such a thing?'

'No, I expected you to say as much. Thank you for your time.' Edmunds left Darley's office and immediately made for the cells.

When he arrived, Butler was asleep, but only just, and he soon woke and sat himself up as best he could. 'Mr Edmunds,' he said.

'Good morning, Frank. I wish I could come here and give you some good news, but alas I cannot. I went to see Judge Darley just now, and asked that the trial be declared a mistrial under the *Extradition Act*, but he was having none of it. Sorry, Frank, but there is nothing more I can do.'

'I appreciate everything you have done for me, Mr Edmunds. It is just my time. It is just my time.'

Edmunds sat down in a chair opposite, reached into his pocket for a cigarette, lit it and placed it between Butler's lips. 'May God have mercy on you, Frank,' he said as he placed a gentle hand on Butler's shoulder.

Butler's response was different to the one he had given Darley. 'Thank you, Mr Edmunds. I hope he does, but I do not expect it.'

Edmunds rose and started to leave, but paused at the cell door. 'One last thing, Frank. You need to have a think about what you would like for your last meal. Any ideas?'

'No, Mr Edmunds. I was thinking of a nice lamb dinner, but I shall think on it today, and let them know of my decision.'

Edmunds then departed, and a few minutes later another man arrived and told the guards that he would like to see the prisoner. When he appeared at the door of the cell, Butler looked up at his unfamiliar face.

'Frank,' one of the guards said. 'There's a journo here to see you.'

'Let him in,' Butler said.

'Hello, Mr Butler, I am from *The Sunday Times*. I was wondering if I could ask you a few questions?'

'Why not, take a seat.'

The journalist proceeded to sit in the same seat as Edmunds had recently vacated, but unbeknown to Butler, the journalist had not come alone, and Governor Herbert soon appeared behind him.

The journalist proceeded to ask Butler various questions about the trial and his treatment in prison, all of which the condemned man answered with good humour. 'Mr Butler, given that you have now been found guilty of murder, I don't suppose there is any harm in telling me how many men you have actually killed?'

'Let's see, how many is it they have against me – three or thirteen?'

Herbert immediately chimed in, 'Three.'

'Oh, no!' Butler boasted. 'It's four. You would have seen the reports in the papers of the discovery of a man called Davis. Well he's another one I killed!'

Having obtained the scoop he wanted, the journalist thanked Butler for his time, and as he rose from his seat he said, 'Mr Butler I promise, unlike some of my less scrupulous colleagues, I will give you fair coverage in my pieces.'

Butler smirked. 'If you don't, I'll come back and fix you.'

Once the reporter had left, Herbert sat down and looked deep into Butler's eyes. 'Tomorrow is the day, Frank. You may be a murderer, but even a murderer is entitled to a few small comforts. Is there anything else I can do for you?'

'You know, I did kill Lee Weller, Preston and Burgess. I have also committed a great many other murders, for which I should have been hanged over and over again – a dozen times if that is possible. Please send word to both Burgess and Preston's families expressing my deep sorrow and contrition for having murdered their sons.'

'I will do that for you, Frank. So, it would seem that your punishment will be a just one. Are you sure there is nothing else I can do for you before the time comes?'

'No, I recognise that my punishment is righteous. I have been fairly treated, both on the way from San Francisco and in Darlinghurst. I did give the detectives a great deal of trouble on the steamer on the way over to Sydney, but they behaved very well towards me. My treatment here has been all that I could expect.'

'You sure there is nothing we can do for you, Frank?'

'The only thing I desire is that you should hurry things along as quickly as you can, then I'll feel alright, but if I spend too much longer here, I fear that I may go mad.'

'I will make sure there are no delays, Frank. I promise you that,' said Herbert.

16 July 1897

Outside Darlinghurst Gaol, the first of the crowd had begun to arrive just after dawn and their numbers had been steadily building all morning. While they waited for the big moment families conversed with other families as they conjectured about what was taking place on the other side of the sandstone walls. The smaller children played in the park, whilst the older ones tried to climb the huge oak trees adjacent to the walls in an attempt to gain a view of the grim proceedings that were about to take place.

Standing next to the flagpole, a prison guard tugged on the ropes attached to the Union Jack. After it had been lowered, he carefully folded it and put it to one side before attaching and hoisting a black flag in its place, pulling on the ropes until the flag fluttered in the gentle breeze.

Outside, the people having now seen the black flag hoisted, the conversations became more excited. Inside the jail, two police officers walked into Butler's cell. Reverend Lane sat at Butler's bedside, whilst the murderer sat with his back propped against the wall staring off into the distance, as if deep in thought. The two officers stopped at the end of the bed and listened to the last of Reverend Lane's words. 'May God have mercy on your soul,' he said to a seemingly uninterested Butler.

'You ready, Frank?' the nearer of the two officers asked.

Raising himself from his bed and standing upright in front of it, Butler turned to face the two officers. 'Yes, I am quite ready. I hope this business will be over and done with as quickly as possible.'

Despite his words, the officer noticed a distinct paleness in Butler's complexion as he removed the straitjacket, attached the leg chains and shackled Butler's hands before the two officers then positioned themselves on either side of the condemned man and led him from his cell for the final time.

In the overcast sky above, several rumbles of thunder echoed around the city as if the Devil himself was whispering in dulcet tones while he awaited the arrival of one of his own. A small group of men were standing in front of the gallows, and turned their heads as one at the sound of Butler's shackles when he appeared at the doorway leading out into the courtyard.

Flanked by the two officers, Butler kept his posture as erect as possible, his gaze firmly fixed on the gallows. After shuffling his way across the courtyard, he was helped up the stairs and placed into position. The two officers then handed Butler over to the executioner and his assistant, the latter removing Butler's leg chains and replacing them with leather straps. Butler gazed out across the small crowd, meeting several people's eyes, some of whom looked away as a chill ran down their spine, whilst others were held transfixed as they stared into the soul of a self-confessed cold-blooded, calculating killer. After scanning the crowd several more times, Butler glanced briefly at his executioner, Robert Rice Howard, known as 'Nosey Bob' the Gentleman Hangman, his eyes then returning for a closer look when he realised that the man dressed in a black frockcoat and white necktie who stood stiffly before him had no nose to speak of.

Transferring his gaze off into the distance, Butler held his arms out in front of him and clasped his hands together. Howard unlocked the shackles that held Butler's arms fast and removed all his chains, then moved behind him and placed a beige hood over his head and affixed the rope around his neck.

'Do you have anything to say?' the hangman asked.

'I have nothing to add to what I have already stated to the authorities,' Butler replied.

Howard moved to the side of the gallows and placed his hand on the lever. The crowd in the courtyard and those up in the trees fell quiet. The wind died down, creating a strange stillness and silence, which was only broken when Butler cried out, 'Let her go!'

The hangman pulled the lever and the wooden floorboards beneath Butler's feet fell away. His body dropped, and the snapping of his neck could be heard echoing through the courtyard.

Epilogue

- Frank Butler's body was left to hang in the courtyard like a slab of meat hanging in an abattoir. The public, hungry for a final glimpse of the murderer, were herded into the courtyard and circled around the body. The newspapers, despite their unwillingness to print words such as "hell" and "damn", were all too happy to publish numerous pictures of the dead man.

- Prominent scientists and criminologists of the era desperately wanted to have Butler's brain removed so that it could be examined, many people feeling certain that a mass murderer would not have the same brain as a normal human being, but the Minister of Justice denied this request.

- With the trial and execution complete, the Attorney-General, Mr Want, and the rest of Australia, were shocked to receive a bill from the American authorities for £6000, or US$28,000, to cover the cost of Butler's incarceration in the States and his lawyers, full details of which are available for public viewing in the State Library of New South Wales.

- For their tireless efforts, John Roche received £6, as did Hector McLean. Conroy, McHattie and other officers who worked on the case received £3 each, and £43 pounds was divided amongst various members of the public who had assisted in the search parties. However, the colonial secretary eventually saw fit to award Roche another £30, McHattie another £25 and Conroy another £15.

- Jack Want, in communications with the Legislative Council, had the final say on the case, concluding by noting, 'If, in the future, we are to be saddled with bills of this nature, I shall deem it my duty in such cases to advise the Government to allow foreign countries to keep our criminals.'

Bibliography

Blue Mountains Organisations

For further information and guided walking tours of the lagoon and of Lee Weller's grave contact the Glenbrook Historical Society (PO BOX 38, Glenbrook, 2773) or the Blue Mountains Association of Cultural Heritage Associations - *www.bluemountainsheritage.com.au/history/*

Books

Travers, Robert, *Murder in the Blue Mountains: Being the True Story of one of Australia's Most Notorious Killers*, Hutchison Australia, Melbourne, 1972

Newspapers circa 1896/97

The Adelaide Advertiser
The Argus (Melbourne)
The Brisbane Courier
The Kalgoorlie Argus
The Mercury (Hobart)
The Nepean Times
The Northern Star
The Rockhampton Capricornian
The South Australian Register
The Sydney Morning Herald
The San Francisco Call
The West Australian

Also written by
Jason K. Foster

SEVEN BONES

Two Wives, Two Violent Murders, A Fight for Justice...

PETER SEYMOUR & JASON K. FOSTER

SO I HIT HIM

Surviving life as an institutionalised alien

Mick Whatham

More titles Available from Big Sky Publishing

The **extreme** life of an **SAS soldier**

Paul Jordan

www.bigskypublishing.com.au